ELIXIR OF KOTTA SATCHIDANANDA MURTY'S LIFE AND PHILOSOPHY

Elixir of Kotta Satchidananda Murty's Life and Philosophy

Editor

B. Sambasiva Prasad
Former Professor & Head
Dept. of Philosophy
Sri Venkateswara University
Tirupati, A.P.

MOTILAL BANARSIDASS
INTERNATIONAL
DELHI

First Edition : Delhi, 2025

ISBN : 978-81-989854-5-3 (HB)
ISBN : 978-81-989854-1-5 (PB)

Also available at
MOTILAL BANARSIDASS INTERNATIONAL
H.O. : 41 U.A. Bungalow Road, (Back Lane)Jawahar Nagar, Delhi - 110 007
4261 (basement) Lane #3,Ansari Road, Darya Ganj, New Delhi - 110 002
Shop No. 6, Luz Ginza Complex, 241 Luz Corner, Mylapore, Chennai - 600 004
12/1A, 2nd Floor, Bankim Chatterjee Street, Kolkata - 700 073
Stockist : Motilal Books, Ashok Rajpath, Near Kali Mandir, Patna - 800 004

Cover Picture:
The Moon Rabbit, a mythical figure associated with the Moon, is beautifully depicted in this painting by Ms. Raaida Hasnain (USA). The artwork was selected by Aarna, Prof. KSM's great-granddaughter, who has the privilege of being one of Mrs. Hasnain's students.

Printed in India
MOTILAL BANARSIDASS INTERNATIONAL

PREFACE

The objective of this work is to expound the personal and academic journey of Prof. K. Satchidananda Murty (KSM), a world-renowned philosopher. It also aims at presenting the substance of his philosophical works.

Dr. M. Rajagopala Rao, one of the old students of Prof. KSM mooted the idea of writing a Biography in Telugu with Prof. K. Ramesh, former Professor of HRM, Andhra University, Visakhaptnam and the youngest son of KSM. Prof. Ramesh after consulting his family members, gave permission to Dr. Rajagopala Rao. He gave all the required material and inputs and encouraged him in every way. Dr. Rajagopala Rao completed the work with the title "Acharya Kotta Satchidananda Murty Jivitha Sangraham" and published in 2013 under Bouddhasahithi Publications, Guntur. Subsequently, with a view to giving this work wider circulation, Prof. Ramesh, requested to write his father's Biography in English by Sri AAV Prasad, Former Executive Editor, India Today (Telugu), currently Consultant, EENADU Central Editorial Board, through Dr. Atluri Gopal Rao. Sri Prasad agreed to do the work but in leisurely way. Ramesh gave all the books, material and information required and made himself available whenever he called. He completed the work in two to three years, but it was shelved by Ramesh the reasons are unknown.

Thereupon, I was asked by Prof. Ramesh, to take up the responsibility of reading and editing the book. I know Prof. Satchidananda Murty, personally. I have worked on some aspects of his philosophy and presented papers in seminars and conferences. With my deep respect to Prof. Murty and his in-depth scholarship, I accepted the assignment, offered by Prof. Ramesh. I took it a great privilege given to me. The Telugu account by Dr. M. Rajagopal Rao and the English version (in typescript) by AAV Prasad, were sent to me by Ramesh. I have gone through them carefully first the work in Telugu, and then its English version. My work is confined to its English part. I have made some corrections to it, wherever I felt needed. I made some changes on almost every page. I gave the book title and the Chapter titles. In Chapter 6 "Native Language Proficiency" 13 books are reviewed. They are arranged chronologically, according to their year of publication. In Chapter 7, " Magnum Opus", a total of 37 works by Prof. Murty were reviewed and arranged in their chronological order. The Endnotes is also given.

I have added five annexes to the book. Annexure I contains the Autobiography of Prof. Murty. Here, we read his life saga in his own words. It is amazing. Annexure II contains Prof. Murty's reminiscences on Andhra University, where he worked for about 35 years. Annexure III refers to Prof. Murty's visit to six West European countries and had the privilege of discussing philosophical problems with distinguished world thinkers. Annexure IV details the non-technical account of Prof. Murty, while receiving D.Litt., from the Martin Luther University, Germany. Annexure V describes the Citation presented to Prof. Murty on the occasion of Honorary doctorate conferred on him by the German University. The information provided in these annexures reflect the great academic commitment of Prof. Murty and ought to be read by a serious scholar in philosophy and hence are appended. While editing the book, I have learnt a lot on the philosophy of Prof. K. Satchidananda Murty. It is a great learning process.

A few words, regarding the exceptional qualities of Prof.Murty. Murty demonstrated rare intellectual abilities from a young age, mastering multiple languages and philosophical texts. By the time, he was 12 years old, he brought out *Śrī Sangameśhaṣhṭakam* along with *Śrī Veṇugopala Stothram*. At 14 years of age, Murty published his Telugu work Hanumad Vijayamu. At 15 years, he started of writing a commentary on *Śrīmad Bhagavad Gītā* in Telugu and completed the work in 1940, at the age of 16. Murty's parents and teachers played an important role in shaping his intellectual pursuits. Murty engaged with various philosophical traditions, including Indian, Western, Chinese, Japanese and Arabian thought, exhibiting inclusive approach. His philosophical inquiry was deeply rooted in spiritual seeking. He emphasized the importance of comparative studies, recognizing the value of diverse philosophical perspectives in understanding complex issues. His philosophy focuses on the social good, advocating for peaceful existence. His travels and interactions with international scholars broadened his philosophical outlook. His works collectively demonstrate his deep understanding of Hindu philosophy, his language skills and his ability to engage with varied spiritual traditions. Murty's work on *Śrīmad Bhagavad Gītā* and the four-fold varna system provide a modern interpretation focusing upon the qualities and actions of persons over their birth. His research papers and books continue to influence Indian universities and philosophical studies. He was known for his simplicity, sense of humour and dedication to duty.

Murty did not hanker after material goods, but spent all his time in reading, writing, thinking and publishing. Out and out he is a great academician. He not only mastered many Sastras, but also at the same time a great administrator. This is obvious from the posts he ably handled like the Principal and Special Officer, Andhra

University Post-graduate Center, Guntur; Vice-Chancellor, Sri Venkateswara University, Tirupati; Vice- Chairman, UGC, New Delhi; Chancellor, Central Institute of Higher Tibetan Studies, Sarnath. Whatever the administrative position he held, during that time, he never left his academic work. That reflects the academic commitment of Prof.Murty.

I thank sincerely Prof. Ramesh, who helped me a lot in preparing this book. But for his constant encouragement and support, this work would have not been completed. He sent me the soft copies of the books of Prof. Murty through WhatsApp, whenever I wanted. I used to converse with him, if I have any doubts in completing the work. I thank him sincerely for offering valuable editorial suggestions. He also helped me in proof reading the text. My health issues interrupted the work now and then. However, I am happy that I could complete the work and hand it over to Prof. Ramesh.

I consider it appropriate to record my appreciation to the work of Dr. Rajagopala Rao. I posthumously thank him. I express my thankfulness to Dr.Gopala Rao, Atluri, President -HR at Ramoji Group, who is instrumental in persuading Sri Prasad to accept to write the Biography in English. I thank profusely Sri Prasad. Also I wish to express my thanks to Prof. K. Pratap, Former Professor of Sanskrit, S.V.University, who helped in inserting diacritical marks in the script. I would like to thank the painter Ms.Raaida Hasnain, USA, for the painting on the jacket of the book. Also I thank Motilal Banarsidass International for neatly printing the work. Additionally, I appreciate the help provided by Mr. V. Rama Prasad and my daughter-in-law, Ms. Y. Gnaneshwari, in typing and computer work. Last but not least, I thank Dr. M. Ramalakshmi for preparing the Index.

Date: 28th August, 2025 **B. Sambasiva Prasad**

Contents

A Time Line of Greatness

Prof. K. Satchidananda Murty

(1924–2011)

Prof. K. Satchidananda Murty's outstanding contributions to philosophy, impressive scholarship, and profound impact on the academic community are underscored by a compilation of quotes and testimonials from esteemed scholars, philosophers, and intellectuals.

Praise from Renowned Figures

Paramahamsa Yogananda: Prof. Murty's books share India's spiritual heritage with the world, positively influencing the globe.

Mahapandita Rahul Sankrityayana: "You (Prof. Murty) have made a good start, and there is much to be done.... Well done, your efforts will be successful in the future."

Dr. C.R. Reddy: Prof. Murty is a "prodigy" and a "creative and dynamic personality."

Dr. S. Radhakrishnan: Prof. Murty's work on Vedanta is "a very learned book" that presents views in a "bold, unfettered way."

Prof. Suniti Kumar Chatterjee: "The mantle of Dr. Radhakrishnan had worthily fallen upon Murty's shoulders."

Commendations from Notable Scholars

Prof. Kalidas Bhattacharya: Prof. Murty's study on Vedanta is a "brilliant study."

Prof. P. Sankaranarayanan: His work is "encyclopaedic" and "the outcome of deep scholarship."

Vera Britain: His book on peace studies is "a comprehensive peace classic."

Recognition for Intellectual Brilliance

Prof. Harold D. Lasswell: Prof. Murty's book on Indian foreign policy evidences emerging policy sciences.

Prof. Wing-tsit Chan: His book on Sino-Japanese philosophies could spark a renaissance of intellectual exchange between India and China.

Prof. Hajime Nakamura: Prof. Murty's syntheses of Eastern and Western philosophy are praiseworthy.

Legacy and Impact

Prof. Murty is considered one of India's top-ranking philosophers, a creative thinker, and a prolific writer.

Prof. Humayun Kabir: "One among the outstanding philosophers of the younger generation."

Prof. D.P. Chattopadhyaya: "One of the foremost creative philosophers and prolific writers."

His legacy continues to inspire and influence scholars, philosophers, and intellectuals worldwide.

Notable Interactions and Praise

Padma Shri Prof. Arvind Sharma: Prof. Murty's philosophical inclinations are noteworthy.

Padma Shri Prof. K.R. Rao: Prof. Murty may have had a transcendental experience.

Dr. Karan Singh: Prof. Murty's articulation of Indian wisdom and civilizational values is appreciable.

Testimonials from Eminent Personalities

Justice A. Sambasiva Rao: Prof. Murty is not only a teacher but also a thinker and writer of outstanding eminence.

Prof. R. Balasubramanian: Prof. Murty is both a scholar and a thinker.

Prof. Sibajiban Bhattacharyya: Prof. Murty is a prolific writer with a vast scope of philosophy.

Prof. Niharranjan Ray: His work on Philosophy of Religion is "a profound book."

Prof. R.C. Zaehner: It manages "to cover an immense ground in so short a compass."

Dr. Margaret Chatterjee: It is "one of the most intelligent works to appear in the field in recent years."

Inspiring Quotes and Reflections

Prof. Vohra: Prof. Murty believed in preserving equanimity without being depressed or elated.

Prof. Srinivasa Iyengar: Prof. Murty was dynamic and wanted to do more than necessary.

Justice Jagan Mohan Reddy: Prof. Murty inculcated a spirit of enquiry, criticism, and analysis in his students.

Overall, Prof. Murty's contributions have left a lasting impact on the academic community, and his work remains a testament to his greatness.

1

Early Influences

Acharya Kotta Satchidananda Murty (1924-2011)- K.S. Murty to his friends and admirers—was born as an Andhraite. He hailed from Guntur district, will surely swell the hearts of the people there, with pride. Yes, we have a physical affinity with him, but intellectually he can't be tied down to a particular space. Having risen to great heights, Prof. Murty earned his rightful place among the world-renowned savants. Prof. Murty's heart was as solemn as the sea, his goals were as lofty as Himalayas. His extraordinary character and deep and contemplative mind still remain unfathomable. Only those who can think and lead a life like Prof. Murty would be able to comprehend him, move closer to him, become dear and intimate companions to him. Prof. Murty never attached much significance to routine, everyday activities, social relations and family bonds. He led a hermitic life- thought not literally but in spirit. Living with family, friends, relatives and neighbours, Prof. Murty remained stoic and untangled with worldly affections- even with his wife and children. He was a loner amidst a crowd. Leading a solitary life, losing himself in a world of deep study, intense contemplation, he was always busy with unveiling novel perspectives.

Hankering after worldly pleasures was not for him. He refused to be trapped in the constant struggle to acquire riches and fame; to provide a luxurious life to his wife and children. Prof. Murty worked for the emancipation of ordinary human beings who are bogged down in timeworn customs and rituals; narrow-mindedly stick to caste, religious and regional divisions; enter into meaningless conflicts, constantly feel the burden of worldly urges, yet arrogate themselves with feelings of achievement. Like so many saints before him, Prof. Murty too dedicated his life to liberate fellow human beings from all these ills, ignorance and grief. Little wonders most of us fail to understand such a great soul. Prof. Murty continued on his path unmindful of brickbats or bouquets; endearment or estrangement. He never bothered to check whether he was understood or misunderstood, and pushed on with his inquiry into human condition. His thoughts and objectives were beyond our comprehension. He was a *Lokottara*[1] (Transcendent), a Superman[2] as conceived by Shri Aurobindo, a spiritualist[3] in the eyes of various Peethadhipathis, a Siddha[4] in Kashmiri Tantrik lingo, a Bodhisatva – particularly a Mahayana[5] Bodhisatva as per Buddhist terminology. To the uninitiated, all these descriptions of Prof. Murty might seem hyperbole and an irrelevant eulogy. But those who are well-acquainted with his efforts truly recognize his greatness.

His way of thought is best revealed in his own words: "Everything is okay. Life is moving on without the feeling of want. I have read all there is to read, yet an elusive pain, an unknown ache frequently haunts me. I dug deep into myself to inquire what was lacking in my life. But, I was unable to find out the source of my nagging pain, I could not discover an answer to the question- how to fill the growing emptiness in me? Whether I was alone or in BA (undergraduate course) class room, this feeling of void constantly haunted me. It haunts me during a walk in the park or among hills. It stalks me in clubs or when I am in deep conversation with my friends. Time and again I suddenly feel the void in my thought. Unless it is somehow filled, life seems like an exercise in futility. I mulled over the growing nothingness inside me and analysed all the schools of thought to get to the bottom of it. Still, I was unable to find a solution". This stream of thought didn't end there. The very first article in his book *Kāru Mabbulu* displays the same tone of spiritual inquiry.

One would think that such a deep contemplation and tireless quest are the hallmarks of a great saint, a revered Swamiji or a very old man. Sometimes a person on the death bed may slip into such an abstract train of thoughts. Some people may even suspect this to be the final distress call of Prof. Murty's anguished soul. But, all such perceptions are wide off the mark. The above-mentioned monologue comes straight out of the first page of his book- *Kāru Mabbulu* published in 1947. The book was the first step in a great mission of analysing the dark shadows over the individual and community lives and on our customs and traditions. The same mission served as the guiding principle to his unique stream of thoughts and became the bedrock of his spiritual quest. If we presume that Prof. Murty might have displayed such profundity at a mature age, and then we are mistaken. You will be surprised to know that he was a young man of just 23 years, when he delved so deep into himself. Normally, eager passions and intense pleasure-seeking behaviour rule the youth of that age. But, Prof. Murty was an exception. It was strange that an existential anxiety should grip him at such a young age. And the same anxiety steered him in later years and moulded him into an unusual person. Over the years, his exemplary character shone like a beacon to one and all. His spirit soared to great heights, forever unattainable to average minds.

His detachment and spiritual quest did not come out of the blue. He displayed these qualities even as a boy.

He got "Maadhyama" certificate in Hindi in the year 1933 and turned "Visharada" in 1936. All this, before he was 10 years old. By the time he was 12 years, he brought out *Sangameśhaṣhṭakam Śrī Veṇugopala Stothram* in Sanskrit. In 1937, at the age of 13, he translated the Hindi work *Nāma Sankīrtana Mahima* into Telugu. At 14 years of age, in 1938, Satchidananda Murty published his Telugu work *Hanumad Vijayam* based on a Sanskrit original. In 1939, i.e., at 15 years, he started writing a Telugu commentary on *Śrīmad Bhagavad Gītā* and completed the work in 1940 by which time, he was 16. The tagline for the book was *The Song Celestial*. As you all know, the *Gītā* was one of the texts of *Prasthanatrayi* – the holy trinity of scriptural authority in Hinduism. Satchidananda Murty brought out Gītā with English meanings and excellent interpretations. He based his translation on many previous authoritative essays like *Gīta Māhātmyam, Bahiranga Parīkṣā, Gītāvaktha Puruṣottama Tatvam, Bhagavad Gītānuṣthana Vidhi, Gītā Pāṭha Vidhi, Gītā Sandeśam and Santa Vani.* While interpreting the *Gītā*, he extensively quoted over 30 world-renowned philosophers, litterateurs, social reformers like Swami Vivekananda, Annie Besant, Hafiz, Plato, Aristotle, Tolstoy, Carlyle, Milton, Shakespeare, Seneca and many others. Satchidananda occasionally quoted the *Bible* also. He revealed an interesting fact that the *Aśwatta Vṛkṣa* metaphor used by Upaniṣads was also mentioned in the *Bible*. Satchidananda Murty had also disclosed that in Greek mythologies, the *Aśwatta Vṛkṣa* was called *Igatrossyl*. It proves that he had embarked on comparative and extensive studies at such a tender age. In his foreword to the *Bhagavad Gītā*, Satchidananda Murty reported that information for his work was gathered from books of 23 authors.

It is still hard to believe that a 15-16 year old teenager had so extensively studied complex philosophical works to come out with an elaborately interpreted *Bhagavad Gītā*. The esoteric knowledge displayed by Satchidananda Murty at such a tender age surely overwhelms us. It is rare for a 16 year old boy to declare himself *Ṣaṭ Bhāṣā Vidura* (master in six languages) by gaining command over Telugu, Sanskrit, Hindi, English along with French and German. Rarer still for a teenager to become proficient in spiritual knowledge and progress on the path of Bhakti. Satchidananda Murty's spiritual evolution was definitely inspired by his father Veerabhadraiah who was a strict adherent of *Sanatana Dharma*. He collected the main scriptures of all major religions and turned his home- "Ananda Ashram" into a small and treasured library. Veerabhadraiah was able to write verse in traditional poetic dialect. Though Satchidananda Murty initially followed his father's orthodox path, eventually he went his own way which was modern and yet spiritual also. Flashes of this tendency were clearly visible in Satchidananda Murty's work *Kāru Mabbulu*.

There were many twists and turns in his progressive evolution. There were many stopovers even in his work life and pursuit of knowledge. He started out as a lecturer at Tirupati and was rapidly promoted first as a Professor and later as a Head of the Department, Vice-chancellor and eventually became the Vice-Chairman of the UGC. Proving himself as an exemplary scholar and achiever, Prof. Murty continued his spiritual quest to win recognition as the able successor to the world-renowned philosopher Sarvepalli Radhakrishnan. Prof. Murty's unceasing efforts, relentless pursuit of knowledge, ability and interest in taking up comparative studies, his exemplary research papers won for him global acclaim. The fact that he published 50 books in a span of 50 years bears testimony to the depth and diversity of his academic research. Such scholarly excellence naturally overawed the intellectuals.

Philosophical studies are usually doctrinarian. This elitist tendency had created a gulf between the common people and philosophers. The philosophical concepts of creation, preservation and destruction of the world; human life, growth and death; the creator and his creation; ways of human perception; the link between the spirit and body; the final emancipation—are still beyond the understanding of common folk. They are beyond the social ambit also. Though we are debating these issues since many centuries and millennia, they still remain inconclusive. With no solution in sight, all those who are of philosophical bent of mind, construct various theoretical edifices and pose as the new age visionaries. But, currently the situation has changed. Modern philosophy works for social good. It seeks to achieve this goal by suggesting guiding principles for man and his life and conduct; It also seeks to evolve modalities for achieving better social interaction, equality, fraternity, comfortable living, public good, world unity and peaceful existence. Prof. Murty gave the clarion call for such a new world order. His studies and analyses were not confined to the Indian and Western philosophical systems and their doctrines. Building better human relations, achieving peace and harmony, ways of promoting social progress- were also his subjects of study. It was for this reason that Prof. Murty won accolades from world's philosopher community, which is rare for modern Indian visionaries.

Prof. Murty categorized the contemporary Indian philosophers into distinct groups and placed himself in the third. As per his classification, the first group delves deep into the orthodox Indian texts to interpret ancient schools of thought. Ganganath Jha and Surendranath Dasgupta et al fall under this group. The second group comprises scholars like TRV Murthi who studied original texts and compared the relevant Eastern and Western concepts. The third group interprets modern philosophical tenets in the light of ancient philosophical traditions. In the process, they also take Western philosophers' propositions into consideration. Prof. Murty put himself in this third group. The fourth group comprises of Indian thinkers like Harilal Haldar, JL Mehta and others. They concern themselves with the issues that Western philosophers wrestle with and interpret their line of reasoning and arguments accordingly. The scholars of the fifth and the last group were seen to be integrators. They strive to achieve a balance between the diverse perceptions of world philosophers. He placed Dr. Sarvepalli Radhakrishnan in this particular group.[6]

As part of the classification, Prof. Murty declared that he interprets modern philosophical issues by combining traditional Indian schools of thought and contemporary Western philosophers' perceptions. It may be recalled that self-knowledge was extolled as the best form of knowledge by both Eastern and Western philosophers. Prof. Murty epitomized that ancient adage. Socrates proclaimed 'Know Thyself', Vedantins declared *'ĀtmānamViddhi'* and the Buddha stated *Athanaava Athana Avakheyya.* Seen in this light, the exemplary quality of Prof. Murty's self-perception becomes all too obvious.

Except atheists, most of the people in the world follow one religion or the other. Everybody thinks their religion is the best in paving the way to emancipation. They claim that their God is the True God, their faith to be the ultimate. Such narrow-minded dogmas create rift among the mankind. By provoking hatred, they lead to conflicts and wars and spread disharmony everywhere. Thus, instead of aiding peaceful coexistence, the world religions are sowing the seeds of discord among the people. Over time the religious beliefs turn into superstitions and unleash the demons of disorder. India is not immune to this unholy tendency. Many faiths were born here, many more came in from outside. Unmindful of this fact, each section argues that its creed is the most orthodox and timeless. But, history proves otherwise. Every religion evolves through the constant exchange of ideas and traditions between various sections of people. When people realize this fact, the dark clouds overshadowing their minds clear away instantly and a friendly atmosphere pervades. In order to bequeath such a realization to fellow humans, Prof. Murty took up intense study of various religions and belief systems. Based on the studies, he concluded that none of the religions of India- including Hinduism retained its original form. The influence of Jain, Buddhist, Islamic and Christian religions over Hinduism can be clearly seen even now. Likewise, he reasoned that Islam has also undergone many changes to evolve into a form that is distinctly Indian. It is the same with Christianity. This line of reasoning definitely promotes meaningful social reformation. He put forward this proposition to promote fraternity among the common folk. If his understanding can inspire people to move on a righteous path, that will be his most satisfying reward. Such altruism was the hallmark of Prof. Murty's intellect.

Satchidananda Murty was relentless in the pursuit of enlightenment. He took to Sanskrit studies during childhood itself and became well-versed in Vedas and other philosophical treatises which are the bedrock of Indian thought and culture. He extended his focus to Jaina texts and the Buddha's teachings also. He acquainted himself with the holy books of Zoroastrian, Islam and Christian religions and delineated the way they attained Indianness. Prof. Murty had also reviewed the influence of Chinese, Japanese and Arabian schools of thought. The fact that he was able to study and evaluate the world's philosophical systems bears testimony to his unmatched genius. Obviously he opted for a solitary life so as to continue his mammoth task. Extolling his unparalleled efforts, the editors of the book *Collected criticism of K. Sachidananda Murty* wrote in the Preface: " Except a very few like Professors S.N.Dasgupta and S.Radhakrishnan, it is difficult to name an Indian academic philosopher who has been more productive than Prof.Murty and whose work has received more notice than his. ... No other Indian academic philosopher has attempted to discuss in such detail problems which belong to so many fields of study---Hindu scriptural exegesis, metaphysics, philosophy of religion, interpretation of Indian culture and history, social and political thought, international relations and Sino-Japanese philosophies." [7]

Most presume that India is synonymous with Hindustan and Hindustan is synonymous with Hinduism. But, Hinduism did not emerge out of an exclusive line of spiritual inquiry. It is a fusion of religions. Many sects, particularly Shaiva, Vaishnava, Shakta and Bhagavatha merged into Hinduism. And these sects contain many sub-sects. Each sub-sect has its own rituals, traditions and armies of disciples. They indulge in fiery arguments. According to Prof. Murty, setting aside our differences, we have to realize that all these sects are rooted in Indianness- Prof. Murty stressed. Ultimately, we have to bring the true *Bhāratīya Dharma* to the fore. He had also stressed that we have to review and revitalize Indian religions and philosophies in the light of other Asian creeds. He analysed the influence of Confucianism and Taoism on China; the syncretic nature of Buddhism and Shinto in Japan; the influence of ancient Arab culture on the development of Islam; the relationship between Christianity and Judaism to envisage a composite culture of Asia. He also advocated that Indian culture should progress hand in hand with Asian culture, facilitating peaceful coexistence of mankind.

Prof. Murty's worldly life and intellect advanced in tandem with deep and extensive studies. He gradually moved away from the ancestral traditions and beliefs to get a grasp of Advaita philosophy. He was engrossed in the texts of Acharya Nagarjuna, who was credited with the founding of Mādhyamika school of Mahāyāna Buddhism. Prof. Murty noted that Nagarjuna's *Sūnya Vāda* inspired the development of Sankaracharya's Advaita. He differed with modern Indian scholars who gave precedence to Advaita or equal importance to both Nagarjuna and Sankaracharya. Along with the inquiry into social, economic, political and cultural issues, Prof. Murty debated and proposed solutions to various national and international issues. This intense effort helped him conceive an extensive system of metaphysics. Given his multifaceted personality, it may be unfair to consider him only as a philosopher.

Endowed with great talent, reason and intellect, he researched the fundamental tenets and texts of Islam, Christianity and those belonging to China and Japan. No wonder, Prof. Murty simultaneously won the blessings of Vedanta Peethadhipatis, Catholic bishops, heads and representatives of Buddhist organisations and Islamic Moulvis. Prof. Murty made a profound study of Greek Philosophers like Plato and Aristotle, French philosopher Descartes and conversed with contemporary thinkers like A.N. Whitehead, Bertrand Russell and J.P. Sartre. With all his devotion to philosophical studies, Prof. Murty never preached any particular system of thought or religion. Except Rāma, he did not champion any particular God or individual as his ideal. He gave credit to the deserving and censured when required.

Hence Prof. Murty was considered by many as an inscrutable philosopher. He was variously described as an orthodox pundit, a conservative, a doctrinarian, a traditionalist, a theist or an atheist. Still others ironically commented that when Prof. Murty can't understand himself, how can we understand him? Yet we should not lose the fact that he had amassed an ocean of knowledge, based on which he wrote over 50 books. Better to listen to his own assessment of himself: "My father, my family life, my teachers, the thinkers, pundits that I have met, my extensive tours and studies had effectively spurred, moulded and helped develop my intellectual life. Though by vocation I teach philosophy, literature was my avocation. I have widely read fiction along with theology, history, political and social sciences, cultural works and books on international relations. While studying Indian and Western; Chinese, Japanese and Arabian schools of thought, I steered clear of narrow minded regional preferences. In a way my mind was hybridised. I can emphasize the fact that I did not attach myself to any one particular philosophical system or sect."[8]

Others, with their limited knowledge might have tried to evaluate him in a limited way. But, his intellect soared beyond their reach. Even after so much study and research, no one knows for sure, whether Prof. Murty was able to quench his innated spiritual thirst and fill the void in his heart. All we know is that his rigorous efforts imparted him an encyclopedic knowledge and made him a world-renowned scholar. We can notice in him an ambition to build a grand unified theory of world philosophy. He himself revealed so: "Recently I have been working on Mahayana Buddhism and Vedānta. Without denying the influence of Western philosophical ideas and adopting some concepts of Advaita and Buddhism, I am exploring the possibility of constructing a modern philosophical system which will not be antagonist to modern science or to the progress achieved so far. I am not sure, how far will I succeed in this enterprise. Because, from Plato to Russell and John Dewey in the West; from Upanishadic seers to Radhakrishnan in India and to Nishida in Japan, no philosophical system has ever gained universal acceptance. That's why I cannot predict the nature of response to the project I wish to take up."[9]

He reminded that the previous efforts of "Whitehead to formulate a comprehensive philosophy was not successful. Likewise the endeavour of Alexander to create a new system of philosophy also failed to take off. All such efforts are doomed in the face of constantly advancing Science and Technology. Yet we should not despair. We have to push ahead with our creative efforts in this regard."[10] With such a spirit Satchidananda Murty continued his work. We are still unable to gauge the extent of his success. Though he was in philosophical pursuit for so many decades, a feeling of discontent still haunted him.[11]

Nevertheless, Prof. Murty did not seem to worry. Having read Valmiki *Rāmāyaṇa* and Tulsi Das' *Rām Carit Mānas* repeatedly, he came to regard Lord Śrī Rāma as his ideal. Just when Rāma was all set to ascend the throne, he was pushed into the forest. Yet he remained unmoved in the face of bad news. He was unconcerned about the fact that he will have to bid adieu to all the luxuries of the palace and lead a very hard life in *Van-vaas* for 14 years. His face did not betray discontent or any other negative emotion. Kalidasa's *Raghu Vaṁśham* described that Rāma was calm and composed even in the face of adversity. Tulsi Das prayed that the serene face of Lord Rāma should stand by him throughout his life. Prof. Murty wrote that Lord Rāma's stoic nature has given him great strength. Surely, Lord Rāma must have inspired him to remain unmoved in the face of joy or grief.

Endnotes

1. Those who lead a supramundane life are called *Lokottara.*

2. Shri Aurobindo explained that the Superman strive to achieve spiritual sachidananda. His evolution proceeds through physical, mental and spiritual levels.
3. *The Sanātana Hindus* believe that human living is guided by *Ātma* and *Ādhyatma*. Those who seek spritual enlightenment are called spiritualists. *Akṣaram Brahma Param Svabhāvodhyātma mucyate* (Gītā 8:3).
4. *Bhagavad Gītā* refers to *Siddha sanghas* and Gaṇas (11:22). *Svakarmaniratah sidhim* (18:45). Siddhas are those who attained extrasensory powers. Kashmiri Saivism counts 80 kinds of powers. Siddhas are those who attain *Aṇimā, Laghimā, Prāpti, Prākāmyam, Mahimā, Eīsatvam, Vaśitvam, Kamaavasayithā*. To gain these powers one has to have Prajñā.
5. Mahāyāna preaches that every person has the potential to attain sambodhi. All the seekers are termed Bodhisattvas. Bodhi means Gyan (Buddha Gyanau), Samyak Gyanam Sambodhi.
6. Murty, K.S.(Co-ed.), *Current Trends in Indian Philosophy*, Andhra University Press, Waltair: 1972, Introduction, p.xiii.
7. Rao, K.R. et al. *Collected Criticism of Satchidananda Murty*, Triveni Publishers, Tenali, 1975, p.1.
8. Murty, K.S., "A Short Survey of My Views" , *Philosophers On Their Own Work,* vol./Band 14, International Federation of Philosophical Societies, H.Lang, 1977, Indiana University, Frankfurt: p.146.
9. From An Interview by Sri G. Suryanarayana Murty, Correspondent, For *Andhra Pathrika* Daily News Paper, published on 09-03-1982.
10. See the essay titled "Towards a New Philosophy" in the book *Towards A New Philosophy: The Unpublished Writings of K. Satchidananda Murty,* Ed. Ashok Vohra and Kotta Ramesh, 2024, Routledge: London.
11. Murty, K.S., *Vedic Hermeneutics,* Shri Lal Bahadur Shastri Sanskrit Vidyapeeth and Motilal Banarasidas, New Delhi: 1993, Preface, p.xxii.
12. Murty, K.S. "A Short Survey of My Views", Op.Cit., p.146; *Āndhra Patrika* Interview, 09-03-1982.

2

Breaking Barriers

Professor Satchidananda Murty, who was very well-versed in the ancient Indian theory of Beeja-Kshethra and modern nature-nurture debate, propounded that man's psychological maturity is shaped by the time, circumstances (economic, social, cultural) and the country he lives in.[1] He knew fully well that modern science contradicts the four-fold caste system and debunks the white supremacism of Western colonial rulers. This perception pervaded most of his writings. Using traditional interpretations, he deciphered traditional literature and simultaneously exposed the anti-traditional aspects contained therein. He clearly recognised that four-fold caste system was introduced to promote the selfish interests of certain classes. He emphatically declared that it is utterly meaningless to apply the anachronistic caste system to the 21st century society which is being moulded by modern science and technology. He expressed such progressive ideas in the first half of the 20th century itself. It would be a true homage to Prof. Murty, if we comprehend the background that shaped his thinking.

We all know that the first half of the 20th century (1900-1950) witnessed a great wave of political, economic and social change which swept through the world in general and India in particular. Western education spread liberal ideas among Indian students. People began to shun caste and gender discrimination and gradually a cultural renaissance dawned in the land. By inculcating nationalistic feeling among Indian youth, the Western education spurred them into joining struggle for independence. Though Sepoy mutiny of the previous century had failed, the establishment of Indian National Congress in 1885 served the educated class as a rallying point. The Congress gradually took over the leadership role of India's Independence movement. The Indian educated class was greatly inspired by the Western Renaissance, Industrial Revolution, French, American, Russian and later by Chinese revolutions. Socialist and Communist ideologies highly motivated them. But, gradually rifts arose among the Indian freedom fighters. They were split into extremists and moderates. While the moderates believed that independence or *Swaraj* can be won through the route of negotiations, the extremist faction debunked such ideas.

In the initial days, many militant movements, local rebellions and sporadic violence broke out. Alluri Sitarama Raju's militant struggle in the Manyam area of Andhra Pradesh was a case in point. The Kathevaram, Kotappa Konda incidents in Guntur district were also among the recorded instances of violence. After a railway line was laid via Kathevaram between Tenali and Madras, word got out that the then Viceroy will be traveling in that route. Lakkaraju Basavaiah of Kathevaram, Chukkapalli Ramaiah of Kancherla Palem got a country bomb made in Tenali and hid it in the bushes along the railway line. But, it was mistakenly triggered by a passerby, killing him in the event. The police booked criminal cases against Kathevaram natives Lakkaraju Basavaiah, Kotamraju Venkat Rayudu and Kancherlapalem native Chukkapalli Ramaiah. Among these three, Ramaiah was awarded life sentence in 1909, which created a sensation in the area. But, recent research shows that the Kathevaram incident was provoked by personal rivalries and it had nothing to do with the Vande Mataram movement. That's why Mamidipudi Venkata

Rangaiah commented: "Whether Ramaiah was a political criminal or not, only God knows."[2]

The Kotappa Konda incident was another sensational event in Guntur district. The natives of the district, traditionally celebrate the Shivaratri festival by riding bullock carts to the shrine on Kotappa Konda (a hill) and offer prayers. In the year 1909, Gade Chinnapa Reddy along with the Reddypalem (Chebrolu) villagers, went to Kotappa Konda in his decked up bullock cart. The situation was tense as those were the days of Vande Mataram movement. The bullocks turned lose in the festival commotion, provoking the police to cane them. Chinnapa Reddy entered into an argument with the police, the villagers protesting police high-handedness retaliated and beat up four policemen. Chinnapa Reddy was arrested and eventually hanged. The people still sing his heroic deed to this day. According to the additional details which emerged recently, Chinnapa Reddy had pushed down a police constable which led the police to believe that the constable was dead. The taking of Reddy into custody provoked the mob to attack and set fire to the police station with slogans of Vande Mataram. The furious mob killed two Government employees. In the melee two boys also died and many constables were injured. The police arrested 45 persons and 21 among them were convicted. Chinnapa Reddy was awarded death sentence. Four of the accused were sentenced to life and the rest were awarded punishment according to the intensity of their crimes.[3]

The above incidents show that the spirit of independence flared up early in Guntur district. In 1915 Gandhiji returned to India from South Africa where he developed his weapons of non-violence and satyagraha in the fight for civil rights. With Gandhi emerging as the undisputed leader, the Indian Independence movement shifted to a high gear by 1920. The freedom struggle which till then was confined to the educated class and a section of revolutionaries had begun to include farmers, merchants, women and various social classes. Gandhiji's sincerity, sage-like attire and speech, the weapons of non-violence and satyagraha perfected by him had motivated and united the common people and brought them into freedom movement. Guntur district erupted against the colonial rule, even before Gandhi gave a call for civil disobedience.

"No tax agitation" in Pedanandipadu led by Parvataneni Veerayya Chowdary, similar campaign in Chirala and Perala led by Duggirala Gopalakrishnayya, and the salt satygraha in Andhra region won laurels from Gandhiji. In the Palnadu region, Kanneganti Hanumanthu who led the no tax movement, was shot dead by the police is revered to this day. These incidents won a distinguished place for Guntur district in the Indian freedom struggle.[4]

Liberalism went hand in hand with freedom struggle. Rationalistic thought overcame superstitions and humaneness became paramount. Caste and creed were increasingly shunned.

Promoting female education, widow remarriages and opposing child marriages became instrumental in women upliftment. Under the able leadership of Konda Venkatappaiah, Gollapudi Sitarama Sastry, Unnava Lakshmi Narayana, Guntur district turned into a stronghold of Indian National Congress. Professor NG Ranga led the farmers of Tenali Taluq. Andhra Rashtra Raithangam was formed in 1923 and took up Raithu Rakshana Yatra from Tenali. In 1931, Andhra Rashtra Raithu Rakshana Sabha was held in that town. A Veda Pathshala was established at Tadiparru by 1924. The Sanskrit Vidya Peetha (Vedic school), established at Amritaluru in 1930 began to churn out Shudra (out caste) pandits well-versed in Sanskrit and Telugu. The Hindi- English School was launched at Govada in 1937 with the explicit aim of imparting education to all. Indian Farmer School was established at Yadavalli in 1938. Chebrolu turned out peace warriors for the freedom struggle. It sent many women into the movement, Mrs. Vasireddy Rajyalakshmi Devi like who ran the newspaper *Andhra Desam*. With such activities, the Guntur district shined like a beacon.[5]

The Colonial British Government was caught in a double blow of violent struggles of extremists on one hand and the non-violent movement of the moderates on the other. No matter whatever the path was chosen, the Indian nation was united in independence movement. And the British began to feel the heat. In such a scenario, the Second World War broke out. As the war proceeded, the freedom movement intensified and India became increasingly ungovernable. So the British had to flee after granting independence to India in 1947. We can rightly rejoice that it was largely a victory achieved by non-violent Satyagraha struggle. Nevertheless we should not disregard the very important role played by the Communists, Socialists, Humanists and social reformist movements. The Communists fought for economic equality right from 1930. The Socialist party worked for social equality. The Radical Humanist party took up the all-important task of analysing and exposing the hollowness of superstitions, caste system and other irrational ideas and practices and worked for the upliftment of humanity. Radical Humanism, an alternative socio-economic-political philosophy formulated by Manavendra Roy (popularly known as M.N. Roy) greatly influenced the educated and intellectual class. Tenali emerged as the centre of Rationalist movement. Kavi Raju Tripuraneni Ramaswamy Chowdary exposed the conceitedness of Puranas in his *Sūta Purāṇam* (1925-32) which was published in four volumes. His other works were *Bhagavad Gītā,* in the backdrop of War of Palnadu, 1940, *Śambūka Vadha* (1922) and *Khoonee* (1935).[6]

The magazine *Radical Humanist* was brought out by Avula Gopalkrishna Murty. It had a long run of publication. People like MV Rama Murty and Ravi Venkatadri also worked for intellectual enlightenment. These movements inculcated anti-Brahamanist rational thought and pushed Guntur district and Tenali taluk ahead on the path of cultural renaissance.

The Theosophical Society launched its Guntur branch around that time. The *Prārthana Samāj* of Keshav Chandra Sen was also established. *Ārya Samāj* of Swamy Dayanand Saraswati spread to Hyderabad from North India. It influenced both Krishna and Guntur districts. Paladugu Seshacharya launched *Sat Purohit Sangham* in Kunderu (Krishna district) to train non-brahmins as purohits and reduced dependence on Brahmin purohits in marriages and other rituals. Anne Keshava Rao (Keshacharya) began translating Vedas and Upanishads into Telugu with *Ārya Samāj* orientation. Later on he had settled in Hyderabad and worked for the growth of *Ārya Samāj*. Working from Kuchipudi (Tenali Taluk), Pandit Gopadeva Shastri helped *Ārya Samāj* movement spread in the district. He promoted female education and organised a school for the propagation of Hindi. By translating *Prasthāna Traya* into Telugu, he contributed to the development of *Ārya Samāj* in the district. All these movements deeply influenced Guntur district in general and Tenali Taluk in particular. Their impact can still be seen on the life of common people.

The visit to India by Śrī Lankan Buddhist monk Anagarika Dharmapala in 1891 gave a fillip to the revival of Buddha Dharma. By 1900, it reached Madras. Ponakala Lakshminarasu, an academic along with Ayothia Das launched schools in the SC, ST areas to work for their upliftment. He had published the book *The Essence of Buddhism* in 1907, which served as manifesto for the social reform movement launched by him. The fact that Anagarika

Dharmapala wrote the foreword to this book was really a great tribute to Lakshminarasu's genius. Even greater was Dr. B.R. Ambedkar's adoption of the book as the standard treatise for his Neo Budhist movement. He also wrote the preface for the fourth edition. More and more Buddhist books in Sanskrit began to influence Telugu land. Tirupati Venkata Kavulu, the Telugu poet duo, translated the Sanskrit work *Saundarananda* of Aswaghosha into Telugu in 1902. Brahmachari Ananda Mohan published Telugu translation of Rahul Sankrityayan's sanskritised Dharma Pada in 1925. Shri Raja Vasireddy Durga Sadashiveswara Prasad Bahadur, the ruler of Munagala principality, published the Pali original of *Dhamma Pada* along with Telugu translation in 1926. Duggirala Balaramakrishnayya, a Hindi pundit from Angaluru (Krishna district) published *Buddha Purana* in two parts which include, *Śrī Buddha Caritram, Śrī Buddha Gītā* (translation of *Dharma Pada*) and *Satya Dharma Prabodha Gītāvali* in 1927. He was honoured with the title—*Bouddha Vāñmaya Brahma.* Meanwhile, the Archeology department has begun the search for ancient Chaityas and discovered many ancient Buddhist sites in Guntur and Krishna districts. Thus the research by Western scholars was vindicated. Awareness of their Buddhist heritage grew in these two coastal districts.

In 1842, Father Heyer, an American missionary arrived in Guntur to establish a Church and ran a small school in its premises. He used to distribute clothes and medicines to the needy. Though Christian missionary activities began in a small way, they eventually expanded. Many schools and hospitals were established by the missionaries. With the indirect support of the British government, the Christian missionaries became catalysts in the development of the poor and depressed sections of Indian society. Alarmed by the inroads being made by the Christian religion, the Hindu community began efforts to save and revive their religion.

They established Hindu schools, colleges and universities. Proponents of Advaita, Viśiṣṭādvaita and Dvaita systems of Hindu philosophy took to popularising their ideas and practices. The first decade of 20th century witnessed Rāma Tirtha Ashram, Ramakrishna-Vivekananda Matts and Nama Sankeerthana Sanghas interpreting Vedanta in modern context. "Śrī Sītārāma Nāma Sankīrtana Sangha" launched in Rāma Nama kshetra of Guntur, "Śrī Rāma Tirtha Sevāshram" in Piduguralla attracted not only the traditional sections but reformist Hindus also.

Thus the cross-currents of independence movement, modern liberalist thought, new economic and political

With his parents Sri Veerabhadraiah and Smt. Ratnanmma.

ideologies, social reform movements and Hindu religious revival began to sweep across the Telugu society.

At such a critical juncture Satchidananda Murty was born to the couple – Kotta Veerabhadraiah and Ratnamma on 24th September, 1924. That auspicious moment filled the couple's life with joy. Their earlier offspring did not survive beyond a few days or months. So, Satchidananda Murty's birth, his event-free growth and development brought immense joy to his parents. They aptly named their house—*Ānandāśram*. Satchidananda Murty vividly recalled the love showered by his parents in his childhood and the care they took on his education, in an article written for *Philosophers on their own work*. It is obvious that the love and affection showered on children, positively shapes up their personality in later years. The accomplished life of Satchidananda Murty bears testimony to this.

He acknowledged in the above article, the influences of his father, family, environment, teachers, the books he studied and the social conditions on his progress.[7] We can clearly discern the evolution of his thinking by chronologically analysing his works in Sanskrit, English, Hindi and Telugu. The winds of change blowing in the nation's intellectual life, moulded Satchidananda Murty's thinking. He gradually broke out of the traditional framework and struck out on his own intellectual path. By grasping the intricacies of international philosophical musings, he dedicated himself to find a way for the spiritual well-being of the mankind.

A look into Prof. Satchidananda Murty's genealogy reveals many interesting aspects. His childhood name was Satchidanand Prasad. The original name of his native village Sangam Jagarlamudi was Chamarla Puri. Satchidananda Murty's ancestors had to migrate from Kodali to this village due to some exigencies. Kotha Bhavaiah Chowdary in his

Sanga Bhūpālīyam (1929), unveiled many fascinating details about the events of 230 years ago. Bhavaiah Chowdary's book was a three part poetic composition. He began his book with the story of Venkatadri Chowdary's dream. The information provided by him about the ruling classes of the day, will be of immense interest to the present day generation. Bhavaiah recounts the way Chamarlapuri became Sangam Jagarlamudi. In the book, the actual history of Kotta lineage starts with Suranna's family, 100 years after Venkatadri Chowdary's dream episode. Appanna was the eldest of Suranna's seven sons. Sanganna was the fifth among six sons of Appanna. Bhavaiah was the second of four sons of Sanganna. The Kotha family tree of Sangam Jagarlamudi began with the offspring of Bhavaiah and his wife Rangamma. The eldest son of Bhavaiah was Sitayya who had to adopt Subbarayudu, because he could not have male offspring. Veerabhadraiah was the son of Subbarayudu and his wife Maha Lakshamma. And Sachidananda Murty was born to Veerabhadraiah and Ratnamma (see the genealogy table).

Bhavaiah explains that Sanganna of Kotta family tree was the contemporary of Raja Vasireddy Venkatadri Naidu (1761-1816), the ruler of Amaravathi and Janganna, the Zamindar of Rachur. The Vijayanti palace built by Venkatadri Naidu in Amaravati was ruined under the onslaught of time. Later the ruins were cleared to give way to a new building. Opposite to the new building, a spacious tiled house named Rajavaari Kota (caste) can be seen on the east side of the road. The old palace of Rachuri Zamindar is still located at Pallekoona village near Repalle in which his successors still live. Kotta family took some villages on mortgage and ruled them as Izaridars. That's why Bhavaiah Chowdary named his book *Sanga Bhūpālīyam.* Kotta family Izara was consisted of the villages—Chamarlapuri, Vadlamudi, Eemani, Parimi, Kuchipudi (Tenali Taluq), Nara

Koduru, Manduru, Chinagadelavarru, Pedagadelavarru, Yamarru, Devarayapalli and some others. They are the Inamdars of there villages to look after the welfare of those who live there and to develop help them. They are in return pay some amount collected as tax from the inhabitants to the jamindars of Raichur and Amaravati.

Venkatadri Chowdary, the ancestor of Kotta family was a native of Kodali village which frequently suffered vagaries of nature. One night, God Sangameshwara appeared in his dream and told him that he is the deity of Chamarlapuri located across the river Krishna, 20 miles away from Kodali. He advised Venkatadri to come to Chamarlapuri as the land and climate was very conducive to agriculture. Following the Lord's directive, Venkatadri shifted to Chamarlapuri and set up family residence under a Shami (Jammi) tree near the Sangameshwara temple. The locals warmly welcomed and gifted them a pucca bungalow. The Kotta family began to prosper there.

It is interesting to note that the above narrative names of the village only as Chamarlapuri without the suffix of Jagarlamudi. The temple is still called Chamarlapuri Sangameswara Alayam. The book *Sanga Bhūpālīyam* was published from Sangam Chamarlamudi. On the cover of the Sanskrit book *Sangameshāṣhṭakam Śrī Veṇugopāla Stotram* written by Satchidananda Murty, he describes himself as *Kartā Kotta Satchidananda Murty Gītā Nidhi, Rashtra Bhāṣa Viśāradaśca, Chamarlapuri*. He dedicated his *Nāma Sankeertana Mahimā* (1937), a translated work, to "Chamarlapuri Sangameswara Swami." This book was published by Śrī Sitarama Nama Sankeertana Sangham, Guntur. The name of the village was again mentioned as Chamarlapuri on the cover of *Hanumad Vijayam* (1938). So it is obvious that Sangam Jagarlamudi was known as Chamarlapuri till recently and later on it changed into Sangam Chagarlamudi and finally Sangam Jagarlamudi. It may be recalled that during Basaveswara's movement (13th Century), Siva temples were called "Koodali Sangama". The same tradition might have reflected in the name of local Sangameswara temple.

Bhavaiah Chowdary explains in his *Sanga Bhūpālīyam* that the word Sangam was derived from the confluence of the rivers Krishna and Tunga Bhadra. But, there is no evidence of river Krishna flowing down here. The construction of the Anicut at Bezwada was completed in 1855. Later the colonial British Government built the Buckingham canal as a transportation route to Madras. The reference to Krishna-Tungabhadra confluence must have cropped up later. Anyway, Sangameshwara temple must have existed since earlier times. The *ijara* quoted by Bhavaiah Chowdary contains the name Chamarlapuri but not Jagarlamudi.[8] He placed the location of the village on the banks of Krishna but didn't say anything about Krishna-Tungabhadra confluence. So it would be reasonable to assume that Chamarlapuri did have a Veera Shaiva Koodali Sangameshwara temple, but as the name of the village changed to Jagarlamudi, it took on the suffix 'Sangam'. Anyway, in contemporary times, the Buckingham canal flowing in the west of Sangam Jagarlamudi and the Kommura canal branching off from it to the north of the village have enabled wet land agriculture and raising of plantation crops.

Kotta Sanganna Family Tree

For the ease of printing the family tree is split into two parts. Keeping them parallelly will give the full picture. (See Page No. 26 and 27)

Endnotes

1. Murty, K.S., *Evolution of Philosophy in India,* St.Michael's Industrial School Press, Guntur; 1952.

2. Hanumantha Rao, B.S.L., *Andhrula Charitra (History of Andhra)*, Vishalandra Publishing House, Hyderabad, 2003, p. 575.
3. Ibid., p. 573.
4. Veerabhadra Rao, M., *Guntur District Independence Movement* (in Telugu; *Guntur Zillā Swārājya Udyamam Document*) 1920-30, Prominent Levels (*Ujvala Ghattalu*), Guntur: 1974.
5. Veeraiah, D., (Ed.,) *Guntur Mandal Sarvasvamu—History Section*, Third Edition 1996, pp. 184-190.
6. Venkata Subbaiah, G., *Kavirāja Jīvitam- Sāhityam*, 1970, pp. 22 ff., https://te.wikipedia.org
7. Murty, K.S., "A Short Survey of My Views", *Philosophers on Their Work*, vol./Band 14, International Federation of Philosophical Societies, H.Lang, 1977, Indiana University, Frankfurt : p.146; *Andhra Patrika* Interview, 9-3-1982.
8. Murty, K.S., *Śrīmad Bhagavad Gītā Savyakhyanamu (The Song Celestial)*, Ananda Ashramamu Grandhamala (self-published), 1941, Sangam Jagarlamudi, Preface, p. XIV.

Family Tree-I

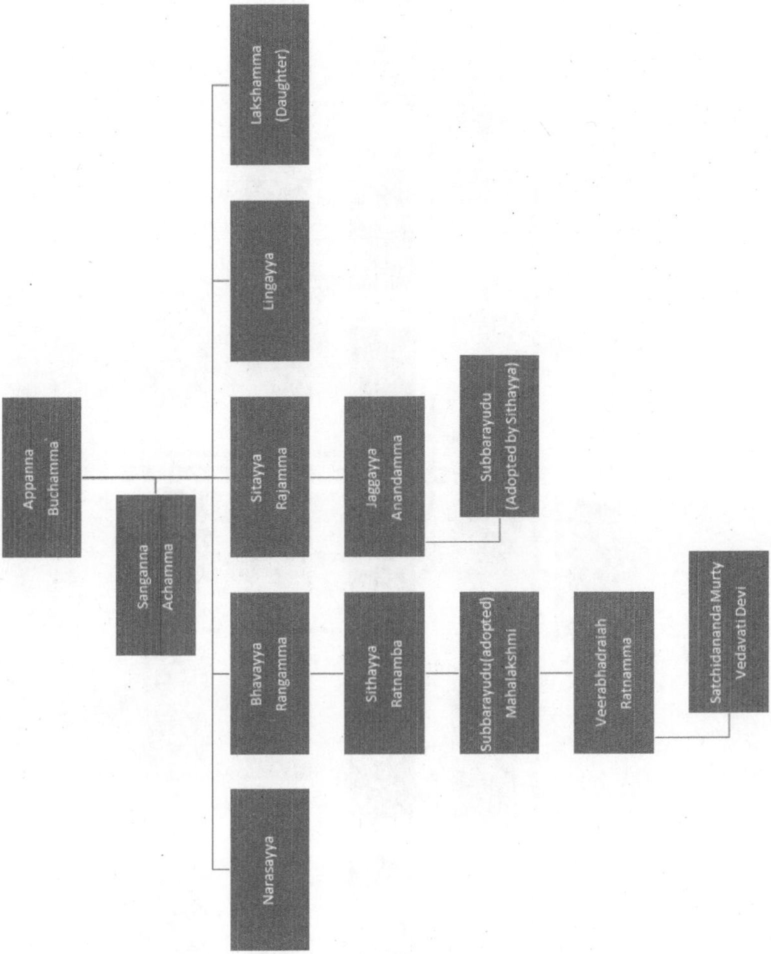

Family Tree-II

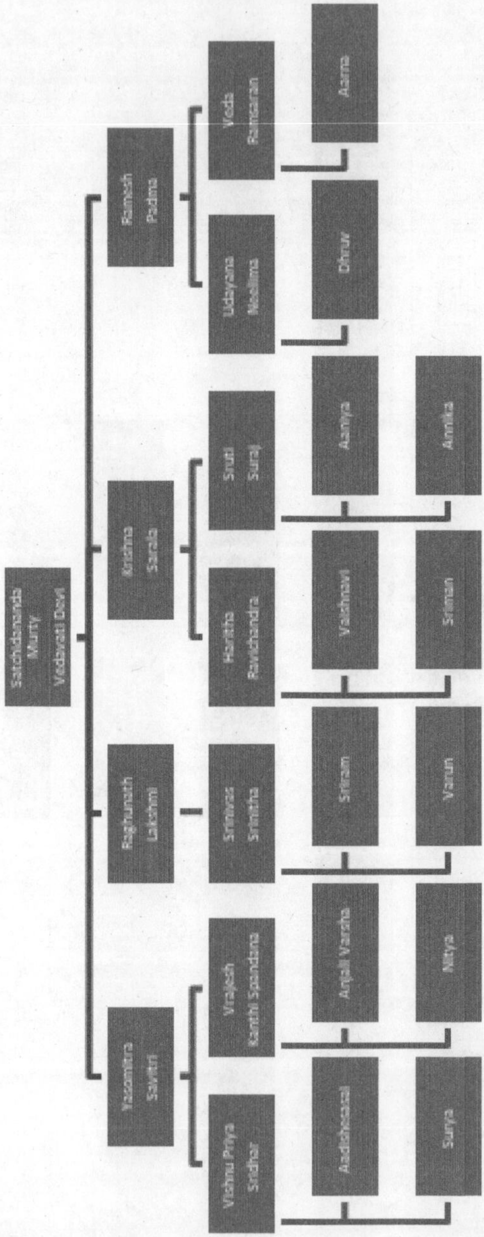

3

Education For Transformation

Professor Satchidananda Murty was a self-educated scholar. His learning activity was not merely confined to the formal classroom, college or a university. It continued in an informal manner also. He was a life-long student who kept on with multidisciplinary studies. He dedicated himself to the acquisition of true knowledge. Education is called *Vidyā* in Sanskrit and it is derived from the root word *Vid*. Those who look with Western eyes can't grasp the true meaning of education. Amar Sinha defines education as *"Vetti yathāvathathvam Jñanam yayā sā vidyā"* meaning that Vidya unveils the basic principles or elements of a particular subject. This follows the Buddha's saying *"Yatha Bhoothoo Jana Dassana"* (*Jñāna Darśana*). Darśana implies internal visualization (Darśana), internally experiencing a deeper truth. According to the Buddha education is synonymous with *Jnana Darshana*. A perceptive mind can instantly recognize how distant modern education is from true education. *Jñāna Darśana* i.e., true education is eternal and without a beginning or end. It cannot be restricted to a particular period of time or a fixed curriculum. Satchidananda Murty embarked on such a quest for true knowledge and little wonder it was such an eternal endeavour.

Jampala Gopal Rao, a relative and Revenue Officer, recalls the childhood of Satchidananda Murty's life. His parents Veerabhadraiah and Ratnamma loved Satchidananda Murty so much that they could not bear to part with him even for a few minutes. So the chubby boy mostly remained indoors and from behind the fortress like walls used to look at the things and people outside diffidently. Satchidananda Murty almost never came out to play with neighbourhood boys—Gopal Rao recalled. Thus, Murty led a solitary life since his childhood. Perhaps, it was due to this love of homebound life, Satchidananda Murty at one time toyed with the idea of dropping out of Honours studies in Andhra University and return home to take up cultivation. This information was also provided by Gopal Rao.[1]

It is a well-known fact that, parents are the first teachers for every student and home is the first school. Satchidananda Murty was no exception. Though his father was not highly educated, having stopped short of secondary education, he made an extensive study of books by Śrī Aurobindo, Vivekananda, Rāma Thirtha and Dayananda. He imbibed the broad outlook preached by these spiritual works. He refused to confine himself to any one particular religion or way of thinking. In short, he shunned narrow mindedness in philosophical pursuits and believed in the equality of all religions. Satchidananda Murty's mother stood by his father always. Such a family

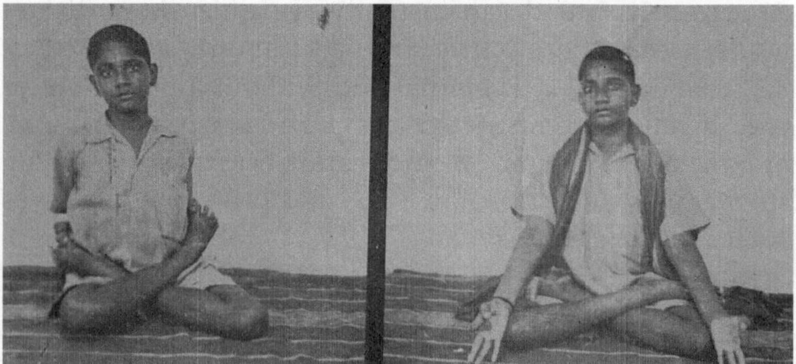

Practicing Yoga.

background naturally helped Satchidananda Murty in attaining intellectual maturity. Following his father's footsteps, he took to book-reading from a tender age and made it a daily activity throughout his life span which helped him greatly.

Murty's father Veerabhadraiah had a good knowledge of traditional Sanskrit books and adequate understanding of contemporary political developments. He obviously recognised the need to groom his son in both these areas. Accordingly, he engaged a Sanskrit teacher and a Hindi

As an Adolescent.

tutor to impart education to Satchidananda Murty as soon as he was 5 years old. He was initiated into education (*Akṣarābhyāsam*) with writing Sanskrit letters in Deva Nagari script. Gadiyaram Shivayya Shastry, a Smartha Brahmin and a grammarian educated in Vijayanagaram was Satchidananda Murty's first guru. The boy's Sanskrit education went on for about 6 years. Thanks to this, Satchidananda Murty was able to read and grasp the meaning of Sanskrit texts in a tender age itself. Later he continued Sanskrit education in Hindu College, Guntur for another six years. Palle Poorna Prajnacharya, a noted grammarian and Dvaita scholar was his teacher. Subsequently, Satchidananda Murty got necessary guidance to further his Sanskrit studies from renowned poet and scholar Kashi Krishnamacharya, the first Prabhutva Asthana Kavi. Following his instruction, he took up daily reading of Valmiki *Ramayana* and also epics and classical plays. Thanks to the grounding in Sanskrit, received during childhood, Satchidananda Murty was able to read and easily understand complex Sanskrit works later in his life.

Satchidananda Murty took up Hindi studies also and got the certificate of "Rashtra Bhasha Visharada". Afterwards he acquired proficiency in English when he completed Faculty of Arts (FA) in Hindu college. Jampala Gopal Rao recalled that Satchidananda Murty was ahead in all the subjects except Maths and Physics. So, it can be safely assumed that Satchidananda Murty opted for humanities rather than sciences in his College education. It must have been a big help when he took up Philosophy in PG studies. Later on, his analytical writings replete with references to Mathematics, Physics, Chemistry, Botany, Zoology, Nuclear Science and Psychology prove that he overcame his shortcomings in Sciences.

During the Second World War (1939-45), when Japan bombed Pearl Harbour, the British Colonial Government temporarily shifted Andhra University to Guntur and Vijayawada. After completing his studies in Hindu College, Guntur, Satchidananda Murty joined Andhra University as a student in B.A Honours (Philosophy). In those days, students after completing two year F.A course can opt for 2- year B.A and later M.A. There was another system in which F.A students can go for 3-year B.A (Honours) and one-year M.A. PG course. Andhra University offered 3- year B.A (Honours). Satchidananda Murty joined B.A (Honours) in Philosophy and attained first class in 1946. One year later he did M.A.

While in B.A (Honours) Satchidananda Murty, opted for Advaita as elective subject. During those days, he made an indepth study of such books as History of Western Philosophy, Indian Philosophy, Logic and Theory of Knowledge, Psychology, Contemporary Western Philosophy (of A.N. Whitehead). Satchidananda Murty lauded two great professors who influenced him deeply. One was Saileswara Sen, a Bengali professor. He was a student of Mr. Fedegan of Holland, a Sanskrit scholar who delved deep into Vaiseshika system of Indian philosophy. Sen did research into Nava Dweepa Logic and Modern Law under the tutelage of Fedegan. Sen analysed the relationship between Modern Law and Mathematical Logic. He taught Indian Philosophy to Satchidananda Murty. Professor P.T. Raju, a student of Dr. S. Radhakrishnan and renowned scholar in the USA was the second teacher who deeply influenced Satchidananda Murty. Raju taught him Logic, Contemporary Indian Philosophy and Contemporary Western Philosophy. Murty wrote very humbly "Thus my initiation into Sanskrit and later day mentoring by these great scholars enabled me to read and understand the original texts of Indian philosophy on my own. After my studies I joined a job in Tirupati, where my colleagues and scholars in Viśiṣṭādvaita viz., D.T. Thathacharya,

K.C. Varadacharya spurred my interest in Mīmāṁsā and Vaiṣṇavism.

It was due to their help and the seeds of knowledge sown by them in my mind, that I was able to pursue my later day efforts. Whatever success I may have attained, I owe it to them to a large extent."[2]

Murty's choice of Advaita as a specialization subject and diligent study of Whitehead's book prove that he was no casual or mediocre student but a serious and diligent one. Little wonder he passed the Honours exam with a first class in 1946. Later on, he opted for Advaita as a research subject. He made an in-depth study of original texts of Advaita and brought out a book *Reason and Revelation in Advaita Vedanta* in two parts (1954). He clearly established the importance accorded to rationality and enlightenment by Advaita and thus won appliance from noted philosophers. He made a deep study of Whitehead's works, one of which was prescribed as a text book in Western Philosophy. After an extensive study, Satchidananda Murty declared that Whitehead ranks as No. 1 among 20th Century Western philosophers. After post-graduation in 1946, he took a position of lecturer in Śrī Venkateswara College, Tirupati for one year. During that time, he taught Rene Descartes' book *Discourses De La Methode* to undergraduate students. His way of teaching mesmerized the students. Subsequently, he translated Descartes' book into Telugu with the help of his friend K.V. Narasimham and published it in 1959 under the title: *Rene Descartes' Pramāṇa Padhati pai Prasaṅgamu.*

Prof. Satchidananda Murty's system of teaching does not restrict itself to fixed curriculum, conferring of academic degrees and help to find employment. It is an unceasing learning process. As we have already seen that Prof. Murty eminently translated *Bhagavd Gītā* and received praise from pundits all over India. On the invitation of pundits he travelled all over the country, addressing the scholars, Peethadhipatis and rulers of princely states in various seminars and conventions. He was honoured with the titles like *"Gītā Nidhi"*, *"Gītā Sāstra Kesari"* and *"Upanyāsaka Ratna"*. Satchidananda Murty, who as a boy spent long hours in the study room of his home to earn the nickname- Book Worm, gradually turned the whole world his library and immersed himself in the study of world philosophy.

Murty did not confine to any particular subject. Starting with the traditional texts, moving on to philosophy and gradually encompassing various topics, he had immensely expanded the horizons of his knowledge. In an interview given to *Andhra Patrika* Murty remarked: "Right from my parents, teachers to intellectuals I met- everybody and every book that I read inspired me to deepen my study and contemplation. I studied many books on religion, history, politics, and social sciences including anthropology, numerous writings on culture and on international relations. Unconstrained by parochial feelings and academic limitations I took up extensive studies on Indian, Western, Chinese, Japanese and other Asian philosophies."[3]

Satchidananda Murty never regarded himself as a philosopher. He described himself as an ardent student of culture and philosophy. He sought answers to the following questions:

- Can Philosophy help us realize the Truth which is inaccessible to the ordinary mind and even scientific knowledge? Can it help us make our lives meaningful?
- Does Philosophy help us reform our ways of thinking, ideologies and values and inspire a novel perspective in the process?

- Can it promote equality and fraternity among us?
- Can it to help integrate individual and the collective lives and promote Unity?

Finding answers to these questions was the purpose of his study and contemplation[4].

After leaving Śrī Venkateswara College Tirupati, 1947, Professor Murty joined at Mayurbhanj (Orissa) as Professor of Logic for a few months. In 1948 he wrote a series of articles for the magazine *Śrī Ramakrishna Prabha* published by Ramakrishna Matt.

He recapitulated the work of ancient, medieval and modern Indian and Western philosophers for the February 1948 Golden Jubilee issue. He classified their expositions into seven groups in his essay 'Tattva Mīmāmsā'. At just 24 years of age, he did a wonderful job of encapsulating the philosophers' quest for answers to the ultimate questions. These questions run something like this:

1. Savants like Adi Sankara in India, FH Bradley in the West pondered over the question whether this dynamic world is real or is there some other Absolute substratum to it? Though they concluded that this world is an illusion springing up from *Avidyā* (ignorance), they did not explain the reasons or basis for this *Avidyā*.
2. Some philosophers refuse to see the world as an illusion and postulate that God is the Creator of this world. But they fail to explain why God created a world so full of suffering instead of a pleasant one? But they hold that the world is the result of human actions and God's play. Madhva and Śrī Chaitanya in India, Saint Thomas Aquinas and Descartes come under this category.
3. It is futile to search for the First Cause of the universe outside of it. That Cause or Elan Vital

should exist within the universe itself. It is the source and driving force of development of all beings. Charles Darwin and Henri Bergson subscribe to this view. Much before them Sāṁkhyā philosophy and Ramanuja's Viśiṣṭādvaita upheld the same view.

4. A certain school of philosophers argue that even Evolution should have a prime cause. Out of nothing, nothing comes out. As the universe is self-originated and self-organizing, it is futile to query about the origins of Creation. Prof. Murty did not name the philosophers who stick to this view.

5. There is another kind of argument which goes something like this: Things are not real. The universe is simply a chain of events. It is a process, changing from one condition to another. In this universe, only change is constant, there is nothing permanent. Buddhist school of thought and modern philosophers like Whitehead subscribe to this view. Abhinavagupta's *Spandana Vāda* also falls into the same category.

6. The Universe and Human life came into being by some chance occurrence...through accidental actions of cosmic forces. It has no meaning or ultimate purpose as such. Indian Carvakas and Western writers like HG Wells held out this argument.

7. The visible universe with all the attendant phenomena is perfectly real. Siddhas through their extra sensory perception (ESP) sense the existence of a transcendental reality. Experiments in USA prove that ESP exists. Those who couldn't attain to such a transcendence are not competent to offer counter- arguments. The eternal substratum gives rise to the visible, ever changing universe.

Sakta Darshana, Bhaskara and Śrī Aurobindo put forward this argument.[5]

How to make our way forward out of this maze? The arguments and counter-arguments regarding the existence of the universe form the subject matter of Metaphysics. Various philosophers advocated a plethora of arguments. Yet none of their views could be proved one way or the other. A true seeker should recognize that all these theories and arguments are products of dry logic and that the Ultimate, Absolute Truth is beyond all logic. This realization should lead us on the path of Yoga and meditation, opined Professor Murty.

Sir CR Reddy detected the solemnity and gravity in Satchidananda Murty's writings much earlier. That's why he invited the young year old Satchidananda Murty and appointed him as Professor of Philosophy, Andhra University in 1949. This provided him an excellent opportunity to deepen his understanding by taking up extensive studies and to meet national and international scholars. In 1954 Professor Murty embarked on a study tour of Europe. He toured Europe again in 1956 on invitation. There he participated in many seminars and conferences. Prof. Murty describes his experiences of foreign visits and interacting with scholars as follows:

"From 1954 till date I toured Europe, USA, Middle East, Soviet Union and China many times. I met noted academics in the inter-disciplinary seminars. In 1954 and again in 1956 I met Betrand Russell at his home. We discussed about Philosophy and the role of India in its development. I already published our discussion as an article in which I put forward two important points. The first one is the threat of Nuclear War and the second one is about the problems posed by overpopulation to India. Though Russell and Radhakrishnan differed in their philosophical outlook, the former was highly respectful of Radhakrishnan."

"I also met another philosopher KJ Pex who was one of the founders of Existentialism. Though born in Germany, Pex left the country during Hitler's time and came to Switzerland where he worked as a professor. The significant quality of Pex was that instead of confining to Western philosophy, he made a deep study of Indian and Chinese philosophies also. He gave prominence to Nagarjuna and Chinese savants in his work — *World Thinkers.*"

"I met many other thinkers in Paris and Switzerland during my study tour and learnt about newer streams of thought. In Switzerland I held talks with Carl Gustav Jung, a student of famed Psychoanalyst Sigmund Freud. By combining dream analysis, religion and poetry Jung developed Analytical Psychology. The long discussions I had with him was really memorable. I also met J.M. Bochenski, a scholar of Mathematical Logic. He posed this question to me: 'India has great philosophers like Sankara and Ramanuja. Instead of pursuing their school of thought, why are you wasting time by going round the likes of Russell, Ryle and Wittenstein.' Bohinski was a Catholic Monk who made extensive studies of Oriental and Western systems of logic to write a book *History of Logic*. I was very much glad for the praise he showered on Indian visionaries." Professor Murty continued: "I toured USA, Greece and Japan to meet noted philosophers there. I have also met religious teachers in Egypt, Turkey and Iran. Participated in many seminars there. All those meetings and discussions had no doubt deeply influenced me, though I can't pinpoint the specific influences."

Professor Murty delineated two distinct streams of thought which gained prominence after the Second World

War. One is existentialism and the second is Humanism that swayed the protestant countries. Thomism (Ideas of St Thomas Aquinas) was prevalent in Catholic countries. In USA, Pragmatism which claims that a proposition is true if it works satisfactorily, gained ground. William James and John Dewy were its proponents. Existentialism and Logical Positivism also spread their influence over America. Marxism is the dominant philosophy in Russia and Eastern Europe. They regarded Dialectical Materialism and Historical Materialism as the true philosophies. At the same time there are Indologists too. Indian Buddhism, Vedanta, Vaishnavism and Shaivism are also being studied both in Soviet Union and China.

Recently Ordinary Language Philosophy, Scientific Philosophy are drawing much interest. Newer fields of study like History of Philosophy, History of Science, Philosophy of Culture are emerging. All these systems of thought regard that the task of philosophy is to find solutions to the contemporary problems. Quest for the Ultimate Truth was long ago abandoned, Prof. Murty opined.

Till the Second World War broke out, Indian intellectuals made extensive efforts to apply Indian philosophy to modern conditions. After the war, our scholars who toured the West began to work in Existentialism and Ordinary Language Philosophy. Along with them study of Vedanta, Buddhism, Jainism, Navya Nyaya were taken up in a big way. But Western Universities are not making any fresh studies into Indian and Chinese philosophies. They are simply confining themselves to the study of a few translated works on Oriental philosophies. Though eminent scholars like Karl Maxford and HH Price advocate that the Oriental philosophies are in no way inferior to Western thought, their advice is falling on deaf ears. Thus Professor Murty provides us with a tour de force of philosophy. His erudition is truly amazing.

Endnotes:

1. Gopala Rao, J., "Śrī Satchidananda Murty and his Contribution to Philosophy", Souvenir Volume, *Institute of Indic Studies*, Santhi Ashramam, Waltair.
2. An Interview by Sri G. Suryanarayana Murty, Correspondent, For *Andhra Pathrik*a Daily News Paper, published on 09-03-1982.
3. Ibid.
4. Murty, K.S., "A Short Survey of My Own Views", in *Philosophers on their Own Work,* Vol./Band 14, International Federation of Philosphical Societies, H.Lang.1977,Indiana University, p.146: Bern.Frankurt.
5. "Tattva Mīmāṃsā", *Śrī Ramakrishna Prabha,* Ramakrishna Mattam, Madras, 1948, pp. 54-60.

4
Family Ties

Rigvedic sages were all householders, i.e., Gṛhasthas- meaning they didn't renounce the world to embrace a celibate life. They enjoyed marital bliss, led a family life complete with kids they owned vast cattle-wealth, wined and dined lavishly on nutritious beef. Those Rishis very frequently performed elaborate rituals and *yajñas* with prodigious offerings to various deities. Individually and collectively they lived full lives – in some cases to more than a 100 springs. The hymns they sung rapturously in honour of the forces of nature, formed the essence of our rich, ancient heritage. These hymns were famously called- Riks. All this goes to prove that Indian culture is basically a Gṛhastha culture. That's why our Brahmanas i.e commentaries on Vedas, regarded family life or Gṛhastha Ashrama as the highest form of living. Stressing the importance of studying Vedas during youth, our ancient Smrithis and scriptures treated Brahmacharya and Garhastya as Ashramas. Our scriptures treated Vedas equal to Brahma- the One God. Brahmacharya means the period in which the recital and study of Vedas is taken up (*Tadadhyanārtham Vratamap*i). Through such studies one will be able to lead a righteous family life—which is the ultimate aim of Brahmacharis, Gṛhastha and Sramaṇas. Here it should be stressed that there are two different kinds of Brahmacharyas. One is defined by Shramana, Buddha and Jain traditions and the other one by the Brahmins. The first kind equates Brahmacharya with leading an ideal and resolute life.

Manu Smṛti reveals that it takes at least 12 years to make a deep study of each Veda. So one requires 36 years to complete the study of 3 Vedas (the fourth one was added much later). Finally it takes 48 years to learn all the four Vedas. Only after completing Vedic studies one should think of entering marital bond- such was the ancient decree. But, it was more honoured in the breach than in actual practice by *Māṇavakas* (Brahmin Brahmacharis). Manu Smṛti itself provides ample evidence of Brahmin celibates rushing into marriage before completing the study of three Vedas. There were many funny characters who jumped into marital bondage after completing the study of just one or a half or even a quarter of Veda. Manu Smṛti too treats *Grihastyāśrama* as the highest among four Ashramas *a la* Vedic smrithis. *Sarveṣāmapi Caitesām Veda Smṛti vidhānataḥ Gṛhastha Ucyate Śreṣṭaḥ (Manu:6:89)*. Just like rivers and rivulets conjoin the Sea, Śramaṇakas also merge in the ocean of Gṛhastha (Manu 6:89). A person, who performs his duties (*Karma*) in the course of life, marries a suitable girl, leads a virtuous family life, properly feeds his servants and makes offerings to gods, ancestors and guests without fail is deemed to be following an ideal *Gṛhastha dharma*—so says Kauṭilya's Artha Śāstra. All those who own houses (Grihas) are not Gṛhasthas, because one may be the owner of a house without marrying or even before that. The word *Griha* has two meanings. One—a dwelling, the other a wife. The person with a wife is called *Grihi* (*Griham Bhāryayā sā asyastīti Gṛhī*). So a *Gṛhastha* is the person who lives in a house along with his wife. Only such a person can fulfill his *Gṛhastha dharma* viz., feeding guests and servants and making offerings to ancestors and gods.

The house of Kotta seems to be deeply influenced by Manu Smṛti. The current generations may find it strange that Kotta Seethayya though a father of four girls should adopt Subba Rayudu. Seethayya was only following the Manu rule 9:69 which states that sons will save fathers from a particular kind of hell *Punnāma Naraka* (*Punnāmo narakād yasya tārāyaate pitaram sutah*). Subba Rayudu and Maha Lakshmi bore a son Kotta Veerabhadraiah who married Ratnamma. The couple gave birth to Satchidananda Murty. Steeped in ancient traditions Veerabhadraiah nurtured his son accordingly. All this acculturation deeply influenced and attuned Satchidananda Murty to our rich heritage. Like Lord Ram who always honoured his father's wishes, Satchidananda Murty married a girl, his father chose for him. The bride is none other than the daughter of his maternal uncle Jampala Koteswara Rao and Seshagiramma of Duggirala village. Satchidananda married 18 year old Vedavati Devi in an auspicious time on 23rd April 1942. Filled with joy Veerabhadraiah blessed the newly weds. His lyrical benediction was a strong blend of nationalism, regionalism, spirit of freedom struggle, and care for women welfare. Reflecting the glory of Telugu language, he went on: "I bless thee on your first big step together in this beautiful and lovely spring. The fame of our lush green motherland flowing with perennial rivers, watering fertile fields and peopled with men of brilliance reached far and wide. While our Northern brothers are renowned for physical strength, we the Southern's are famed for our mental acumen. The great works of Andhra poets fill our hearts with joy forever. Andhra kings always nourished this creative spring. Lovers of Telugu poetry are men of refined tastes. Andhra womenfolk are marching ahead in literature, social reform and national movements. Historically Kamma people gained name and fame as military commanders under Kakatiya rulers. But right now our homeland is reeling under foreign rule and mired in poverty. Unlike the common and average couples, educated couples like you should help our land reach great heights once again. Long live Mother India."

Satchidananda Murty's wedding was held in April, 1942 i.e., during the summer vacations right after he completed FA at Hindu College in Guntur, but before he joined BA Honors course in Andhra University during 1943. He graduated in 1946, got into teaching which enabled him to further his studies, conduct research and finally earning him a doctorate. Later he held many higher posts with distinction. It should be noted that his married life while in no way impeding him, in fact helped him with his studies. No bonds or burdens can hinder a man moving ahead with a steely resolve. Thanks to an understanding life-partner, Satchidananda Murty's

At the time of his marriage.

marital ship sailed on blissfully. The couple had their first son on 7th October 1946 around the time Satchidananda Murty completed BA Honours. He requested Mr. Saileswar Sen, his professor, to name his son. Accordingly Professor Sen named the child 'Yasomitra' after the great Mahayana Buddhist philosopher. Later Satchidananda Murty fathered three more sons- Raghunatha (13-07-1948), Krishna (1-07-1949) and Ramesh (12-11-1950). Even while his family was expanding Satchidananda Murty never let it affect his studies. His writings, musings, the process of finding solutions went on unbroken. While it was his father who shouldered all the family responsibilities till Satchidananda Murty's marriage, it was his wife who did the same after the event. Thus both kept all the distractions away from Prof. Satchidananda Murty. This was recounted by Professor Murty himself in one of his books. Little wonder that he dedicated the book to his wife Vedavati Devi in 1971 with deep love and affection.

All along their 60 years long marital life (i.e., till 27-10-2002 the date of Vedavati Devi's demise) Professor Satchidananda Murty was always busy with study tours, giving lectures in universities and academic forums in India and abroad. He toured England, Germany, France, Switzerland, Italy, USA, Russia, China, Japan, Arabia and numerous other countries. He gave talks and submitted many papers. Every research paper published by him was rich in detail and displayed deep understanding. Later he developed many of his talks into books with valuable additions and suitable references. All of Satchidananda Murty's works are regarded as classics and serve as reference books to this day. His master works like *Indian Spirit, Far Eastern Philosophies, The Realm of Between, Hinduism and its Development* and *Vedic Hermeneutics* exerted deep impact on later-day researchers.

Satchidananda Murty's thought continued to have a major influence on Indian Universities, Peethas of

Sanskrit and other languages and Centres of Philosophy studies which used to invite him to grace numerous special occasions. He played a crucial role in shaping up Indian Philosophical Congress as its Chairman. He visited, addressed and submitted important papers in almost all distinguished universities in India like: Osmania University, Śrī Venkateswara University, Dr. B.R. Ambedkar Open Varsity, Śrī Padmavathi Women's University, Madras University, Annamalai University, Bharathiyar University, Marathwada University, Thilak Maharashtra Vidyapeeth, Ravindra Bharathi University, Viswa Bharathi University, Gulbarga University, Vikram University, and Banaras Hindu University, Rajasthan University and Kashmir University. All this shows the vast amount of time and effort he put into deep research and writings.

"The ideal house-wife will cook and serve a thousand guests even if they arrive late at midnight"- so described Allasani Peddana- the great poet of Vijayanagara Emperor Krishna Deva Raya's court. Vedavati Devi, the better-half of Prof. Satchidananda Murty was exactly such an ideal wife. She took the family responsibilities upon her shoulders so that her husband can devote himself to philosophical studies and research. The couple moved from Sangam Jagarlamudi to Waltair (Vizag), Guntur, Tirupati and Delhi during the course of Satchidananda Murty's career. Getting along with such unfamiliar environs was no easy task for Vedavati Devi. Yet she used to go out all by herself into the market to buy groceries and other home needs, attend to the guests who visited the couple very frequently and above all taking care of children and their education.

The Philosophy of Samkhya states that in the silent presence of *Puruṣa* (Consciousness), *Prakṛti* (matter) evolves and creates the universe through three *Guṇas* (qualities) and 25 *Tattvas* (true principles). Professor

Satchidananda Murty's and Vedavati Devi's marital bond can be likened to that of *Prakṛti* and *Puruṣa* relationship. She effectively led the family with tacit approval of Satchidananda Murty. Without hankering after riches and luxuries, preserving the ancestral properties, she was content to live with what they had and concentrated on children's upbringing. All the four sons completed higher education, settled in good careers, making their parents very happy. The eldest son Yasomitra did B.Sc., took up agricultural and commercial activities and is now settled in Guntur. The second son Raghunatha was a M.A., Ph.D. He is living in Vijayawada after retiring as Professor in the Regional campus of Dr. B.R. Ambedkar Open University there. The third son Krishna, after he did M.A., in Social Work is serving as General Manager, Administration wing in KCP Ltd, Vuyyuru. The last one Ramesh did M.A., Ph.D., in Industrial Relations. He settled in Waltair after working as a Professor in Andhra University.

Yasomitra and Savitri had two children—Vishnu Priya (daughter) and Vrajesh (son). Śrīnivaṣ was the only son of Raghunatha and Lakshmi. The third couple Krishna and Sarala had two daughters—Haritha and Sruti. The last couple Ramesh and Padma had a son Udayana and a daughter Veda. All the offspring are employed in suitable occupations and are leading contented lives. Vide the Family Tree-2, given in Ch. 2 of this book.

5

A Life of Purpose

Traditionalists still regard *Manu Smṛti* as the ultimate treatise on Hindu social law. They steadfastly follow four Varna system enunciated in that timeworn text and believe that the sole duty of Śudras is to serve their overlords.[1] Pity, we come across such stupid characters even to this day. Professor Satchidanada Murty recounted such an encounter with a narrow-minded, intolerant family.[2] According to that dogmatic family Prof. Murty should not have taken up the studies of ancient texts, much less teach them. They also declared that he was not at all fit to be a Professor.

Eventually Prof. Murty made mincemeat of their retrogressive beliefs through his outstanding academic achievements and by winning numerous awards and accolades in India and abroad. He attained all this by dint of hard work and loads of merit. *Shrimad Bhagad Gītā*, which inspired him right from childhood stood as the constant guide and companion in all his endeavours.

Lord Krishna, while approving four-fold Varna system, completely reworked and redefined the basic framework saying that he created four varnas in accordance with humans' intrinsic nature and qualities[3]. He explained to Arjuna: "I revealed the secret of four-fold varna system first to the Sun who in turn disclosed the same to Manu and he passed it on to Ikshvaku. Over aeons the secret remained undiscovered. Now I chose to divulge the same to you—my devotee and my best friend.[4] Lord Krishna went on: "The basic nature of Brahmana Varṇa should be *Upaśamana* (assuagement), *Damana* (suppression), *Tapas* (deep meditation), Swachata (purity), *Kṣamā* (fogiveness), acquisition of *Gyāna* (wisdom) and striving to attain higher Truth.[5] And the *Kṣatra* qualities are: valor, courage, fighting, never showing one's back on the battlefield, adroitness, generosity and self-control.[6] The Vysya varna's basic qualities are: farming, cattle-rearing and trade. And lastly- service is the nature of Shudras.[7] Thus according to Śrīmad *Bhagavad Gītā*, Varṇa Dharmas are not set in stone. They are dynamic. They are not socially fixed or fossilized in a particular caste or castes. A person born as a Shudra may display Brāhmaṇa or Kṣatriya qualities and vice versa. Therefore Lord Krishna affirms that *Varṇa dharmas* change according to the demands of times and social needs. He provided an entirely new and liberal framework for the four-fold varna system. Thus he rejected certain basic Manu's tenets viz., *Ācāraḥ Paramo Dharmaḥ* (Manu 1:77), the customs and traditions of castes are irreversible, so they should be sustained as such. (Manu 1:78). But, by proclaiming *Sva Dharmo Nidhanam Śreyah Para Dharmo Bhayāvahaḥ*. Lord Krshna approves that one should practice the Dharma spurred by his/her inherent qualities. This was indeed a revolutionary social ideology. Does the orthodox section who religiously chant *Gītā* realize this?

But Satchidananda Murty surely internalized the essence of *Gītā* as enunciated by Lord Krishna. Applying the same to current social conditions he expounded that *Karmas* are variegated by intrinsic qualities. The way he modernized and applied teachings of *Gītā* to the four-fold varna system of Hindu religion is truly ingenious:

- Those worthy souls who excel by the power of intellect, control over oneself, deep study of various sciences and arts so that they can help others broaden their understanding are called *Brāhmaṇas* Ex., Sage Vasishta.

- The courageous and valorous persons who rule over men with power and tact can be termed as *Kṣatriyas*. Ex: Bhishma.
- Those who virtuously trade in various goods required by the society and also take up occupations like agriculture and cattle-rearing are known as *Vaiśyas*. Ex: Thuladhar.
- Those, devoid of intellectual acumen but being physically strong, take up hard labour benefitting the wider society are termed as *Śūdras*, Ex: Dharma Vyādha.

Applying Lord Krishna's precepts to the modern age, one can discern that those who serve the nation by their intellect, who enlighten people by their talks and writings along with the ministers of state can be reckoned as Brahmanas. The soldiers, policemen, Government officers and other law-makers can be considered as Kṣatriyas. The Vaisyas can be those who trade in paddy, turmeric etc., The manual labour, peons and other servants can be classified as the Śūdras.

"Nobody is a Brāhmin by birth. The varṇa can be delineated only according to the qualities he or she acquires while growing up. So if one distinguishes himself by virtue of his brains he can be termed a Brāhmin, if one shines by his martial vigour he is a Kṣatriya, if one earns riches by taking up business he is a Vysya. And lastly those who devoid of any of these qualities live by doing manual labour can be treated as Śūdras."

"So a man's Varṇa is defined by his qualities and actions (*Gītā* 4:13)"

"By this reckoning a Brahmin may give birth to a Kshatriya or a Shudra. Perhaps he may beget a Brahmin also – because the ultimate deciding factor is a man's real qualities and actions spurred by them. This is the view held by *Gītā*."[8]

With this commentary Prof. Murty applied Lord Krishna's elucidation of four-fold Varṇa system to modern conditions and envisaged an ideal social order free from regional and linguistic divisions. This universal and timeless truth is clearly conveyed by Lord Krishna's teaching—*Swadharmo Nidhanam Śreyam.*

Born in a traditional agricultural family belonging to Kamma caste of Guntur district in the state of Andhra Pradesh, India, Satchidananda Murty was groomed by his father in the timeless tradition of Hindu culture and religion. As he grew up Murty became a well-versed scholar in philosophical studies. He imbibed modern thought and contemporary spirit. This growth process had shaped up Murty to a great extent. Recounting his personal evolution, Prof. Murty stated: "I was born as a Viśiṣṭādvaitin. In M.A., I intensively studied Advaita Vedanta. I learnt Sanskrit under the tutelage of a Dvaita acharya. Thus I developed a close affinity with all the three schools of Hindu religious practice. While at Tirupati I made a deep study of Viśiṣṭādvaita books like *Śrī Bhāṣya, Śruta Prakāśikā, Vedānta Sāram, Vedānta Dīpam, Vedārtha Saṅgraham, Tattva Ṭīkā, Tattva Muktākalāpam, Sarvārtha Sidhi* and *Nyāya Parishuddhi*. Also I was fortunate enough to meet the scholars of various schools of Advaita and other saints. It is said that God's grace makes even a mute to speak fluently (*Mūkam Karoti Vācālam)*. Likewise I too gained fluency in Vedantic thought, thanks to the grace of saints."—These words show Prof. Murty's mental maturity[9].

The great souls of our age- Vivekananda, Gandhiji, Dayananda Saraswati, Ramaananda, Radhakrishnan *et al* while declaring themselves as Hindus, tried to establish the monotheist, non-idolatrous Advaita as the real Indian spirit. Viewed in this background one finds it strange that Prof. Murty, while admitting the influence of Advaita, Viśiṣṭādvaita and Dvaita on himself, declares himself as Viśiṣṭādvaitin by birth. It makes us pause to ponder over the greatness of Viśiṣṭādvaita.

It is common knowledge that Śrī Ramanujacharya was the proponent of Viśiṣṭādvaita. It can be described as a qualified Advaita and is a sub-school of Vedanta. While Sankaracharya of Advaita school expounded unqualified monism by saying that *Brahma Satyam, Jagan Mithya, Jīvo Brahmaiva nāparah,* Ramanujacharya propounded that Brahman and Jagat are separate entities with a special relationship between them. The same relationship exists between God and Man. Ramanuja's revolutionary philosophy propounded a modern egalitarian world-view. It spurred a social movement opposing varṇa and caste discrimination. Even if his Guru resented him and his wife deserted him and many other impediments came up in his path, Ramanuja (1019-1139 AD) in his 120 year-long highly fruitful life never turned back from his revolutionary ideals. Single-mindedly and single-handedly he strove to enlighten Indian society by bestowing "Aṣṭākṣarī mantra"—*Om Namo Narāyaṇāya* to one and all. Ramanuja was instrumental in turning Tirumala—Tirupati as the world- renowned Vaishnavaite shrine.

The winds of social awakening soon spread far and wide and turned into a social movement. Śudras and Paraiahs took to Ramanuja's teachings and thus became Vaishnavaites. Eventually it was Vaishnavaite school which crystalized into Hindu religion[10]. Though many puṇḍits try to push the antiquity of Hinduism into far reaches of time and space, the fact is that our ancient scriptures like Vedas never mentioned the word—Hindu. Though traditionalists state that Hinduism is the oldest religion, the word Hindu does not appear anywhere in Vedic scriptures. Neither can it be found in the eighth century text—*Ṣaṭ Darśana Samucchaya* nor in the 13th century index of religions viz *Sarva Darśana Sangraha*. During Satchidananda Murty's childhood, group discussions on Ramanuja's teachings were used to be held in almost all villages. Those venues of discussion were widely known as Ramanuja Kootams or Koshtams. They can still be found though they are no longer bustling with group activities. Śrī Vaishnavism led to the rise of Sūdras as Vaishnavite saints and gurus. Out of a total of 12 Alwars (supreme devotees) Perialwar and Nammalwar were born Sūdras. They are worshipped in Viashnava temples till this day. Sāthāns were the descendants of those Śudra Vaishnavas. Ramanujamma, Ramanujayya, Venugopal Rao... Reddy ... Chowdary etc., have become common names among Sūdras. From olden days Vaishnava Acharyas used to dine along with Sūdras. Dining on Mat (Chaapa Koodu) of Palnadu area of Guntur was, nothing but a continuation of that tradition. Back in Prof. Murty's childhood i.e., seven decades ago Vaishnavite preachers used to come to his village in bullock carts.

His elders tell him that those pot-bellied preachers with Vaishnavite sacred marks on forehead used to partake non-vegetarian food along with Sūdras. Resenting this, Vaishnava Brahmins developed their own sect -Śrī Vaishnavism separately. Followers of Ramanuja took to building Venugopala temples all over the Telugu country. The temple built by Prof. Murty's ancestors (Veerabhadraiah's father and uncle) still stands loftily in Sangam Jagarlamudi of Guntur district. We have already seen how Prof. Murty wrote hymns to Sangameswara and

Venugopala. Now we can see why he described himself as Viśiṣṭādvaitin by birth. Murty's disciples who are spread far and wide bear testimony to this.

After completing his studies in Guntur[11] , he served as a lecturer at S.V. College, Tirupati, for a year and thereafter worked as a Professor in Philosophy at Mayurbhanj, Odisha before returning to Sangam Jagarlamudi. During those years he extensively wrote essays on Indian philosophy in various magazines. Later, on the invitation of Sir Cattamanchi Ramalinga Reddy (C.R. Reddy), Vice-chancellor of Andhra University, Murty joined as a Lecturer in Hindu Religion and Philosophy Department, Andhra University. In those days he wrote many books and submitted research papers in national and international seminars. One of those books was *Ramanuja Darshanamu*, which displayed Murty's unique way of thinking. He divided his time between teaching and writing books and taking up national and international academic tours. He became one of the world-renowned philosophers. He distinguished himself in various official and honorary positions.

Except for 5 years of childhood, he devoted all his 87 years of life to unceasing studies and philosophical inquiry. If one goes strictly by the definition of *Śrīmad Bhagavad Gītā*, one can find no greater brahmin than Prof. Murty anywhere in India at that time. We can only take pity at the ignorance of those who arrogate themselves as brahmins simply by birth but not according to *Gītā*. Prof. Murty served for four years as the Principal and Special Officer of Andhra University's Post Graduate Centre at Guntur right from its inception in 1967[12]. Later he was the Vice-Chancellor of Śrī Venkateswara University, Tirupati for three years (1976-78). After retirement he served as Vice-Chairman of UGC for three more years (1986-89). Also served as the Chairman (Chancellor),

Central Institute of Higher Tibetan Studies, Saranath, Varanasi, during 1988-95. While discharging these duties ably and honestly for ten years, Prof. Murty continued his philosophical studies. He drew inspiration from S. Radhakrishnan in this regard[13]. By relentlessly pursuing knowledge and tirelessly practicing what he believed, Professor Satchidananda Murty transformed himself into a modern-day Rishi.

Working as a lecturer in Andhra University (1949-58) he published many notable books and toured Italy, Switzerland, France, Great Britain, Greece and Egypt at his own expense to meet illustrious academics, intellectuals to learn about their diverse views about philosophical issues. He expanded his horizons of knowledge by following distinct academic standards set by world-renowned universities. In 1956, as a member of General Education Committee, Prof. Murty visited the universities in US and UK which enabled him to provide valuable suggestions for the advancement of the educational standards of Indian Universities. Concurrently he continued with the study of the great Sanskrit works on Advaita Vedanta and submitted his research thesis *Revelation and Reason in Advaita Vedanta* to Andhra University in 1956. It won him a Doctorate (Ph.D). He got promoted as Reader that year and published his thesis in 1959 by Columbia University Press, USA.The same year he went to USA to serve as the Visiting Professor and Senior Fellow of the Council of Humanities at Princeton University for a semester. On his return Prof. Murty was promoted as a Professor and the Head of the Department. He continued in that position till he retired in 1984.

Before that he served in many positions. In 1963, he was invited to visit notable universities of Pakistan, Turkey, Iran, UK and Austria, where he delivered talks and submitted lecture papers. He visited USA, Japan and

South East Asian nations in 1966. Toured USSR in 1967. All these foreign visits enabled him to appreciate finer aspects of diverse cultures, religions and philosophies. While functioning as Chairman, Faculty of Arts in Andhra University, Prof. Murty was conferred with University Grants Commission's National Fellowship. After serving as Vice-chancellor of Śrī Venkateswara University, Tirupati, he returned to his alma mater. For 35 years, Prof. Murty continuously amassed four kinds of professorial wealth—deep study, teaching, research and publishing before he retired in 1984 from Andhra University. Even later, he continued with endless research, talks and writing. His fame reached far and wide. Many universities awarded him honorary positions. Famed institutions like People's University of Beijing, Ucha Tibbati Sansthan of Varanasi and Andhra University of Waltair benefited from his distinguished services by appointing him as honorary professor. For over half a century, Prof. Murty served as a Lecturer, Reader, Professor, Special Officer, Vice-Chancellor, Vice-Chairman of UGC and Chancellor. All the honours and high positions did not deter him from continuing with philosophical studies. His quest for knowledge was never-ending. He inspired students to strive for reaching ever higher heights. He encouraged research personally; he continued with research and publishing.

In 1947, while he was at Śrī Venkateswara College, Tirupati, Prof. Murty published his classic work-Hinduism and its development- in two parts. During the same time he also translated *Ṣad Darśana Samucchaya* of Hari Bhadra Suri into English. This work is considered by scholars as the gold standard for understanding the parting of ways between various Indian philosophies and religions. This book was published by Tagore Publishing House, Tenali in 1957. Prof. Murty also translated into Telugu, Edwin

Lein's 'The Character before Pilate' and published it under the title *Divya Jīvitam* in 1948. He took up a lecturer position in Religion and Philosophy Department of Andhra University in 1949. Two years later, in 1951, he published two books—*Thought and the Divine (Chintana-Divyatvam) and The Rhythm of the Real (Yathadrthatha Avrithi)*. Prof. Murty published *Evolution of Philosophy in India* in the year 1952. It should be particularly noted that the book carried a foreword by world- renowned radical humanist MN Roy[14].

Prof. Murty interacted with many world- famous philosophers even before he was elevated to Professorial position in 1960. He published *Studies in the Problems of Peace* in 1960 with the joint authorship of AC Bouquet. When Telugu Bhasha Samithi of Madras undertook the publishing of encyclopedias, Prof. Murty took over the editorial responsibilities for the section on "Religions and Philosophies" of the seventh volume. That was put in print in 1962. Around the same time Prof. Murty took up the editorship of *Samakālīna Bharatīya Darśan (Contemporary Indian Philosophy)* which was published by Bharatiya Darshan Parishad, Faridkot, Punjab.

In 1963, Murty came out with *Metaphysics, Man and Freedom* – a deeply contemplative philosophical work. Later in 1970 he translated the same book into Telugu under the title *Manishi-Mukti*. He came out with another book- *The Indian Foreign Policy* in 1964. Next year, he followed up with another work *The Indian Spirit*. Prof. Murty was invited and toured many countries in 1963, 1966 and 1967. He submitted many research papers and returned home with many honours.

During the four year period 1967-71, while working as the Principal and Special Officer of Andhra University's PG Centre at Guntur, Murty delved deep into the life and teachings of Acharya Nagarjuna. He also undertook correlative studies of Indian, Chinese and Tibetan Buddhist traditions, Great Philosophers and finally published his work *Nagarjuna* in 1979. Prior to this Murty returned to his alma mater Andhra University to publish *Current Trends in Indian Philosophy* with the joint-editorship of Prof. K. Ramakrishna Rao.

With the appointment as Vice-Chancellor of Śrī Venkateswara University, he went to Tirupati for a period of three years (1975-78) and continued philosophical studies, in spite of his administrative responsibilities. He published *Far Eastern Philosophies* in 1976 based on the talks delivered by him in 1966 on the development of Asian cultures, religions and philosophies at Mysore University. He finally returned to Andhra University in 1978 and continued there as a professor till 1984. It was really unique for Murty to take up professorship at Andhra University long after serving as a Special Officer at Guntur and Vice-Chancellor of Śrī Venkateswara University. By showing to the world that the field of education has no place for any kind of discrimination or prejudice, Prof. Murty set a fine academic precedent. He continued his writing activity with the same youthful enthusiasm. He came out with *Andhra Contribution to Budhist Thought* in 1980, *Indian Philosophy Since 1498* in 1982, *Naisreyasa Dharma* in 1984. His writing activity continued even after retirement. He published *The Advaitic Notion* in 1985 and *Quest for Peace* in 1986 which was an improvement on his previous work. Prof. Murty was appointed as Vice-Chairman of University Grants Commission (UGC) in 1986. He fulfilled many responsibilities in various capacities till 1989. Even in the thick of work pressures he published *Radhakrishnan- His life and Ideas* with the collaboration of Professor Ashok Vohra in 1988. Before that he published *Atha Deepaa Viharatha* (Be a lamp unto yourself) based on Buddha's teachings in 1987.

Even after he returned to native village on completion of his term at UGC, Prof. Murty continued his writing activities. In 1993 he published *Vedic Hermeneutics.* He also served as the editor to the books *"Ethics, Education, Indian Unity and Culture"* (1991), *The Divine Peacock* (1995), and *The Perennial Tree* (1996).

All this was just one facet of Prof. Satchidananda Murty's personality. The other one was his dedication to duty and administrative acumen. Lecturer, Reader, Head of the Department; Chairman, Faculty of Arts; Special Officer and Principal, Andhra University P.G. Centre; Vice-Chancellor, SVU and UGC Vice-Chairman—whatever was the post or position he carries, he gave out his best, fulfilling his duties without fear and favour. His deep understanding of education system, clarity of purpose and the valuable insights gained through the visits to various national and international universities helped him vastly in discharging his duties. Spotless character, moral uprightness- were his inherent qualities. Prof. Murty was a person who represents dignity in a complete and exemplary way. While he might have looked flamboyant, he was actually simple at heart. Though a lover of solitude he was also outgoing. Seemingly easy-going, he was actually unflinching in the pursuit of his goals. Only those who gained proximity to him could understand this distinct quality. Hypocrites who touch his feet expecting something in return could never understand it. Little wonder, while some people were deeply annoyed at him, those who could understood were highly charmed by his personality. Righteousness was the underpinning of his life. Praise or criticism- he remained unaffected. Following Lord Buddha's teaching he dedicated his life and career for attaining self-enlightenment, helping others and the whole wide-world[15]. Those who were his colleagues and students at Andhra University during the initial days of his career still remember his scholarship and impeccable character. Just a mention of his name brings forth vivid memories of him. They happily reminisce about the way he looked, walked and taught.

Prof. Murty was naturally fond of the spacious home in his native Sangam Jagarlamudi village. Wherever he worked Prof. Murty naturally chose houses almost as big and with a leafy courtyard. The bungalows at Andhra University premises, Guntur and Tirupati were large. In Delhi he used to live in an MP's bungalow. Guests were received very warmly by him at all these places. Wherever he lived, he always sported a distinct style. Chewing supari or smoking cigars made with country tobacco, Prof. Murty used to make rounds in the university[16]. Loose-fitting pants, long shirt upto his knees, wearing sandals, the six-foot tall Satchidananda Murty used to pace around his office, department of philosophy and his class room. The image of Murty wearing black shades over prescription glasses, lost in deep thought is still etched in the memories of his former students. Accepting greetings from his students, friends and acquaintances, wishing them well, hurling jokes- he always presented a jovial personality. There are many people who can recollect his typical ways even to this day. They are still in awe over his venerable character. Soon after Prof. Murty entered his spacious office in the department of philosophy, students and fellow- professors flocked around him, seeking help in clearing doubts, or to discuss about some complex points in research or just to move closer to him. Moving into classroom, leaning against the edge of table, he opens his lecture with catchy introduction and delivers it by striking a balance between depth and breadth of coverage. Never letting go of his sense of humour, Prof. Murty used to encourage bright students, make sarcastic remarks against inattentive ones and reprimand those who miss classes frequently.

Enunciating clearly, spurring interest in students with deep and pointed questions, letting out sense of humour, Prof. Murty delivered his lectures. Students used to feel as if time simply flew away in his classes.

In those days the subject of Philosophy in Andhra University was consisted of eight papers: 1. Indian Philosophy 2. Western Philosophy 3. Logic 4. Ethics 5. A special study of works of one of the contemporary philosophers like AN Whitehead, Henri Bergson 6. Contemporary Indian Philosophy 7. Essay writing-constituted the compulsory papers. 8. In addition to them, students ought to take an optional paper from Vedanta, Psychology or Sociology. Prof. Murty taught Indian Philosophy and Contemporary Western philosophy. After he got promoted as Reader and Professor, Prof. Murty also shouldered the responsibilities of guiding the research scholars and organising academic seminars along with the usual teaching duties.[17]

The University's Philosophy department consisted of a limited number of professors who could provide research guidance.[18] Among them Satchidananda Murty's guidance was the most enthusiastically sought out. Students believed that those who do Ph.D., under him can easily get teaching positions in other universities. Prof. Murty encouraged his students to strike out on an independent path in research, he made them grasp the fundamentals. It was considered an honour to do research under his guidance[19].

Prof. Murty set a precedent of holding national and international seminars every year at Andhra University. Scholars and academics enthusiastically participated. Students and Professors found those seminars highly informative and useful. Intellectuals like TRV Murti, Debiprasad Chatopadhyaya and his spouse Mrs Amala, Nihar Ranjan Ray, Lalmani Joshi, the great logician

Rajagopalan, S.S. Barlingay, G.C. Naik (Orissa) and Pullela Śrī Ramachandrudu used to attend those seminars.

Prof. Murty never imposed the research subject of his choice on the students. Usually he tried to ascertain the aptitude of a student first. He did this by chatting with him for a few days. Only after getting a measure of the student he recommended a suitable research subject to him. He never allowed the students to lift and incorporate material from other texts in their thesis. The world-famous magazine *Readers Digest* once quipped: 'To copy from a single work is called Plagiarism and to copy from many more works is called Research.' None of the research theses supervised by Prof. Murty fall under these categories. He always encouraged the students to study source books. If they were unable to understand the originals, he suggested them to read their translations. He strongly advised them never to depend on secondary sources or third rate works. If a student badly needs urgent assistance, Prof. Murty was always ready to help him out by elaborating various aspects personally. Such an integrity is definitely lacking in most of the universities today.

The Department of Philosophy, Andhra University is world-famous. Scholars used to enquire about Andhra University and Prof. Murty. It is not exaggerating if we say that the then philosophy department, Andhra University, was identified with Prof.Murty. The entire academic world held him in great esteem. His reputation spread far and wide. That's why all the illustrious people who used to visit Telugu country (Andhra) made it a point to meet him either at Vizag or at Sangam Jagarlamudi village.

When Andhra University (A.U) decided to set up a PG Centre at Guntur, it chose Professor Meenakshi Sundaram to lead it. Prof. Sundaram was working on lien somewhere else. The A.U. officials appointed this highly capable professor as the Special Officer and Principal of Guntur PG Centre. True to the trust put in him by the A.U, Prof. Sundaram made hectic efforts and launched the Centre on schedule. But unfortunately he died of heart attack just days after the launch. Giving temporary charge to Prof. Ramachandra Rao, the varsity officials began to search for an alternative. Prof. Śrīnivasa Iyengar, the then Vice-chancellor of Andhra University finally zeroed in on Satchidananda Murty because he was the senior most professor and hails from Guntur district. Iyengar called him up on 26-08-1967 and informed him of his decision. Satchidananda Murty asked for some time to think it over. As he did not respond even after a month, Prof Iyengar finally called him again. In fact Satchidananda Murty was deeply considering the nitty gritties of the new job. He focused his attention on the likely hurdles and opportunities in store for the PG Centre. He was also trying to devise a plan to develop the Centre into a highly useful hub of higher learning for the students of the region. When Prof. Iyengar summoned him again, he was finally ready to don the mantle. He took charge of PG centre on 17 January, 1968. Whatever little funds the state government allocated to this centre, they were routed through the Andhra University. Same curriculum was followed at both the places meaning there was little freedom for experimentation, for trying something new. So soon after taking over the PG Centre Prof. Murty decided that he has to go back to the mother university once he fulfils his duties here. He made a deep study into administration affairs so that he can do justice to his new job. After observing the working of various universities he identified five flaws.

- Indian Universities still follow the obsolete policies imposed by former British colonial rulers. They give little scope for innovation. This situation must change.

- Under the centralised administration all the universities confer all the powers to the Vice-Chancellors forcing the professors to run after the V.Cs even for getting small things done.
- Our universities still blindly follow the curriculum set by the British. They do not care to devise a syllabus suited to the needs of contemporary society. They are unable to impart purposeful education.
- Unmindful of today's needs our universities stick to moribund and mechanincal educational policies. Failing to inspire the research scholars and professors to strike boldly on a creative path, they push them into deep despair.
- Most of our universities have failed to gain autonomy.

Professor Murty took it upon himself to set things right as far as he can. He earnestly tried to shake off the deep inertia in our university educational system. He strove to change the old practices and evolve a holistic structure and to set it on the path of all round development.

Murty himself revealed this in the valedictory function held in his honour when he was returning to Andhra University after ably discharging his duties at PG Centre, Guntur.[20] He came here and worked on his terms. When he realized that things are not shaping up in the way he liked them to be, Prof. Murty decided that he will give his best within the limits imposed by the system. He tried to open History and Archaeology department at the PG Centre and even got positive response from Andhra University. But in the last minute it slipped away. But Prof. Murty was not the one to give up easily. Next, he tried to set up the department of Asian Philosophy and Culture but again disappointment awaited him. Prof. Murty tried to develop Education with Production Project to enable students to gain a foothold in life. But higher authorities dodged the issue with meaningless queries and sought numerous nonsensical explanations. Realising that all of his efforts were to no avail, Prof. Murty focused on reforming the administration system in the P.G. Centre. Finally he decided to do away with this system which forced the Professors and Department Heads to run to the Special Officer for each and every need. Thus he helped them to think and act independently. To this end he formed a committee with all the heads of departments and set the precedent of discussing and thrashing out a solution to the problems encountered in the running of P.G. Centre. This system promoted camaraderie and co-operation between the members, thus spurred single-pointedness in achieving objectives—he himself revealed these points in his farewell speech.

The notable thing here is that he didn't confine this approach only to the faculty. He used to discuss with the President and Secretary of the students' union about the issues which affect the future of student community. His policy instilled a sense of responsibility in the student community. Prof. Murty used to encourage the students who come out with useful suggestions. He launched Telugu Association, Games and Sports committee, Dramatic Association, Fine Arts Association etc., with the active participation of the faculty and the students. He did also arrange medical camps for them with the help of the local doctors.

Prof. Satchidananda Murty strove to bring higher education within the reach of all sections, regions—particularly villages. He dedicated his career to make it meaningful and useful to society. Towards this end he took up many experiments. When people from Guntur district requested Andhra University to establish rural colleges, those appeals were referred to a committee set up under the chairmanship of Prof. Murty as he was the special officer of Guntur P.G. Centre. Following this, he toured the backward areas of district viz Pedanandipadu, Tadikonda and Amaravathi to explore the possibilities of establishing a college there. Finally he sent a report to the university recommending that a rural college can indeed be set up there, because of the enthusiasm being shown by the local elite to provide all necessary support. Opening up these colleges will greatly help the rural students who wish to avail the benefits of modern education. Thus he paved the way for the launching of Pedanandipadu Arts and Science College, Bhagvan Satya Sai College at Tadikonda and Raja Vasireddy Venkatadri Nayudu College at Dharanikota.

Though the requisite facilities to establish a college were lacking in those villages, it was the sheer will and enthusiasm of the local elders that led to their establishment. Prof. Murty frequently spoke of the initiative taken by Pamulapati Venkata Krishnayya Chowdary, the then President of Guntur district board in this regard. In those days even high schools were few and far between. Only Taluk headquarters housed them. Students had to travel long distances all the year and cross overflowing streams in monsoon season to reach the schools. What little transport available was disrupted by the rains. Such were the hardships faced by the students. Determined to change this, Venkata Krishnayya Chowdary helped the village elders in setting up local high schools. But lack of buildings and other basic facilities, the reluctance of teachers to go to villages proved to be dampeners. It took nearly a decade to overcome these teething troubles. Gradually local bigwigs came forward to help with the construction of school buildings and other amenities, played a key role in getting them off the ground. Their philanthropy helped thousands of students and contributed to the revolutionary development of education in Guntur district.

Like-wise Prof. Murty never let financial constraints to derail his efforts in developing academic and infrastructural framework for the Guntur P.G. Centre. Dedicating his time and energy for the P.G. Centre he soon reached a point where he felt nothing more could be done from his side. After successfully completing his term at Guntur he moved back to Andhra University in 1971 with a sense of fulfilling his duty well.

Taking over the university's Philosophy department once again Prof. Murty devoted his multi-faceted genius for the advancement of his students. Ever available to help research students, he set out writing a philosophy work. With Prof. K. Ramakrishna Rao serving as joint editor, he published *Current Trends in Indian Philosophy* in 1972. Two years later in 1974 be brought out the classic *The Realm of Between*.

Meanwhile, recognizing his matchless contribution for the development of Guntur P.G. Centre, the state government appointed him as Vice-Chancellor of Śrī Venkateswara University in 1975. Prof. Murty accepted the orders because he believed that he could function independently and make a difference in this new position which was lacking at Guntur P.G. Centre. Taking charge in October 1975, Prof. Murty served till 1978 as the VC of SVU during which time he enriched the academic programme by improving it with necessary changes. He adopted and refined his system of participatory democracy by inviting and taking suggestions and assistance from academics from all over the nation and the world. He spurred creativity among the university faculty and students by involving them deeply in this system.

Moreover Prof. Murty had a special relationship with Tirupati. It may be remembered that his career started in Śrī Venkateswara College of Tirupati. This attachment further motivated him to strive for all round development of S.V. University. He infused life into the decking Oriental Research Centre (ORC) in the varsity. He made arrangements to preserve the ancient manuscripts and books. He named a new building in honour of Tiruppan Alwar of 8th century who was one of the two Vaishnavite saints. It must be noted that Tiruppan hailed from a lowly caste. Observing that the professors of ORC were sticking only to traditional studies, he began to invite modern philosophers and arranged get together with students and faculty. These discourses were popularly known as Philosophical Collegium. Professor Murty used to organise these collegiums every year. They stretched from 15 days to one month. He also invited noted philosophers like Nihar Ranjan Ray and T.R.V. Murti as visiting professors to S.V University. They used to stay for a period of 48 days interacting with and instructing the faculty in

With Sri Sanjay Gandhi, Sri Jalagam Vengala Rao, CM of AP, Sri Kotha Raghuramaiah, Cabinet Minister and others at SVU, Tirupati.

modern trends. Without limiting this practice only to the department of Philosophy, Prof. Murty extended it to other departments also. In those days no other university made such a revolutionary attempt anywhere in India. All this goes to prove Prof. Murty's synergism, his passion for knowledge and modernity and his dedication to the advancement of student community.

Prof. Murty strove to change not only university academic policy but executive policy also. He gave freedom to the university Registrar, Dean and Heads of departments to formulate and implement suitable policies independently, which in turn contribute to the all round development of students and the university. The faculty was always free to discuss with him on policy issues. He provided the students a conducive environment for research. He ensured student participation in all the matters having a direct bearing on them. He made himself available to the students who wished to meet him whenever a need arises.[21]

Prof. Murty realised that the meaningless practices and thought processes long entrenched in the university had to be shaken off. Otherwise they will adversely affect the students hindering their progress. So he tried his best to spur them into new ways of thinking, helped them to push limits. The constitution of our Secular, Socialist Republic institutionalized liberty, equality and fraternity. It envisaged a society unburdened by caste, creed and community. In a way these principles were based on Buddha's teaching—*Athahita, Parahita, Ubhayahita, Sabbalokahitameva.* Though Indian constitution allows everybody to practice their own traditions and beliefs, it disallows them to impose their whims and fancies over others. It has zero tolerance towards deception. Prior to Prof. Murty taking charge, it was an established custom to open schools and colleges with a prayer. All the Hindu, Muslim, Christian and Parsi educational institutions followed this. Students belonging to other faiths found this practice highly uncomfortable. Considering this recitation as a blot on the modern education system, Prof. Murty banned it in SV University (SVU). But as Tirupati and SVU were Centres of Vaishnava tradition, many people expressed disapproval over this. Finally Prof. Murty relented and reinstated the prayer session but with a condition that students belonging to other faiths should be allowed to recite their own prayers. This practice continues to this day in SVU. I can confidently say that no other educational institution in India follows this admirable tradition.

Though he devoted much time to discard the old and set up new precedents, Prof. Murty never neglected his fourfold duties: making deep study, teaching, research and book-publishing. Concurrently he assisted the teaching staff in their advancement and inspired students to do research. Many students including myself from AU frequently visited Prof. Murty at Tirupati for his valuable guidance. It is hard to find an ideal and altruistic professor like Satchidananda Murty these days. His exemplary services brought renown not only to the university he served but to him also. He frequently convened seminars to spread traditional knowledge among our people. Experts in Indian philosophical tradition used to attend them. Prof. Murty published the collection of their talks with a foreword written by him.[22] He provided the readers an opportunity to understand our ancient heritage with the help of modern scientific thought. That was truly an admirable endeavour. As Vice-Chancellor of Sri Venkateswara University, he paid tribute to his Sanskrit Guru, Sri Palle Purnaprajnacharya, by conferring upon him an honorary doctorate, showcasing his deep reverence and gratitude.

After serving in Śrī Venkateswara University for three years, Murty laid down his office of Vice-Chancellor and returned to Andhra University in 1978. There he served as a Professor of Philosophy till his retirement. Recalling his experiences and feelings at S.V.U. he remarked: "I served as head of Kendriya Sanskrit Vidya Peeth at the varsity for a year which accorded me the opportunity of interacting with great professors Śrī Krishna Sharma, Sankara Narayanan of S.V.U and pundits like Balasubrahmanyam and Ramanuja Thathacharya. These discussions broadened my understanding. While Professor Śrī Krishna Sharma and Sankara Narayana were adept at Veda Patha, Nyaya Darshana and history of Epigraphy, Ramanuja Tātācārya was well-versed in Nyāya, Mīmāmsā and Viśiṣṭādvaita. Whenever I had any doubts in understanding of Vedas, I used to take their help. In my three year term as V.C of SVU, among other things, I reinvigorated the Oriental Research Centre and published Telugu translations of Madhavacharya's *Vivrithi* his interpretation of 40 initial suktas of Rigveda- and *Mantrārtha Mañjari* of Raghavendra Swamy in 1978".[23]

Even after returning to Andhra University Prof. Murty continued with his relentless academic activities. In 1986 he was appointed as Vice-Chairman of University Grants Commission (UGC). Thus his valuable services, which till then confined to institutions based in Andhra Pradesh were made available to all Indian Universities. Though Professor Yashpal Sharma, a famed scientist served as the Chairman of UGC during 1986-89, he was more interested in scientific pursuits than in leading the organisation. He took over UGC because of the Union Government's decision. Prof. Murty was widely recognized as a man who fulfils his duties dedicatedly, impartially and with integrity. Yashpal was very much pleased with Murty's appointment as his Vice-Chairman. Whenever problems cropped up in the commission he used to call up Murty and ask him 'Murtyji, Aap dekhiye' (Mr. Murty, please look into this). So it ultimately fell upon his shoulders to look after each small and large problems, faced by the UGC. And he carried out his responsibilities very ably. As Vice-Chairman of UGC, Prof. Murty bestowed autonomy on all the universities in making academic policy decisions. He reoriented the university administration towards achieving all round development of students and faculty. He also allowed the Universities to make necessary changes according to the local needs.

As UGC Vice-Chairman Prof. Murty gave valuable suggestions and provided necessary financial and other assistance to various universities, *Vidya Peethas* and other educational Centres which greatly helped them scale new heights in teaching. He provided financial and other infrastructural resources to set up new universities and Chairs in areas where they were lacking. He was instrumental in establishing Veda Vidya Schools in Northern and Eastern India and providing an interface with the modern educational system. This linkage went a long way in preserving our ancient Indian culture and literature, gave a fillip to comparative studies. Prof. Murty constituted Chairs on Mīmāṁsā philosophy in various North Indian universities. He thus paved the way for interpretation of the ancient philosophy. He once again established the pre-eminence of ancient Vedic literature. In the endeavour of achieving a cohesion between ancient and modern educational systems, he was eminently successful.[24]

In those days heads of the departments usually appointed the faculty from among the research scholars who were their proteges. This practice of inbreeding and appointments done on the basis of caste and creed were shunned by Prof. Murty. He realised from years of experience that it was best to go in for out-breeding viz., inviting foreign scholars as the visiting faculty. In order to achieve high standards in teaching he designed National Talent Test, which is being followed even to this day.

Prof. Murty served as a member of the Committee for "Review of National Policy on Education" (NPE) 1986. The NPE, introduced by the Rajiv Gandhi government, aimed at significant reforms in the Indian education system. As Murty was known for his philosophical insights and expertise in comparative philosophy and education theory, his views on the philosophy of education, advocating for aspects like free universal education and higher studies in Science and Technology, influenced policy discussions during this period, particularly through his writings, some of which are now collected in his books like *On Education and the Philosophy of Education* (2024).

During Rajiv Gandhi time particularly through his role in establishing the Indian Council of Philosophical Research (ICPR), he fostered philosophical inquiry and provided intellectual guidance, reflecting a broader effort to shape educational and policy directions.

Prof. Murty also was an office bearer of the International Federation of Philosophical Societies (FISP). It is a global organization that brings together national associations and organizations in the field of philosophy. One of its key activities is hosting a World Congress of Philosophy every five years, which takes place in a different country each time. Notably, FISP is recognized by UNESCO and serves as a representative for philosophy in international forums. The organisation's activities are funded through membership fees from its affiliates and grants from UNESCO and other sources. FISP holds elections for its office bearers every five years. In the 1993 election, a notable lineup was elected, featuring a President from Latin America, a Secretary General from Turkey, and Vice Presidents from the United States, Russia, and India.

Prof. K. Satchidananda Murty was elected as the Indian Vice President, marking a significant milestone as the first Indian to hold this position.

The FISP executive committee meets approximately once a year, often in a different country, to conduct business and typically organize a seminar or symposium. For instance, in September 1994, the committee met in Kyoto, Japan in which he participated.

He was known for his commitment to high principles and provided dignity and moral authority to the offices he held.

Endnotes:

1. *Ekamevatu Śūdrasya Prabhuh karma samādiśat*, Manu.1:60.
2. Random Reflections, a record of last talks of Prof K.S. Murty in the Dept of. Philosophy, Andhra University, during Dec 2001 — January 2002, unpublished.
3. Murty, K.S. *Śrīmad Bhagavad Gītā,* Ananda Ashramam Grandhamala: Sangam Jagarlamudi, 1941: 4:13, 41.
4. Ibid., 4:1, 2, 3.
5. Ibid., 18:42.
6. Ibid., 18:43.
7. Ibid., 18:44.
8. Ibid., 18th Chapter, pp. 418:20
9. Murty, K.S. *Ramanuja Darshanamu,* Śrī Rāma Tirtha Seva Ashram, Guntur: 1951, Foreword, p.2.
10. Prof. Satchidananda Murty clearly stated this in Sanskrit and English languages in the forward to *Śrīmad Bhagavad Gītā.*
11. During the Second World War (1939-45) Andhra University was shifted from Waltair to Guntur and Vijayawada. So Murty was able to complete B.A., Honors in Guntur.
12. This P.G Centre later grew into Acharya Nagarjuna University.

13. While stressing the importance of ceaseless studies in research endeavour, Prof. Murty told that Dr. S. Radhakrishnan while serving as Vice-chancellor, Andhra University used to read books lying under the big tree behind his official bungalow.
14. Noted Rationalist Manavendra Nath.
15. The actual teaching in Pali language was Atha Hitha, Para Hitha, Ubhaya Hitha, Sabba Loka Hithameva. Words like Athadeepa viharatha, Atha Sarana in Pali literature denote Athma and Self in Sanskrit. Damma Patha has sentences like Athanachodayathanam Patimaase Athamathana (25:20), Sudassum vajja majnosam Athanopanadudaasam (18:18), Athanaava katham Paapam, Athajam Athasambyhavam (12:5). Pundits who try to stress Buddha's Anatha (Anaathma) Vaada should note the above lines.
16. Prof. Murty used to smoke thin cigars for a long time. He gave that up later. When he was the Head of Department of Philosophy, other professors frequently imitated him by smoking cigars to display a sort of kinship.
17. Prof.Murty's students like Gajula Sekhar, Annapureddi Venkateswara Reddi, Sakhamuri Raghava Rao and Surapaneni Vimala Devi recollected this valuable information.
18. Those who did Ph.D., or who had 13 years of teaching experience were considered as the qualified guides.
19. M.Rajagoala Rao did M.Phil under his guidance.
20. Valediction-farewell speech of Prof. K. Satchidananda Murty carried in the magazine of A.U. P.G. Centre, Guntur 1971.
21. Professor C. Ramaiah who worked as the Head of Philosophy department, Śrī Venkateswara University shared these reminiscences with me over phone. Though he was convalescing at his son's home in Bangalore, he was kind enough to share these memories with me.
22. *Teacher & Student relations: Ancient Ideals and Current Situations*, Śrī Venkateswara University, Oriental Research Publications, S.V.University, Tirupati: 1978.
23. Murty, K.S., *Vedic Hermeneutics*, Op.Cit., Preface, p. xx.
24. Ibid.

6

Native Language Proficiency

Ascertaining the total number of books written by Professor Satchidananda Murty is no easy task. Most of his books are in English. Some are in Telugu. Still others are bilingual. Some of his longish talks were incorporated into the compilations of his articles. About thirteen such special works are in Telugu. The current chapter confines itself to these Telugu works.

The following analysis of Prof. Murty's works proceeds according to a chronological order rather than the order of importance. It is hoped that this particular order will enable us to better understand the evolution of Prof. Murty's thought and style of Telugu used in his writings. We all know that the relationship between language and thought shows us the the organic evolution of a writer's personality. One can discern the influence of his father- linguistically and conceptually in Prof. Murty's childhood writings. As a child all his writings revolved around the family worship of Śrī Sangameswara, Śrī Venugopala Swamy and Prasanna Anjaneya. His language was highly pedantic, full of archaic words. It should be recalled here that his father Veerabhadraiah published *Śrī Kūḍali Sangameśwara Māhātmyam* much earlier by combining prose and poetry. It consisted of Sangameśāṣṭakam and Śrī Veṇugopāla Stotram. He individually built a temple for Lord Hanuman in the village. Before that Veerabhadraiah's father and brother constructed Śrī Venugopala Swamy temple. These details were recounted by Satchidanada Murty himself.[1] All this proves that his family was deeply devoted to the worship of God. We have already seen Veerabhadraiah's love of pedantic language in the way he blessed Satchidananda Murty and Vedavati Devi on their wedding ceremony (See Chapter 4). The same can be witnessed in the very first Kanda poem in his *Śrī Kūḍali Sangameśwara Māhātyam* which opens with a prayer to Lord Gaṇeśa. Quoted below is the Kanda poem:

> *"Śrī Lalara Sangameśwara*
> *Śailendra Kumāri Hṛdayalālana Catura*
> *Śūladhara Lōka Nāyaka*
> *Pālimpumu Vṛṣabha Vāhana Pramadādhipatī"*

1. Śrī Sangameśāṣṭakam (1936)[2]

As noted earlier, Satchidananda Murty followed in his father's footsteps—devotionally, linguistically and conceptually. Accordingly he wrote *Śrī Sangameshashtakam* along with *Śrī Venugopala Stotram* in 1936 when he wrote just 12 years old. It was the same age in which he got Rashtra Bhasha Visharad (Hindi) certificate also. At that tender age, he opened the book with a Sanskrit prayer in Telugu script.

> *"Kavitābhyāsa Sidhyartham*
> *Krottānvayabhuvāmayā*
> *Satchidananda nāmnedam*
> *Sangameśāṣṭakam kṛtam"*

He then adds Śrī Veṇugopāla Stotram containing 12 ślokas and he ends the stotra with a hymn to Hari and Hara and by chanting five times the letter "Śrī". Such was his religious ardor.

2. Nāma Saṅkīrtana Mahimā (1937)[3]

Murty's devotion to customs and traditions was more

vivid in his work *Nāma Saṅkīrtana Mahimā*. It was a Telugu translation of Hindi speeches delivered by Śrī Śrī Śrī Prabhudatta Brahmachari at Rāma Nama Kshetra, Guntur. Explaining the context Prof. Murty said: "Having deeply felt that Prabhudatta Brahmachari's talks should be translated into Telugu, I took up the task. Though it was written for theists who strictly follow our Vedic and Puranic traditions, modern youth may also find it useful.

That's why 'Rāma Nama Sankirtan Sangha' brethern took up the responsibility of publishing this compilation. I am very much grateful to them."

> *"Ihānvaya Mukhenaiva Sarvam vyākhyāyate mayā |*
> *Nā mūlam likhyate kiñcit*
> *nānapekṣitamucyate."*

Murty wrote "I followed this advice by Mallinatha Suri and took every care not to lose sight of the original meaning. Even after this, if pundits find some errors I request them to bear with me and drink up the nectar of the Great Lord's name." Further Prof. Murty observed:

> *"Apa Śabdumbula gūḍiyun haricaritrālāpamul sarva pā*
> *Pa parityāgamuseyu gāvuna Harin bhāvincu baḍucun*
> *Japamul seyucu vīnulan vinucu nashrāntambu gīrtincucun*
> *Dapasul siddhulu dhanyulouduru gadā! Tattvajña! yūhimpumā".*

He explained thus in Mathebhavritha poem and dedicated it to Chamarlapuri Sangameswara Swamy. He even provided some financial assistance for its publication. He prayed Lord Kodandarama Swamy to shower his blessings on the Sangha which published the book in 1951. Satchidananda Murty was 13 years old then.

3. Śrī Hanumad Vijayam (1938)[4]

When Satchidananda Murty was 14 years old, he published *Hanumad Vijayam*. Mrs. Lakshmi Narayanamma, daughter of Rao Saheb J. Venkateswara Chowdary B.A, convinced her parents to finance the publishing of the book. Kaviraja Tripuraneni Ramaswamy Chowdary commended the book and blessed Satchidananda Murty to write many more in future. Vyakaranacharya MadhvaŚrī Palle Poorna Prajnacharya, who was Satchidananda Murty's teacher in Hindu High School, carefully examined his work. He praised the way his student gained command over Sanskrit, Telugu, Hindi and English. In order to write *Hanumad Vijayam*, Satchidananda Murty had gone through many reference books. It is a wonder that at such a young age he wrote the book after going through Rigveda, Valmiki Ramayana, Tulsi Das Ramayana, Bala Ramayana, Satha kantha Ramayana, Sahasra Kantha Ramayana, Vamadasu Andhra Ramayana, Paparaju Ramayana, Andhra Bhagavatham, Hanumantha Charithra, Kumara Sambhavam and other Puranas. The way he divided the book into three chapters and the narration he provided under catchy headlines is nothing short of a wonder at that tender age. The first chapter had fifteen sub parts- the birth of Anjaneya, the boons he got, his schooling, Hanuman becoming the minister to Sugriva, Maha Vishnu incarnating as Rāma, Śrī Rāma and Sugriva becoming friends, the killing of Vali, Hanuman flying over the seas, Maruti killing Akshaya Kumara, Hanuman conveying message to Ravana, the burning of Lanka and giving Chooda Mani to Rāma, Śrī Rāma invading Lanka with Ape army and slaying Ravana, Sita and Rāma blessing Hanuman, Hanuman becoming Chiranjeevi, the extraordinary role of Hanuman. Thus Satchidananda Murty provided complete history of Hanuman in the backdrop of *Ramayana*.

Second chapter recounts under 10 sub-heads the marriage of Hanuman and Suvarchala Devi, Hanuman tearing Mukta Haara, Hanuman writing *Ramayana*, giving a boon to Pangu, slaying of Sahasra Kantha Ravana, killing of Shatha kantha Ravana, slaying of Mairavana and slaying of Kalanemi, Hanuman appearing before Bhima, philosophy of daśāvatāra of Hanuma.

In the third chapter Satchidananda Murty recites Anjaneya Dhyana mantras. He ends the chapter traditionally with a prayer, upasamhara and Phala Sruthi.

4. Śrīmad Bhagavad Gītā (1941)[5]

Satchidananda Murty developed a special bond with *Śrīmad Bhagavad Gītā* at a very young age of 13 years (i.e., in 1937). "The Great Lord gleaned the nectar of *Gītā* by churning the ocean of wisdom. It embodies the essence of all branches of knowledge. The confusion arising from differing interpretations is cleared away and a synergy emerges from the profound meaning of *Gītā* provided by the Great Lord himself. Various schools of thought converge in *Gītā* which serve as a guiding beacon for all the inquirers into philosophy and various doctrines. *Gītā* promulgates the highest ideal for man and shows the easiest way to attain it. That's why the great little book containing just 700 ślokas is treated as equal to *Kāma Dhenu and Kalpa Valli* (the wish fulfilling divine cow and tree). Many a great soul penned erudite interpretations to *Gītā* and won esteem as outstanding teachers. "The ultimate gain one could get from good education is to be able to read and understand *Gītā*."[2] Its a wonder that Satchidananda Murty should declare this at a very tender age, that too years before he became a university professor. He himself revealed that the Great Lord inspired him to translate and interpret *Gītā* when he was just 13 years old. Though he began to carry out Lord's command on 20-03-1939, he had to discontinue the task due to some unforeseen circumstances. He resumed the work in January 1940 and finished it by May. On the whole he took 5 months to complete the translation and interpretation of 536 page *Gītā*. He was16 years old by then. His great work consisted of 26 pages of foreword, 454 pages of *Gītā* with interpretation, 6 addenda totalling 54 pages and 2 pages of Mangala Harathi. That he could present the *Gītā* running into 536 pages in just 5 months is nothing but a wonder. His superhuman concentration and tireless efforts helped to achieve this feat at such a tender age. Satchidananda Murty's achievement reminds us of young Adi Sankaracharya's accomplishment. By the time Murty attained 16 years of age, he already completed reading of interpretations of *Bhagavad Gītā, Brahma Sūtras*, eleven *Upaniṣads* by Sankara (788-820 AD), Ramanuja (1019-1139) and Madhvacharya (1199-1330). Satchidananda Murty's rendering of *Gītā* reveals his knowledge of Vedas, Brāhmaṇas, Smṛtis, Epics and Purāṇas.

Satchidananda Murty in his foreword to *Bhagavad Gītā* stated that he consulted about 20 to 30 books before writing the book. "I have maintained objectivity and steered clear of bias towards traditions. This book addresses very young readers. Those who have a rudimentary knowledge of Sanskrit can finish reading in just two hours. So I urge all the sections of readers to take up the book. As Aravind Ghosh advised, *Gītā* reading is not intended to evaluate the intricacies of the language used, or to critically analyze it or even to decide its place among Dharmic texts. It is solely meant for knowing the right path to be taken in life." Satchidananda Murty agreed with Tilak's dating of *Gītā* as 3132 BC which was the beginning of Kali age. Prior to this, in Dvapara age Lord Krishna delivered *Gītā*.[7] He presented the book "at the feet of Śrī Venu Gopala Swamy at Sangam Jagarlamudi with utmost devotion."

In the first chapter of sixth addendum to his commentary Satchidananda Murty addresses the reader: "To tell you the truth I have nothing more to write and you have nothing more to learn about *Gītā*. Because the glory of Bhagavad *Gītā* and its analysis was already widely known. Many simple, effective and unbiased interpretations are available for the seekers. They contain complete explanations regarding the importance of action and inaction. The Great Lord's intent was clearly enunciated in all those works. Yet the mystery of *Gītā* is profound. My interpretation is all encompassing. This addendum is written for the benefit of devotees who practice daily recitation of *Gītā*."[8]

Satchidananda Murty also appended additional information in his explanation to *Gītā*. He gave simple Telugu meanings to the complex Sanskrit words and sentences. With his wide knowledge of Sanskrit, Satchidananda Murty

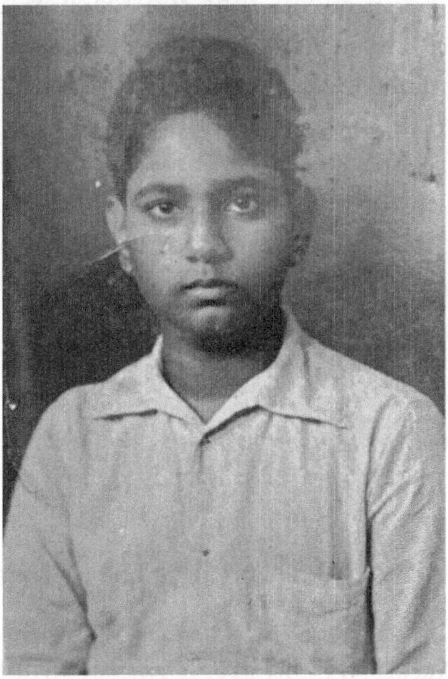

The age at which he wrote commentary on Śrīmad Bhagavad Gītā.

while explaining the renditions of ancient Acharyas, he never hesitated from offering his own opinion when it was necessary. In offering the true meaning and purpose of *Gītā* he often struck an independent path. Take for instance the 12th Śloka of second chapter of *Bhagavad Gītā*:

> *"Natvevāham jatu nāsam na tvamneme janādhipāḥ*
> *Na chaiva na bhaviṣyāmaḥ sarve vayamataḥ param"*
> *(Gītā 2:12)*

The way he had pointed out the imperfections in previous explanations of this śloka and the way he elucidated the *Ātma Gȳana* was truly amazing. He went on like this: "The plural used here should not confuse us into thinking that Atmas or Souls are innumerable. The words Me, You and Others, frequently used by Lord Krishna while teaching *Gītā* to Arjun were merely conversational terms. They shouldn't be misunderstood as inferring many Atmas. It does not mean that the teacher has a different Atma from the disciple and other humans. Yet there are some who declare that the Great Lord's Soul is entirely different from all the beings. Nothing can be farther from truth. Lord Krishna declared that Soul or Atma is eternal. He did not differentiate between Paramatma and Atma". The soul residing in a human being's body is nothing but God himself. Just like the Great Lord all beings are eternal.[9]

Also, note the way Satchidananda Murty had interpreted the 15th śloka of second chapter.

> *"Nāsato vidyate bhavo nābhāvo vidyate sataḥ Ubhayorapi dṛṣhṭo sthvanayo statva darśibhiḥ" (Gītā 2:15)*

The gist of this śloka: The false has no existence, It is the Truth that exists forever.

Various Acharyas had given various interpretations for this śloka- depending on their philosophical traditions. Yet we have to understand this as Lord Krishna intended it to be. According to Krishna, Truth means *Brahman* which is unbound by space and time. Untruth means the physical world which has a form and name.

"What is true has no end. So it is pointless to lament that Atma will end one day. What is untrue will surely come to an end. So it is stupid to rue about those untrue things that have a form and name. It is foolish to lament about the loss of things which give pain and pleasure. "Aśocyā nanvaśochastuam" meaning Ātma which is the ultimate Truth is never destroyed, the body which is untrue will surely end one day. It is meaningless to rue about it's loss".[10]

See the meaningful way Satchidananda Murty interpreted the 38th Śloka in the same chapter.

> *"Sukhaduhkhe samekṛtvā lābhālābhau jayājayu*
> *Tato yudhāya yujyasva naivam pāpa mavāpsyasi"*
> *(Gītā 2:38)*

"Treating pain and pleasure, gain and loss, victory and defeat as one and the same, do your battles. This equanimity will put you beyond the pale of Sin." Satchidananda Murty further elucidates the śloka- "In the Kurukshetra war, Arjun was ready to lay down his arms and embark on the path of renunciation. But Lord Krishna pointed out that the very path of renunciation asks us not to cry about impending end of either the body or soul. It teaches us to treat pleasure and pain as two sides of same coin. So a Kṣatriya has to fulfil his duty i.e., to fight his battles. Sin will not touch him if he fights righteously with a detached mind. You may say that as you are going to renounce everything on any given day, you refrain from fighting today. You may also say that as you have already received self-knowledge from me, it is time for renunciation. But the truth is even after receiving self-knowledge one has to keep on doing actions with a detached mind. Lord Krishna termed it as Karma Yoga. Thus the Great Lord enunciated the Advaitic Yoga concept in his *Gītā.*" One should note that Satchidananda Murty's explanation differs with Sankara's Advaita.

> *"Ahamātmā guḍākeśa sarvabhūtāśayasthitah*
> *Ahamādisca madhyamca Bhūtānāmata Evacha"*
> *(Gītā, 10:20)*

Satchidananda Murty rendered that the Great Lord revealed that there is no difference between him and the universe. Both are one and same. Advaita also propounds the same principle. One attains emancipation by realising that *Vasauda Sarvam.* Satchidananda Murty's rendition is closer to Visishtadvaita than Advaita. Though he did not use the word Advaita directly, his monotheistic beliefs show through his renditions. But one shouldn't presume that Satchidananda Murty opposed Sankara's Advaita.

> *"Karmaṇyakarmayaḥ paśye dakarmani ca karma yaḥ*
> *Sa budhimānmanuṣyeṣu sa yukth kṛtsna karma kṛt"*
> *(Gītā 4:18)*

Satchidananda Murty states that the meaning of this śloka is deep and mystifying. He asks "how can one see non-action in action." Who can say that he is not acting while acting?

People in general equate non-action with inaction. But in reality, no man or woman can be inactive all the time (*Gītā* 3:8; 5:12 page 125), because every being has to sleep, lie down, sit, stand and move about in the course of life. So what does Lord Krishna mean by action and non-action?

"One has to determine action and non-action by its good or bad effects. In fact all creation is one great action. So as long as the creation continues, action never leaves man. The action which does not affect self has no source. Thus one has to discern true action from non-action with a detached mind. Such action or non-action is what *Gītā* instructs us to do. That action which doesn't bind one is the true action. It is in reality a non-action". (page 126)

"The man who sees action in non-action and non-action in action is called a Yogi. One who does all actions with this mindset is a sensible and intelligent person. By following the definitions *Yogah karmasu kauśalam, Samatvam Yoga Ucyate* he is considered as an intelligent person or a Yogi and Yukta (an intelligent and detached person)." I do not recall any other pundit who explained difficult terms like action and non-action in such a simple Telugu and with so much ease.

Karma Yogis are liberated souls. Like the *Sanyāsis* they need not depend on others for sustenance. They entirely rely on God for everything. A true *Karma Yogi* is always content, free and does actions without seeking results. (page 129)

> *"Nehābhikramanāśosti pratyavāyo na vidyate Svalpamapyasya dharmasya trāyate mahato Bhayāt" (Gītā 2:40)*

By quoting this śloka, Satchidananda Murty enunciates that *Bhagavad Gītā* stresses Karma Yoga which can be practiced easily by common folk even. Lord Krishna highly favoured this Yoga of action (page 53). *Karma Yoga* is also termed as *Karma Sanyasa Yoga* and *Niṣkāma karma yoga i.e.*, yoga of result—foregoing action.

> *"Ye me matamidam nityamanutiṣthanti mānavāḥ Śradhāvantos nasūyamto mucyante tespi karmabhiḥ" (Gītā 3:31)*

Those who dedicatedly follow the path instructed by me will be liberated from the bonds of karma- the Lord promises. "The path propounded by *Gītā* is a combination of Gÿāna (higher knowledge), Bhakti (devotion), Vairāgya (renunciation) and Niṣkāma karma (action without seeking the fruits) yogas. So Satchidananda Murty prefers to call this path as Lord Krishna's yoga or religion. Those who follow this path should be devoted to the Great Lord Krishna till death. It can be followed by both commoners and yogis. Thus Lord Krishna bestowed the mankind an equitable path of liberation.

But a problem arises here, because Lord Krishna himself declared earlier that there are only two paths – Gyana and Karma Yogas.

> *"Lokessmin dvividhā niṣṭhā purā proktāmayas nagha!*
> *Jnāna Yogena sānkhyānām karmayogena yoginām"*
> *(Gītā, 3:3)*

"So *Gītā* propounded two paths: Samkhya Niṣṭa and Yoga Niṣṭa. Among them Yoga Nishta which was given more prominence is nothing else but Karma Yoga," Satchidananda Murty explained.

Lord Krishna while clearing doubts expressed by Arjun, shows him the way to understand him also. (*Asamsayam, samagram mā yathā gñasyasi tacruṇu- Gītā* 7). Satchidananda Murty explains that the first six chapters of *Gītā* articulate *Karma Yoga*. Following six chapters instruct *Bhakti Yoga* and *Gyana Yoga* exposition is delivered till 18th chapter. Here Yaamunaacharya's *Thrishashti* comes to mind.

"Following Gyana Yoga's Samkhya Nishta, should I give up battle or jump into this terrible war? If I do so, how can I be free of the sins committed in war?"— Arjun was haunted by such doubts. To allay his doubts Lord Krishna explained Sāmkhya and Karma Yogas in the first four chapters of *Gītā*. But after being quizzed by Arjun as to the best yoga of them all (page 196), Krishna declared Karma Yoga to be the best.

"Lokessmin dvividha niṣṭha purā proktāmayānagha" (*Gītā* 3:3). This śloka makes it clear that *Gītā* propounded only

two independent yogic paths. Yet interpreters argued that Bhakti yoga also is an independent path — Satchidananda informs us.

"Without Gyana, one can't attain *Moksha* (liberation from birth and death cycle). One can attain Gyana in whichever he chooses. Once attaining Gyana he becomes liberated. Should he continue to do karma even after that? This was the principal question in *Gītā*. It describes only two yogas—one is Karma or Kevala Yoga, and the other is Samkhya or Gyana Yoga. So *Gītā* infers that there is no third path meaning Bhakti Yoga. One can attain Gyana through devotion (Bhakti) also. After attaining Gyana, one can still continue actions (karma) and be known as a yogi. If a Gyani chooses not to do karma, he will become a Samkhya Margi. Though both are liberating, taking up karma or action is clearly superior. The 5th śloka of 5th chapter in *Gītā* reveals that Moksha (liberation) can be attained both by Samkhya and Yoga. Now the Lord states that by doing action (karma) one gets Gyana and finally Moksha. He declared the same in the 1st śloka of 7th chapter: "I am not going to teach you about Bhakti (devotion), but I will reveal how you can gain Gnana by doing actions while always keeping me in your heart and mind . (page 197)

By scrutinizing such ślokas, Satchidananda Murty rejects the contention that *Gītā* prefers Bhakti over Gyana. He declared that the essence of *Gītā* is Karma Yoga and fulfilling of worldly duties (Pravṛtti Marga) but not renunciation and turning back on the world. It may be noted that though Samkara accepted both Gyana and Karma Yogas, he gave more prominence to Gyana (Samkhya) Yoga. Ramanuja, Madhva et al stressed Bhakti over other yogas. They affirmed that the relationship between individual soul and Universal Soul can only be understood through Bhakti. In *Gītā* one can find many ślokas asserting Bhakti. Prominent among them is:

"Pathraṁ pushpaṁ phalaṁ toyaṁ yo me bhaktyā prayachathi tadaham bhaktyupahṛta masnāmi prayatātmanaḥ" (Gītā 9.26)

The 17th and 18th chapters in *Gītā* emphasize Bhakti. "Lord Krishna declared that he deems Bhakti as the most important in 2:49 śloka. He repeated the same in these two chapters"—Satchidananda Murty feels. The Great Lord proclaimed that even sinners, women, Vaisyas and Sudras will attain to him if they worship with utmost devotion.

"Mām hi Partha vyapāśrītya yepisyuḥ pāpayonayaḥ Striyo vaiśyāstathā Śūdrāste'pi yānti parām gatim" (Gītā 9:32).

Satchidananda Murty reminds us that Bal Gangadhar Tilak also quoted this śloka to conclude that the essence of *Gītā* is to combine Gyana and Bhakti yogas. But it should be noted that Satchidananda Murty, having sublimated one into the other, did not regard Bhakti as a separate yoga. Karma is entwined with Dharma. That's why *Gītā* exhorts us to fulfil our own Dharma which is another way to say that one has to do his own karma. If we stick to the traditional interpretations of *Gītā*, a confusion arises on the nature of one's Dharma. Satchidananda Murty identified this problem at a very young age and set out to solve it in his own way.

Manu Smṛti divided the society into various castes and gothras and imposed *Varṇa Āśrama dharma* meaning duties to be followed by various castes. But Lord Krishna stated that it was he who classified men according to their intrinsic qualities.

"Cāturvarnyam mayā sṛṣṭām guṇa karmavibhāgaśaḥ
Tasya kartāra mapi mām viddhya kartāramavyayam" (Gītā 4:13)

Here a question arises as to which comes first: whether the division of men according to their caste and gothra or the division based on intrinsic qualities. Lord Krishna revealed in the fourth chapter of the *Gītā* that it was he who instructed this perennial yoga first to Sun god who in turn revealed this to Manu and who passed it on to Ikshvaku.

> *"Imam vivasvate yogam proktavānahamavyayam*
> *Vivasvān manave prāha manuriksvakave bravīt."*
> *(Gītā 4:1)*

It is evident that *Manu Smṛti* was laid down much later than Lord Krishna. The division of men according to the inherent qualities is much older than the one by caste and gothra. We have to take into account his instruction that one should better follow his own Dharma than others.

> *"Śreyān svadharmo viguṇaḥ paradharmātsvanu ṣtitāt*
> *Svabhavaniyatam karma kurvannāpnoti kilbiṣam"*
> *(Gītā 18.47)*

However flawed one's innate actions may be, they should not be abandoned. Conveying this, Lord Krishna stated *"Sahajam karma kaunteya sadoshamapi na tyajet"* (*Gītā* 18:48). Affirming that the actions of various varnas are intrinsic to them, He defines Brāhmina, Kṣatriya, Vaiśya and Śūdra karmas.

Krishna explains in the following śloka that self-control, overcoming temptations, meditation, cleanliness, forbearance, simplicity, knowledge and understanding are the innate qualities of the Brahmin Varna.

> *"Brāhmaṇa, Kṣatriya, Viśām Sūdrāṇām ca paramtapa!*
> *Karmāni pravibhaktāni svabhāvaprabhavairguṇaih"*
> *(Gītā 18:41)*

He defines Kṣatriya qualities as valour, fearlessness, fortitude, resourcefulness, and also, not fleeing in war, charity, and the ability to rule, are the natural duties of a Kṣatriya.

> *"śauryam tejo dhṛtirdākṣyam yuddhe cāpyapalāyanam dānamīsvarabhāvasca kṣātram karma svabhāvajam" (Gītā 18:43)*

Vaiśya varṇa natural occupations are farming, cattle-rearing and commerce. And service the quality of Śūdra varṇa.

> *"Kṛsi Gorakṣa vanijyam Vashyamkarma svabhāvajam Paricaryātmakam karma Śūdrasyāpi svabhāvajam" (Gītā, 8:44)*

Thus Krishna proclaims that one will attain liberation by doing actions natural to one's own varna. *"Sve Sve karmaṇyabhiratāssamsidhim labhate narah"* (*Gītā* 18:45) meaning one attains emancipation by worshipping the omnipresent God from whom all creation came forth. That's why Lord Krishna declared doing one's own karma is sure path to Moksha.

> *"Yataḥ pravrittirbhūtā nām yena sarvamidam tatam Svakarmaṇā tamabhyarcya siddhim vindati mānavaḥ" (Gītā 18:46)*

It is truly surprising that Satchidananda Murty at so young an age could explain and apply such a complex dharmic analysis to the contemporary society.

He acknowledges that the śloka *"Cāturvarṇyam mayā Śṛṣṭyam guṇakarma vibhāgaśaḥ"* (*Gītā* 4:13) is highly controversial. Satchidananda Murty wants us to ponder over the question-why the Great Lord did proclaim such an inflammatory statement.

The 9th śloka describes God's actions (page 121). But it didn't say anything about the divinity, distinctiveness and nature of his karmas. So 13-14 ślokas gave us that discourse. The distinctiveness of God's karmas is that he will remain a non-actor even after acting. How is it so?

"There are three Guṇas (qualities or attributes) that have always been and continue to be present in all beings and things in the world. They are called: <u>sattva</u> (goodness, constructive, harmonious), <u>rajas</u> (passion, active, confused), and <u>tamas</u> (darkness, destructive, chaotic). A person who has more of Sattva guṇa is known as a Brahmin, And a Kshatriya is one who has more rajasic qualities with a mix of sattvic. One who is more dominated by tamo guna is a śūdra. And vaishya is one who has predominantly rajasic qualities mingled with tamasic guṇa. All humans are Śūdras by birth. It was by education one develops various guṇas and acts thereby. Any man can become a Brahmin through education and meditation. So *Gītā* proclaims that a man who chooses appropriate actions in accordance with his intrinsic qualities and fulfils them dispassionately is sure to attain Mokṣa." (page 122)

The following śloka explains action and non-action.

> *"Karmaṇyakarma yah paśyedakarmani ca karma yaḥ*
> *Sa budhimānmanuṣyeṣu sa yuktaḥ kṛtsna karmakṛt,"*
> *(Gīṭā, 14:18)*

"A person who sees action in non-action and non-action in action is the most intelligent one, He alone is brilliant and takes up proper actions." Satchidananda Murty says that the meaning of this śloka is deep and mysterious. Who could see non-action in action? Who can say that he is not acting while acting?"

Generally non-action is taken as inaction. But no man can be inactive forever. This was made clear earlier (3:18; 5:1). Sleeping, lying down, sitting are all part of life. So what the Great Lord means by "non-action."

Here Satchidananda Murty explains: "We have to decide action and non-action by their results whether good or bad. When creation itself is action personified, man can never be free of action as long as creation exists. The action whose outcome is not detrimental to man can be termed as non-action. So non-action is not synonymous with inaction. True karma is not binding. In order to shake off bondage of action, one has to take up non-action with tact and equanimity. Such non-action is reckoned by *Gītā* as real action. Non-binding actions are non-actions.

"When we exclude such dispassionate and desireless actions (Niskama Karma) we will be left with two kinds of actions. (1) *Vikarma* and (2) *Kevala Karma* (or karma). *Vikarma* is the karma, done out of ignorance and infatuation. *Kevala Karma* or karma is the outward action done in the pursuit of *swadharma.*

In the end, actions done due to *āsakti* (stake), *phale ca* (seeking benefit) *mamata* (affection) and *ahaṅkāra* (ego) lead to pain and pleasure and eventually to rebirth (page 126). Such actions, at times, turn out to be distorted actions or Vikarmas.

"One who discerns between various kinds of actions and acts dispassionately and without desire is truly wise. *Yogaḥ karmasu kauśalam, Samatvam Yoga ucyate* (page 27) meaning a person who does karmas with tact and composure is a resourceful and reflective one. He is the Yogi.

After examining action, non-action and distorted action, Satchidananda Murty sets out to explain *Bhagavad Gītā's* four fold Varna division.

"Brāhmana Kshatriya Viśām Sūdrānām ca paramtapa Karmāṇi pravibhaktāni svabhāva prabhavairguṇaḥ" (Gītā 18:41)

O Arjun! The actions by Brahmin, Kshatriya, Vaishya and Shudras spring from their nature which in turn are dictated by Gunas. Hindu Dhrama Shastras divided men into four varnas.

- Brahmins are those who by virtue of intelligence and self-restraint make a deep study of various Shastras and spread knowledge. Ex: Sage Vasishta
- A Kshatriya is one who is brave and courageous and is skillful in deploying men in various duties. Ex: Bhishma
- A Vaishya does business righteously, fetches and sells various goods from near and far, takes up agriculture and cattle-rearing. Ex: Thuladhar
- Lacking mental acumen but full of bodily vigour a Shudra takes up physical labour and serves the society. Ex: Dharma Vyadha.

Satchidananda Murty applies these principles to modern conditions and says "In these days, persons who serve the nation by their intelligence, spread knowledge through their writings and discourse can be termed as Brahmins".

Soldiers, Police, District Collectors and various lawmakers are modern Kṣatriyas. Those who engages in trading of various goods and services are Vaishyas. The manual labour and various kinds of servants can be counted as Shudra.

Nobody is a Brahmin by birth. All men acquire differing qualities. If one distinguishes himself with knowledge and intelligence, he is surely a Brahmin. If one makes himself renowned by valour, he is a Kṣatriya. A man who shines in business is a Vaiśya. And finally the person who ekes out a living by doing hard labour is a Śūdra" (pp 419-420).

The way Satchidananda Murty debunked Manu Smṛti's definition of four-fold varṇa system is laudable. Not content with that he sets out on an independent path to unveil Lord Krishna's interpretation of Gunas and Karmas. He differed with the traditional *Gītā* interpretations to declare that one can be a *Sthita Prajñā* (steady and one-pointed) and still be a *Gṛhastha* (page 14). But he has to:

- Maintain self-restraint
- Control his emotions
- Control his senses.

"Sanyasi, Grihastha, Vyadha or Shudra-who ever has these qualities is the real *Sthita Prajñā*. Such a man doesn't care for differentiations of caste and status. He attains serenity of mind."

> *"Yaḥ sarvatrānabhisnehastatprāpya śubhāshubham*
> *Nābhinandati na dveṣṭi tasya prajña pratiṣṭhitā"*
> *(Gītā 2:57)*

Meaning "He who is without attachment, who neither rejoices nor laments in the face of good and bad experiences, is of a firm mind and fixed in perfect knowledge."

"Lord Śrī Ram was the ideal *Sthita Prajñā*. He was free of attachments. He was the perfect Karma Yogi because he neither exulted on being coroneted nor bemoaned on his exile into forest" (page 69). Such independent interpretations abound in Satchidananda Murty's version of *Gītā*. See his explanation of *Gītā* 1:10:

> *Aparyaptam tadasmākam balam Bhīṣmābhi rakṣitam* I
> *Paryāptamtvmeteṣām balam Bhimābhi rakṣitam* II

It means "Our army protected by the strength of Bhishma is unlimited. Whereas the army of Pandavas protected by Bhima is limited." This was a comparative estimate by Duryodhana. But it is a highly controversial interpretation because there are differing meanings for *paryapta* and *aparyapta* which confound us. The word *Paryaptam* has two contradictory meanings—whole and limited. Like-wise

Aparyaptam has two opposing meanings—limited and not holistic. So Duryodhana must have intended to say that though the Kaurava army under Bhishma is a large one yet it is insufficient to face Pandava might. Whereas Bhima's Pandava forces while being limited in numbers is powerful enough to deal a death blow to Kauravas (page 7).

Such unique renderings abound in young Satchidananda Murty's writings. One can savour these by reading his interpretation of *Gītā*.

5. Saptaslokī Bhagavad Gītā (1943)[11]

This seven śloka work was published three years after Satchidananda Murty's interpretation of *Gītā* i.e., in 1943. By that time he was 19 years old. Satchidananda Murty specially chose seven ślokas from five chapters of *Gītā*. He obviously believed that these ślokas unveil the essence of *Gītā*. This little book explained the beneficial effects of reading the seven ślokas.

6. Īśopanishattu (1946)[12]

This is also called Iśāvāsya Upaniṣad because it starts with the mantra *"Iśāvāsya midam sarvam."* It forms the 40th chapter of *Shukla Yajurveda*. Coming at the end of Veda it has become renowned as Vedanta. Though all Upaniṣads are termed as Vedanta, *Īśopanishad* occupies a singular place among them. Monotheistic in character, it is also known as the First Upaniṣad. This must be the reason for Satchidananda Murty to choose the study of this particular Upaniṣad.

In 1946, the very first year of taking up a teaching position in Śrī Venkateswara University, Professor Murty began work on interpretation of *Īśopanishad*. The unusual feature in this 86 page work is that it contained a 51 page introduction. Prof. Murty explained the meaning of Upanishad, omniscience of God, spirituality, the way to attain it, meaning of Deva pada, nature of Time, the way ancient rishis attained the ultimate Truth through meditation (*Dhyān Yoga*), Man's relationship with God, and finally assures that one can attain the omnipresent Truth through *Brahma Vidyā*. Rejecting that *Brahma Vidyā* is reserved for only higher varnas i.e., the Twice born, he affirmed that it is attainable even by normal *Gṛhastas.* He reminded that almost all the Vedic Rishis were *Gṛhastas*. Taking a wholly new perspective Prof. Murty declared that *Brahma Vidyā* is universal and can be learnt by anyone. He saw faith in God is necessary and explained the effectiveness of Devotion (Bhakti) and exhorted that all religions should be respected equally. God, Śrī Krishna, *Parameśwara, Paramātma* or the Ultimate Cause or Purpose — all are one and the same. The *Jīva* (human being) should realise that he is a part of the *Paramātma* and strive to reach him through attaining *Brahma Gyan* or through *Dhyāna,* Bhakti Yogas. At a time when worship of Avatars and Gods was being ridiculed, he strongly advocated it. His Vishitadvaita beliefs played a crucial part here.

7. Kāru Mabbulu (Dark Clouds) (1947)[13]

Prof. Murty published this book in 1947 from Sangam Jagarlamudi. He explained the background to this eight-article compilation in a foreword titled 'Notes'. He said "I have collected my recent articles about political, social and philosophical topics into this book. The first four articles were already published in *Bharatha Mitramu*—a Guntur publication. I have endeavoured to discuss a specific topic in each essay from a particular viewpoint.

The eight articles in this collection: 1. Vetukulāṭa (the Seeking) 2. Yemi Ceyāli? (What is to be done?) 3.

Abhyudayam (Progress) 4. Marxism 5. Anaatha (The Orphan) 6. Bhāva Sangrāmam (the clash of ideology) 7. Neṭi Samasya (The Contemporary Question) 8. Kāru Mabbulu (Dark Clouds).

By taking the title of the last article as the cover title, Prof. Murty indicated its importance. Each article is a standalone one. His angst and search for solutions for life's problems form the theme of the book. For the first time he diverted his attention from spiritual quest to worldly and secular affairs in this collection. The way he incisively analysed contemporary problems unveils an unknown aspect in Murty. It serves as an eye-opener to those who tried to pass judgment on his personality without realising his broad outlook. Prof. Murty likened the problems faced by modern society as dark clouds and offered sensational solutions to them.

The first article 'Vethukulāṭa' (the Seeking) flows like a self-introspection. He examines human nature and ponders over man's duty. He wonders whether it is man's fate to be ceaselessly tortured by useless thoughts. Should he be always troubled with a scattered brain? Prof. Murty also points out that there is a fundamental difference between men, cattle and trees. He queries: "Should I be content with mere money-making, eating, drinking and sleeping like the calf in our backyard? Should I learn to live like a buffalo, simply eating and ruminating? Is going through the motions of living, man's only purpose?"

He sets out to answer the query in the following manner: "I understood one thing quite clearly. There is an abysmal emptiness, a limitless imperfection in human life. Till that emptiness is filled and imperfection straightened out, the perpetual craving in man's heart won't be satiated. So what to do? That I do not know. But one thing is sure. Attaining great riches, beautiful women, fame and good food can't fill that limitless whole in our hearts. It is like an incurable disease. Then how can we get rid of it? Now religion steps forward and asks us not to worry and assures us of a solution.

The next article 'Yemi Cheyāli?' (What to be done?) elaborates on this concept. Most of us don't have time for this type of philosophical inquiry. Yet we find people living in hills and forests leading a simple and contented lives. So we have to ask ourselves what's the use in leading such a harried and restless lives? Do we need such a pompous and destructive development just to feed ourselves? Are we happier with our lives than our ancestors?

Yet some moderns predict that as we are on the path of endless progress, man will be like a God soon and heaven will be brought down to earth. Prof. Murty debunks this by saying, "We, the simple folk can't understand these tall claims. All we know is that modern man is making a fool of himself. The present day world is turning into hell."

"Some people say that Russia has everything. When we go deep into the truth we will come to know that to put faith in Russian system is like sowing seeds in Sahara desert, trying to gather flowers in Gobi desert. On the other hand Churchill declares that Anglo-American culture is the best. While people of their own countries are themselves in utter confusion, they go on lecturing others about the virtues of their system. None of them will ever work. Though people like Gandhi, Wallace, Einsteirn, Pearl S. Buck, Bernard Shaw et al., suggest there are better ways, their words are falling on deaf ears. The threat of Third World War is hovering above our heads. Is there no other way to save mankind?", Prof. Murty asks. He declares that politics can't answer this questions but Prophets can.

The third article titled 'Abhyudayam' (Progress) poses the question- What is Progress? Following Darwin's evolution theory, can we term every change as progress? Is every transformation good? Won't it ever turn out to be dangerous? Theorists conclude that the higher stage is always better than lower stage in biological evolution. Why so? Is it because of higher energy expended? Such were the questions posed by Professor Murty. To say that no one knows the answers is nothing but stupidity (page 10). He concludes that progress is also an action which has no actor. So if we agree to the idea of Progress we will also have to the moving force behind it. That force may be called God or some other thing. So the theory of progress or evolution is an empty one. In the end, Evolutionary theory is a misnomer- Murty contends (page.11) and rejects it.

"The meaningless theory of evolution is being taken as the standard one in each and everything. If we believe that an unseen conscious power is driving the world, then we can be sure that it will gradually lead us into progress. But if we deny the existence of such a force, we may well say good bye to the idea of progress". Thus Prof. Murty asserted the predominance of the unseen omnipresent force.

If there were two or three different paths to a goal, we can choose the reliable method among them and achieve progress. When we lack such diverse methods, the question of making a choice doesn't arise. "The world is undoubtedly evolving. It is changing everyday. Darwin asserted that evolution always proceeds towards progress, which is totally false. And Marxist dialectical materialism is based on this delusive notion of ever increasing progress (page 12). This counterfeit argument firmly took hold amongst the modern thinkers.

The fourth essay in the collection is titled 'Marxism'. Today, a confusion prevails over the meaning of Marxism. There are many hues of Marxists, each providing their own interpretation of the theory. Marxism dons many garbs-

as a logical system, philosophical, historical and cultural system- all at the same time. Satchidananda Murty tried to understand this theory in his own way and provide a simple explanation to the common people.

"There are two kinds of interpretations to Marxism. One was provided by Trotsky and the other by Stalin. As Russia bowed down to Stalin, the ideas of Trotsky disappeared from the scene. Currently Marxism as interpreted by Stalin has possessed the communist parties all over the world. Yet Trotskyism still survives in our country. The Radical Democratic Party adheres to this particular ideology. But they lack sufficient cadre or financial resources. It may eventually disappear just like Justice Party did"- Prof. Murty captures the early phase of Marxism in India in these words.

"Though Marxism wielded a wide influence over political, economic, social and moral fields, it is not a sound theory either scientifically or logically. This fact was long ago established by Russell et al.," he continued.

He explained this argument further: "Marx declared that the world moves forward according to a dialectical formula. This forward movement or progress is inevitable and inexorable. The driving force behind this inevitable development is nothing else but Matter i.e., Nature. The Nature or Matter in Marxian jargon is nothing like the one defined by Indian Samkhya philosophers. It is also contrary to the definitions provided by Western philosophers like Aristotle. According to Marx the subject and object; the percipient (one who perceives) and the object known are in a continuous process of mutual adaptation, which is being dialectical, is never completed fully. In Marx's view all perception is an interaction between subject and object.

"Marx also says that it is the interaction between man and the physical world that determines the material world.

Man's methods of production form the most important part of this interaction. The future of the world is determined by how we are acting on the material world and how the world in turn is acting on us. This in essence is Marxism"

"Marxism declares that it is man's methods of production which change the world. It sees the world through these glasses only. It also declares that it is this dialectic which brings the labour into power. Marx believed that each step taken forward in the dialectical development is Progress which can only be achieved by revolution. That's why people who follow his path hail the revolution on the streets"- Prof Murty explained.

But he differs with Marx: "His dialectical theory doesn't stand before logic even for a minute. In fact, it is the interaction between subject-object; knower-knowledge that determines the nature and progress of the world individually and collectively. Evidently it is man's methods of production that are causing wars and pestilence, famines, storms, earth quakes and crop failures. There is no greater superstition than believing that our civilization, culture, arts, music and literature- all have man's mode of production as their base (page 17)".

"Let us agree with Marx's dialectical progress for argument sake and accept that the kingdom of Labour will dawn on us one day. Marx assures us that the rule of labour will be ultimately beneficial to us. But who is he to decide what is good for us? Socialism may truly take the place of Capitalism one day. But how can we be sure that it will be the most welcome development? If socialism is good for labour, the landlord will feel bourgeoisism is of utmost benefit to him. If oppressing the land lord is of advantage to the coolies, the land lord may deem it necessary to exploit the coolies.

Marx felt that every forward step in dialectical progress is great and highly desirable. As Marx vows that the next phase of Bourgeoism is Bolshevism, he feels it is the best way forward. But who is Marx to choose the future for us, how can he judge which is good and which is bad? That is just his own opinion. It is just his imagination. If Marx holds an opinion, I may harbour a contrarian one. How can anybody decide which is the better one among these two? Marx answers this by declaring that the world always and inexorably moves towards progress. So socialism inevitably follows capitalism. He avows that socialism is good for all. But those who deny the existence of an Unseen Conscious Power have no right to profess that the world always move forward and forever scales new heights (page 18).

"So the contention that Socialism is synonymous with Progress is just the personal opinion and belief of Marx. To launch an armed revolution and subjecting the society to untold hardships just to achieve this fantasy is nothing but a superstition and height of stupidity" (page 19). Every body has seen how blind beliefs lead to religious tensions and communal riots. Those who believe that Marxism is the ultimate truth and commit themselves on the path of revolution are no different than those swayed by religious fanaticism. Every one or every section fights for power. Once they grab power, no distinction remains between them and those who lost it. Till the time they lay hands on power, they remain enemies of the society. That's why Russell equates Marxism with power politics. Murty remarks:

"Yet I don't mean that Marxism doesn't contain truth at all. I also don't wish to say that it is a meaningless movement. All I want to convey is that Communism based on Marxism is nothing but castles built in sand."

Thus Satchidananda Murty concluded that Marxism is a fantasy which has no firm ground to stand on. Change the world- this in short is the dream of Marxism which is yet to become a reality.

The fifth article *Aanaatha* (the orphan) proceeds from his personal experiences. It starts with evaluation of the role of unmarried women employees, moves to compare Eastern and Western systems of marriage, accepts that man and woman naturally want to be together, supports traditional family system and finally cautions modern youth against the perils of blindly following modern trends.

Satchidananda Murty knew about Miss Manorama Goyanachi, a beautiful unmarried woman who took up a job to support her family. In this article he takes a sympathetic view of her and proceeds to probe the conditions of women employees, the plight of rural women, the differences between Eastern and Western women employees, domestic disharmony. He advised against infidelity and warned the straying males about the dangers of sexually transmitted diseases. Extolling the greatness of Indian marriage system, Satchidananda Murty stresses that just the thought of being a man and wife fills one with satisfaction and sweet memories. The institution of marriage is just not simply meant to fulfil sexual desires, it is meant to serve as a bedrock during hard times. Under the wedlock, the affection and the bond between man and woman grow forever. Thus we can see that the article titled *Anātha* (the Orphan) is not really about orphans per se. It is about unmarried women who by serving others take care of their families. An encounter with such a lady spurred Satchidananda Murty to write this article.

In the sixth article *"Bhāva Sangrāmam"* (Clash of ideologies) he analyses the impact, merits and demerits of the two opposing ideologies dominating modern world. These mutually exclusive theories are dividing mankind into two conflicting camps, sow dissensions among them, increase hostility in their hearts and minds and finally lead to civil war and war between nations. Prof. Murty counsels that we should not give way to the destruction of the world.

Contemporary world is divided into Marxist- Communist camp and the capitalist camp led by Anglo-American liberals. Meanwhile, the proselytizing Christian missionaries are endangering national identities, ancient Indian, Chinese and Japanese cultures. The efforts of Mahatma Gandhi and Jawaharlal Nehru to build an alternative was laudable.

Though Capitalism and Communism appear to be difficult, deep down both are one and the same. He explains that both these systems incite class antagonism. "They build palaces of so called peace on the foundations of disharmony using bricks of hate and cruelly cement them with blood and sweat of the people. Trying to install peace and fraternity through revolution is like seeking a child from a barren woman (page 46). Just a look at the totalitarian policies followed by Communist countries makes us realise that the revolution's promise of bringing heaven to earth is an empty one. At the same time he approves Anglo-American system of governance which follows electoral democracy and equal opportunities to all. It also honours majority opinion and pays compensation in cases where individual property is taken over by the state. "Now we have to choose the better of the two systems. Both Communism and Capitalism assure that everyone will earn in accordance with their abilities. Persons of merit can make it big in Russia and US as well. But rabble-rousers, hypocrites and fraudsters can become dictators both in Russia and India (page 55). Stalin and Patel are the best examples here. The dim-witted lowly people cannot hope to rise either in Russia or in India. In Russia such people will be made to work hard and paid something in return. But in India there is nobody bothers to do so. Choosing Russian system for such a small mercy is like jumping from a frying pan into fire. Choosing between the two systems is like opting between the devil and deep sea (page 56).

"Marxists set out to turn hell into heaven. Though it is a laudable goal they don't know how to go about it. As a result all communist countries have turned into living hell. Those who don't subscribe to Communist ideals are sticking with the status quo. Currently there is a clash between these two ideologies. If it degenerates into war all hell will break lose" (page 57).

In this way Prof. Murty surveyed the situation obtaining in his time. Today, the world has changed. Soviet Union collapsed long ago. The days of US dominance seem to be numbered. Like Mao, Je Dong said many other ideologies are blossoming in the present day world. How these developments are going to shape up—nobody knows.

"The Contemporary Question" (*Neti Samasya*) is the title of the seventh article. In every age every country faces many problems. Many temporary problems simply disappear in the currents of time. "The main question in the present age is related to individual freedom. How can political democracy help bring out economic equality—this is the main issue now" (page 60).

"When man is not free to think, teach and do things in a way he deems fit, even if the whole nation attains freedom it will remain meaningless. When people are deprived of basic necessities like food, shelter and clothing, then also we can't call ourselves a free society" (page 60).

Russia wants state control over each and every aspect of society. Dictator Franco's Spain wants trade union control. Both nations lack individual freedom. In countries like USA and India which are under Capitalism, rich people exist. But here all the material wealth is concentrated in the hands of a very few people or corporations. In these capitalist countries countless peasants and coolies are reduced to slavery. They are lorded over by big land owners. So many people facing dire straits is a blot on capitalist system. "So concentration of wealth and power either in the hands of a few rich men or the Government is equally bad. Adding trade union dominance completes the triad of power. As long as three arms of the triad are equal in strength common people can breathe easy. But if any one of the arms is longer than the other two, individual freedom is lost and society will suffer" (page 62). "Our common objective is to ensure individual freedom along with providing basic necessities to one and all" (page 63). Yet the society is divided into rich and poor with the latter reduced to deprivation. We need a government to protect the poor. Rich, poor and the Government-all should work together instead of working at cross purposes. This is the only way peace and harmony can be protected in our society. Though we have created money as a means of development, it ultimately became a cancer on the society. Only by destroying toxic money culture, we will be able to live like human beings. "The palace of superior culture should be constructed with a fresh viewpoint and novel objectives. Rousseau, Gandhi, Einstein, Aurobindo and centuries before them, the Buddha- all gave the same call. Building a society without desires is what Buddha exhorted (page 66).

What all man really needs is a fistful of food, a glass of water and a shelter from rain and sun. All else is nonessential. They don't give happiness. None of our scientific and technological inventions which are considered as the true standards of our civilization can give us peace. Rousseau emphasized that unless we destroy this false and toxic civilization we can't attain peace and happiness (page 67). We have to bid adieu to all falsehoods and return to Nature. Only by leading such a virtuous life that man can be truly happy. Everyone will produce things to fulfil his needs, the surplus will be bartered. Because of such cashless transactions, man's acquisitive nature disappears, disparities and clashes between men will become things of past. The rise of such ideal societies all over the world will bring about happiness to the mankind. How and when can such a society emerge? It can only happen after man's basic nature changes for the good. This can be achieved not through physical means but through knowledge. Gandhi and Aurobindo made it a mission to spread this higher knowledge all over. Thinkers like Henry Wallace, Bertrand Russell, Pearl S Buck and others were also dedicatedly working with the same objective (page 71). In olden days Indian villages used to rely on barter and stood as the epitomes of peaceful co-existence and co-operative spirit. Every village and social group enjoyed an independent life. Gradually the poisonous concept of modern development had destroyed this idyllic life where there was no one to lord over all others. The ultimate saviour was the Soul. That's why Upanishads exhorted that man should firmly be fixed in his soul. The Buddha asked us to be our own helmsmen. These teachings were meant to achieve an ideal society.

"Such a society will make every one's life happy. There won't be a place for violence, crisis, anarchy and chaos. Every individual sees himself in others. In fact he realises all human beings are one and the same. He recognises that he is a part of the whole universe and knows that he is a symphony in the Universal Orchestra. Devoid of coercion, instigation and dictatorial fiats, such a co-operative music will be full of melody and reflects Gandhi's happy dream."

"But some people may ridicule all this as the dreams of an Idealist. They may dismiss the efforts of building a Republic based on spiritual principles and trying to transform human nature into divine nature as vain. They may advise us to give up these futile attempts and concentrate on practical and realistic endeavors for the benefit of nation (page 77). But I want to remind that there were so many dictators who turned ordinary human beings into demons and pose this question: When it is possible to turn man into a devil, then why can't we transform him into a God? This may sound illogical but it is not. With strong resolve, discipline and dedicated learning one can achieve this goal. It may not be possible in a day or two. Instead of wasting our time and energies on fulfilling basal desires and to indulge in immoral activities, we can strive to reach this noble goal. We may be nothing in the scale of universe, we may lack resoluteness to implement our intents. But we should remember that history was not made by heroes and great leaders. It was made by ordinary folk (page 78). Knowing this fully well, Gandhi is ardently moving towards his goal boldly and courageously. He may or may not reach the goal. Perhaps he may never reach it. Yet his efforts will never go in vain (page 79). Taking an optimistic view of Gandhi's path, Prof. Murty expressed a strong belief that only through rural self-rule can India build for itself a glorious future. He exhorted that Indians should wholeheartedly and energitally participate in this grand mission of nation building. He reminded us that we hold our future in our own hands.

The last article *Karu Mabbulu* (Dark Clouds) lent its title to this compilation. Our country still carries old baggage. Everything seems to be in a broken and dilapidated condition. We have to throw out the old and renew ourselves. But we have to remember that much valuable knowledge is buried deep under our fossilized culture. The wisdom of our ancestors, spirit of action, the quality of striking out in ever new directions and skillfully adopting various customs and traditions to everyday life were lost in time. Crushed by the weight of superstitions we gradually lost contacts with outside world. We have to unearth the ancient gems of wisdom from under the age old debris and break out of isolation and self- imposed constraints. We shouldn't fall into the trap of believing everything in the past is glorious. We should not either accept the past in toto or reject it altogether.

Truth is many faceted and reveals itself in many ways. It is expressed through religions also. There is no denying the fact that world religions have done much for human progress. But over time many superstitions have crept in and turned the religions into narrow creeds. We should rediscover the socially relevant aspects in them. It is utterly wrong to think that in ancient India sciences were separate from spirituality. Indian sciences were socially useful. Though Western science and technology has much to its credit, the fruits of such knowledge led to two world wars. Fear of a third world war haunts us now.

Under the impact of philosophy, Western science had undergone reforms to some extent. In the end we shouldn't blame scientific method for all the evils of modern world. In order to derive maximum good, we have to use science and technology wisely and properly. It should be stressed that science and religion are basically different from each other.

Religion concerns itself with the otherworldly things. It completely depends on emotion and insight which lie beyond the reach of science. A religion which promotes superstitions is no religion at all. As the body of human knowledge grows, the unnatural and extrasensory elements in religion go down. So while continuing spiritual quest inwardly, we should lead our lives relying on scientific knowledge in the physical world. In this way we can bring Indian culture- which for ages was lost in spiritual wilderness- back on tracks. In this way, the Indian culture will be able to shake off the dark clouds looming not only over itself but also over the whole world. It will once again be able to race ahead on the path of progress.

8. Divya Jīvitamu (1948)[14]

This book is a Telugu translation of the English book

"The Church before Pilate" written by famous spiritual writer Edward Lean. In the foreword, Satchidananda Murty explains: "This book is not only useful to Catholics, Protestants and other Christian denominations but also to Hindus and Muslims. This book talks about God, the ways to achieve his grace and about the incarnation of Jesus Christ in a highly inspirational manner. Recognizing that such evangelical works help us comprehend deep meaning of philosophy, Prof. Murty earnestly took up the translation. He believed that 'it will be highly useful to the followers of other religions also' (Introduction, Page 1). He also explained that while translating the book, he wholeheartedly followed the dictum of Mallinatha Suri: 'None of the points in the original work should be left out, nor extraneous things be added' (Introduction, page 2).

It may be rude, but we have to admit that the translation style adopted by Prof. Murty in this particular book is pedantic and artificial. On the contrary, his work *Kaaru Mabbulu* (Dark Clouds) published very next year ie 1948 contained an easy flowing, natural style. *Divya Jeevitham* being a religious work might have influenced Murty to adopt an artificial and preachy style. Moreover his choice of Telugu words for English ones doesn't always find our approval. For instance translating the word Church as 'Matham' (religion); communism as 'Sansarga Vaada'; Bible as 'Veda', Offering as 'Bali',' Sacrifice as 'Yagna', Kingship as 'Nripatva' and calling Saints as 'Rishis' sound odd. One can't help but term these as goof ups. Perhaps he might have adopted these words from Catholic translations into Telugu.

Divya Jīvitamu has four chapters. The first one tells us about the rise of Christ, divine teachings of Christianity, opposition of misguided souls, Christianity's boon to common folk, the laudable efforts of Catholics to convey Christ's teachings without any distortions. The second chapter recounts the way the then rulers abused and tortured Jesus Christ. The third chapter recites the compassion and love showered by Jesus Christ on all of us, even while he was carrying the heavy load of crucifix on his shoulders. It brings forth the divinity of Jesus in a highly effective manner.

> *The way Roman rulers distorted the truth regarding Jesus and the brutal manner in which they tortured him were recounted in the second chapter.*
>
> *Even while being crucified Jesus did not condemn his torturers. He was ever compassionate and loved one and all. The third chapter narrates his unique personality.*
>
> *God created Man, so that he can free himself of the sins of this world and attain God's grace. The fourth chapter recites Jesus teachings which show the way in which man can free himself of worldly pleasures and attain divine bliss.*

This book proceeds with the sole purpose of establishing the distinctiveness of Catholicism and the services it provided for the emancipation of humanity. Though Prof. Murty was not a Christian, it is laudable that he shouldered the responsibility of translating this particular book for the sake of Christians.

9. Rāma Teertha Vedanta Darśanamu (1950)[15]

This was the Telugu translation of Rāma Katha, a collection of English articles written by Puran Singh of Punjab who was the prime disciple of Śrī Rāma Teertha (1873-1906). Like Vivekananda, Swami Rāma Teertha also toured the world to propagate ancient Indian values. He died young i.e., when he was just 33 years old. Prof. Murthy's work was published by Rāma Teertha Seva Ashram, Pigudurala (now Pidugu Ralla) who for some reason forgot to mention the year of publishing. But Keshava Teertha Swami of the Ashram who had published the book and wrote the foreword, hinted that the book might have been published during 1950-52.

Professor Murty recounts Rāma Teertha's biographical details and introduces us to his US talks. It can be inferred from the book cover that he translated this work while he was working as a professor of Philosophy. This book is a collection of 13 talks: 1. Synthesis of Idealism and Materialism 2. Idealism and Materialism 3. Answers to some questions about Vedanta 4. Origins of Maya or Jagat 5. When did the world start? Hypnotism and Vedanta 7. Vedanta and Socialism 8. Man is the maker of his Fate 9. After Death or Synthesis of all religions 10. Answers to some problems 11. Various dialogues 12. Rebirth and Family Connection 13. The problem of Sin.

These articles help us to understand the singular qualities of Rāma Teertha. Yet neither the Rāma Teertha Ashram of Piduguralla nor the propagation of Rāma Teertha's spiritual concepts seem to have continued for long.

10. Rāmānuja Darśanamu (1951)[16]

Śrīmad Ramanujacharya occupies a distinctive place in Indian philosophy, social and religious thought. Indian philosophy sees the God Almighty everywhere and every time in the animate and inanimate universe. It also propounds that all individual souls ultimately merge in the Universal Soul which has many names- God, Eshwar, Brahma, Vishnu or whatever. Ramanuja declared that this omnipresent, omniscient and omnipotent can be reached by utmost devotion. He rejected all the differences between men and stated that all men are equal. Immediately after his Guru whispered Taraka Mantra in his ears, Ramanuja climbed onto the roof and shouted the mantra so that every one can learn it. When the angry

Guru cursed him that he will go straight to hell for this sacrilege, Ramanuja replied that he is prepared to go to any number of hells for common good. He declared that even untouchables can attain Gyana. Combining Gautama Buddha's teachings with traditional Vedic knowledge, he heralded a social transformation. Yet sadly neither Ramanuja nor the universal Vaishnavaite religion he propounded got due recognition. Satchidananda Murty took it upon himself to spread Ramanuja's teachings and the essence of Visishtadvaita far and wide. He adopted an easily comprehensible style so that his book can reach a wider audience. Prof. Murty stressed same point later by clearly stating that he intended the book not for pundits but for common folk. He specifically wrote *Bala Bodhaka Granth* for this purpose (*Vigyana Sarvasvam*, 17th volume, "Philosophies and Religions", Vedānta Prasthānamulu, page 139). This 39 page booklet makes the readers wonder, 'Is understanding Viśiṣṭādvaita so easy?'

Many modern reformers, who were deeply influenced by the non-ritualistic Western culture tried to counter it with Sankara's Advaita. But the *Apa Sudrādhikaraṇa* in Sankara's *Brahma Sūtra Bhāṣya* threw a spanner into their works. Later Ramanuja's Viśiṣṭādvaita with its reformist zeal successfully came along to take up the challenge. Satchidananda Murty was born into a family which imbibed such a progressive outlook. "I was by birth a Viśiṣṭa Advaitin. I made an intense study of Advaita," Prof. Murty said in the foreword to this book (page 1).

Vedas refer to a deity named *Bhaga*. The cult of worshipping *Bhagawan* is renowned as *Bhāgavata*. The *Vaiṣhṇava* sect had sprung from *Bhagavatha* cult. The ancient *Pānca Rātra* concepts are the source of Vaishnavism. Their essence can be found in Rigveda's Purusha Sukta and *Sathapatha Brāhmaṇa* also. Jayadhya, Vishnu, Satwata, Āhirbhudhnya Saṁhitas are the most important ones among the *Pāñcharātra Āgamas*. While many other ancient texts branded Pāñcharātra as non-Vedic and inferior, *Bharata, Bhāgavata* and *Viṣṇu Purāna* praised them as authoritative works. *Vedānta Desika* quoted Veda Vyāsa who termed the *Pāñcharātra* as helpful to understand Vedas. Prof. Murty mentioned the relevant śloka found in *Seśvara Mīmāṁsā* in the initial pages of his book. Thus he established the antiquity of Viśiṣṭādvaita. Differing with Shankara's Advaita which termed *Brahman* as the only Truth and the world as unreal, Ramanujacharya had declared that there is nothing else but *Brahman* who contains the whole Universe in itself. *Jīva* (beings) and *Jagath* (the world) are the body of Brahman. *Jīva* and *Brahman* are one and the same. *Brahman, Jīva* and the *Jagath* truly exist. *Brahman* is the whole of all the three. As *Brahman* is real, the other two are also real. So the world can never be unreal. *Brahman* is *cit* and *Acit*. He is *Viśiṣṭa* meaning Unique. Ramanuja propounded non-dualism between Brahman and the World. Thus he put forward Qualified Monism. That's why his philosophical system came to be known as *Viśiṣṭa Advaita*. Brahman of Ramanuja's conception is of uniform goodness. All sentient and non-sentient beings emanate from him, sustained by him and eventually enter into him. Nature and Ātman exist in him. Just like Ātman drives the body, *Brahman* is the driving force of *Ātman*. That's why Vedas describe *Brahman* as the Primal Cause of Creation. While all beings undergo the processes of birth, growth, decay and death, *Brahman* is free from them all. He is detached and is pure bliss. The World runs according to his will.

Thus Prof. Murty gave a fine description of Ramanuja's Viśiṣṭadvaita philosophy which was republished by Tirumala Tirupati Devasthanams (TTD) in 1995. In the preface he made this odd remark: "If I have to write a book again on Ramanuja's philosophy, it will be completely different from this one." Sadly we will never get the opportunity to go through such a book, because Prof. Murty passed away shortly later.

11. Pramāṇa Paddhati pai Prasaṅgamu (1959)[17]

This was a Telugu translation of the 'Discourse de la Methode' by the French philosopher Rene Descartes (1596-1650). Prof. Murty with the aid of KVR Narasimham delivered this in 1957 and the same was published by Andhra Vishwa Kala Parishad, Waltair in 1959.

Rene Descartes is regarded as the Father of Modern Philosophy. Generally Western Philosophy is divided into Ancient Philosophy, Medieval Philosophy or Modern Philosophy and Contemporary Philosophy. Bertrand Russell in his *History of Western Philosophy* had added Catholic Philosophy also into this scheme. There are many sub-divisions among these broad ones. Ancient Western Philosophy stretches from 6th Century BC to 15th Century CE i.e., upto Descartes era. The time period of Medieval or Modern Philosophy ranges from Descartes to John Dewey (19th Century). Later developments are regarded as Contemporary Philosophy. The Frenchman Descartes was the first among those who were deeply influenced by Renaissance. Differing with the age-old Idealistic spiritual quest, adopting the modern scientific insights, Descartes strove to develop an empirical modern philosophy. Denying the theory of Creation and faith in God, Descartes tried to find clear-cut rules of life like those found in Mathematics and Geometry. By declaring that ' I think, therefore I exist,' he gave an entirely new direction to Western Philosophy. Descartes published *Discourse de la Methode* in 1637 in which he described his thinking mode and empirical methods.

Satchidananda Murty, when he was a Lecturer in Venkateswara College, Tirupati, used to teach from this book as it was a text book for Degree students. It was at that time Prof. Murty decided to present it in Telugu. After coming to Andhra University as Professor, he took up the translation aided by K.V.R. Narasimham and completed it in 1957. Written in a simple but pedantic style, this book running into 118 pages was published by Andhra University in 1959.

Prof. Murty added a six-page listing of English terms and an introduction of Descartes' life and work in 70 pages. The introduction was divided into six chapters: 1. Overview of Philosophy 2. Principles of Standard method 3. Morals derived from them 4. Proving the existence of God 5. Understanding the human and animal behaviour 6. Inspiration for his enquiry into Nature.

Those who want to know and understand Descartes' life and contributions should definitely read this book.

12. Vijñāna Sarvasvamu (1962)[18]

Telugu Bhasha Samithi, Madras, which used to publish encyclopedias on various subjects had assigned the responsibility of editing one on Religions and Philosophies to Prof. Murty. It was to be the seventh encyclopedia to be published by the *Samithi.* Prof. Murty successfully completed the job and the book was published in 1962. To prepare this book he consulted the writings of many pundits. In the foreword Prof. Murty defined: 'An encyclopedia is really a reference book where all topics are explained briefly and authoritatively.' He also states: "It is said that only a *Rishi* should write an epic. In the same way, editing an encyclopedia is not for ordinary minds. Yet sometimes we may not find independent and capable thinkers who can shoulder such a big responsibility. Sometimes such great intellects may not exist at all. Under such circumstances, ordinary people may have to come forward to fulfil the task.' These words prove how humbly Prof. Murty took up the editorship of this encyclopedia.

He also submitted that 'By virtue of travelling all over the world; having deep interest and experience in the study of various religions; by maintaining wide interactions with people belonging to other cultures and religions; acquaintance and friendship with modern Eastern and Western philosophers- the editor of this work has imbibed a balanced outlook enabling him to fulfil his duty. (page 8). A 198 page review of the encyclopedia written by him and attached to the book reveals the balanced and careful way Prof. Murty completed the job.

The encyclopedia begins by informing briefly the outlines and the nature of philosophy. It contains chapters on definition, sources, qualities and importance of philosophy; the relationship between religion and philosophy; various schools of philosophy. It also captures the historical evolution of the Vedic, Lokayatha, Tirthankara, Jain,

With Pandit Sri Jawaharlal Nehru on the occasion of releasing Telugu Encyclopaedia Edited by him, others seated are Sri Neelam Sanjiva Reddy, the then Chief Minister and Prof. Humayun Kabir, Central Cabinet Minister.

Buddhist philosophies, Bhagavad *Gītā*, six Darśanas, Vedanta Prasthānas, modern Indian philosophies. Later it moves on to explain Chinese, Greek, Christian, Jewish, Arab and Modern European philosophies.

The encyclopedia further takes up the definition and review of religion. It delves into the essence, sources and character of it. Later it looks into the objectives, qualities, evolution and the beginnings of the idea of religion, its relation to sciences and philosophies. Prof. Murty competently narrates the following topics in an alphabetical order: *Acintya Bhedābhedam*, Budhist *Anāthma Vādam*, Jain *Anaikānta Vādam*, Arabic philosophy, Alexander Samuel, A. Richard, Ashwapathi Kaikeya, *Ārambha Vādam* (Nyaya), Upasana, Uma Swathi, Miguel, Elysian mystic processes, Kant's philosophy, Pascal and *Vivarta vaada* of Adi Sankara (Theory of Causation).

The final product shows Prof. Murty's intense understanding of philosophy, his talent for finding inter- relationships, consulting international pundits and rendering Telugu translations of their works. We can't but wonder and take delight in his unparalleled endeavours. The encyclopedia which was published in 1962 has many years of dedication and ceaseless efforts behind it. Apart from editing, Prof. Murty also provided original articles to the book. So I took the liberty of including the encyclopedia in the body of his writings.

13. Manişi-Mukti (1970)[19]

On the invitation of Annamalai University, Tamilnadu, Professor Murty delivered 3 lectures in a distinguished gathering. The exclusive meet was attended by university professors and research students particularly in the stream of philosophy. Prof. Murty unveiled novel perspectives developed by him in the study of philosophy. Later he elaborated on the three talks and compiled them as the book- *Manişi-Bhowtikata-Freedom* (*Metaphysics, Man and Freedom*). It was published by Andhra University, Waltair in 1963. In order to reach a wider audience Prof. Murty got these English talks translated by Medepalli Varaha Narasimha Swamy, a scholar in Telugu and Sanskrit and vetted it. Perhaps finding the translation a little pedantic, Prof. Murty engaged Ramakrishnacharya to render the book in an easy, informal style with the title *Manishi-Mukti*. Even after taking so much care, Prof. Murty clearly understood that his work won't be understood easily by common readers.

"Just like the English original that may not be understood by those well-versed in English, this Telugu translation may not be easily understood by native Telugu speakers. It should be noted here that though there are many books available on Nuclear physics, Maths and Geology not everyone could grasp their content. Likewise only those readers who are acquainted with philosophy will be able to understand this work," Prof. Murty stated in the foreword (page no. XI-XII). Little wonder Dr. S. Radhakrishnan, the renowned Indian philosopher was highly appreciative of this work. In the foreword he showered applause on Professor Murty. He said "Prof. K. Satchidananda Murty's book *Metaphysics, Man and Freedom* is written with wide learning and deep understanding of metaphysical problems. He discuses the objections to the possibility of metaphysics from the intellectual, linguistic and psychological stand points" (p. IX).

Prof. Murty said, if those who are somewhat acquainted with philosophy, linguistics and psychology, make a patient and intensive study, they will be able to find gems of spiritual knowledge in this book. In order to help such people, I am providing explanations for certain complex concepts to the best of my ability.

This book is divided into three chapters. In the first chapter Prof. Murty states that only by understanding the interdependent relationship between himself, society and the whole wide world, Man will be able to grasp the essence of his own personality and lead a fulfilled life. Murty explains that metaphysics will be a big help in this endeavour. He also avers that there is a metaphysics of linguistics. He rejected the view that modern sciences have turned human life into a mechanical existence and affirmed that it was human creativity that gave birth to all the sciences and technologies. The same creative consciousness is driving man into ever new directions.

It is by questioning himself and his environment Man acquires knowledge. But there is always something which exists beyond human comprehension. Metaphysics is nothing but the quest for such transcendence. We try to find out attributes and qualities of various objects in the everyday world and try to draw generalized conclusions. By applying such generalizations to the concrete, objective world we construct an abstract form in our minds. We derive many abstract forms in various ways. Those forms are not visible physically. But the common qualities among these abstract mental concepts lay the basis for our understanding of the Unity, underlying the objective world. This helps to form an idea of universal man which extends to all the human beings. Without such a concept it is impossible to envisage the unity of human beings.

The second chapter affirms that efforts to achieve human unity proceed in various ways. It is believed that human soul forms the basis for human personality and the soul is deemed transcendental. It analyzes the quest for Supreme Soul through Yoga and Gyana methods. In this chapter Prof. Murty declares that soul is not confined to human body but pervades one and all. The third chapter defines Freedom as evolving a universal perspective to breakout of limits imposed by physical existence.

Reading *Manishi-Mukti* earnestly with serene contemplation enables us to gain an insight into Prof. Murty's thoughts and help us to understand them.

In the next chapter a review on his English and Hindi works is given.

Endnotes:

1. Murty, K.S., *Śrimad Bhagavad Gītā,* Ananda Ashramamu, Sangam Jagarlamudi, 1941, p. XV.
2. Murty, K.S., *Sangameshashtakam,* Ananda Ashramamu, Sangam Jagarlamudi, 1936.
3. Murty, K.S., *Nama Sankirtana Mahima,* Guntur: Sri Rama Nama Kshetram, 1937.
4. Murty, K.S., *Hanumad-Vijayamu,* Tenali : Janakirama Press, 1938.
5. Murty, K.S., *Śrimad Bhagavad Gītā,* Op.Cit., pp. XVI-XXII.
6. Ibid., pp. XVI-XXII.
7. Ibid., pp. XXII-XXIII.
8. Murty, K.S., 6 addendum, chapter 1, p. 31.
9. Ibid., pp.25-26.
10. Ibid., 29-30.
11. Murty, K.S., *Saptasloki Bhagavad Gītā,* Samgam Jagarlamudi: 1943.
12. Murty, K.S., *Ishopanishattu-Sa-vivaranmu,* Tenali: Sundaram and Sons, 1946.
13. Murty, K.S., *Kaaru Mabbulu,* Tenali: Krishna Book Depo. 1947.
14. Murty, K.S., *Divya-Jivitamu,* Guntur; St.Michael's Press, 1948
15. Murty, K.S., *Rama Tirtha Vedanta Darshanamu,* Guntur: Sri Rama Tirtha Seva Ashram, 1950.

16. Murty, K.S., *Ramajuja Darshanamu*, Guntur: Sri Rama Tirtha Seva Ashram, 1951.
17. Murty, K.S., *Pramana Paddhati Pai Prasangamu*, Waltair; Andhra University, 1959.
18. Murty, K.S., *Vijnana Sarvasvamu* (Matamulu, Darshanamulu), Madras: Telugu Bhasha Samiti, 1962.
19. Murty, K.S., *Manishi-Mukti*, Vijayawada: Navodaya Pub. 1970.

7

Magnum Opus

The previous chapter "Native Language Proficiency" looked into Prof. Satchidananda Murty's original Telugu works and his translations from English. The current chapter consists of reviews of Prof. Murty's writings in English and Hindi. These reviews were written in other languages. The reviews are arranged in the chronological order.

1. Hinduism and its Development (1947)[1]

This book contains a series of five lectures that Murty delivered under the religious education scheme of the S.V. College, Tirupati. It was addressed to graduate and undergraduate students. These lectures were compiled in a book form by Sundara Ram & Sons of Tenali and was published under the title *Hinduism and its Development* in 1947.

In the Preface of this book, Prof. Murty writes: "Amidst the clash of rival ideas and ideologies, fundamental issues have been forgotten without being detrimental to individual views and ideals, Hinduism was built up a unity of spirit which has survived the ravages of time. A recapture of this spirit, so unique to our religion and culture, is the essential need of these times of strife and tension. I shall be delighted if this brochure could attract the attention of some of our young men and women in the colleges towards that ideal."

In the first lecture on "Vision", Murty emphasizes upon "global outlook" which must be essentially spiritual in character as contradistinguished from the Global outlook which is frequently referred to the contemporary political terminology, that is pre-eminently economic and socio-logical. In short, the vision is a vision of identity between man and the universe. (2) In the second lecture titled "The Rise of Religion", it is contended that religion is neither the pursuit of a ritualistic programme nor an adherence to blind belief in dogma, but is essentially "Experience of the Boundless, the unlimited, the Absolute, the Divine, The Mahan or the Brihat" (p.23). (3) In the third lecture titled "The Vedanta", a brief exposition is attempted of the different systems of Vedanta with special reference to the system of Sankara. (4) 'Practice of Dharma' forms the subject matter of the fourth lecture on "Religion in Life". Conformity to the law of one's own being, one's own essential nature would constitute the practice of religion. (5) In the fifth and final lecture Murty discusses the "Evolution of Hinduism". Here, he provides a brilliant account of the emergence of Hinduism, and its development through successive stages of evolution under influences – internal as well as external . The way Hinduism has been moulded at different periods by the influences of the Greek and Arab contacts, by the Turko-Afghan invasions and later by the impact of the West on India has been analyzed in a masterly manner.

2. The Rhythm of the Real (1951)[2]

This book consists of five essays titled: Beauty, History, Causality, God and The Good. All of them unveil varied facets of Truth and provide a basis for philosophical quests. This work which reflects the depth of thought displayed by Satchidananda Murty in his earlier years was published by Andhra University, Waltair in 1951. It provides insights into many familiar concepts. Taking cues from Indian and Western philosophies, Prof. Murty offers general and specific meanings to supposedly common ideas and themes.

Prof. Murty begins the first article 'Beauty' by furnishing the dictionary meaning and captures the evolution of the word in various phases. The Namalinga Anushasan of *Amara Kosham* describes Beauty as the most valuable. It lists various synonyms like radiance, melodious and charming. On attaining it, one feels mystifying bliss. According to Upanishads, beauty is not subjective, it is transcendental and eternally satisfying. It is auspicious. Subjective beauty is transient. Ramanuja who regarded the animate and inanimate world as the body of the God, stated that beauty is nothing but God's love. We generally discriminate between beautiful and ugly. But devotees of God see beauty everywhere.

The second article 'History' examines the underlying viewpoints of history-writing. Many people defined History in their own way. Their versions are not complete. Ascertaining the beginning or end of any historical phenomenon is no easy task. One has to break out of mythical accounts, divide time into various eras and centuries and systematically study various events and personalities. We have to always remember that no event happens suddenly and in an unconnected manner. The fact that humans are affected by various forces has to be borne in mind before embarking on history writing. Evolution doesn't proceed in a linear way. Lots of jumps occur during its course which are called mutations in Darwinian theory. History is no exception. Yet some people see history as linear while others declare that history repeats itself. These interpretations ultimately depend on differing viewpoints. No one can predict the future course of history. Such predictions are just imaginary-Murty declared.

The third article is 'Causality' which narrates Indian 'cause and effect' theory. It describes that specific effects are derived from specific causes. *Prakriti* is unmanifest, only its properties are manifested. This led some to argue that those properties are real. Yet properties or *Gunas* are not independent of *Prakriti*. Both are inter-related. Cause occurs earlier invariably and effect follows. That's why Westerners regard Cause as the antecedent and effect as consequent. They see an eternal and consistent relationship between these two.

Indian Nyaya philosophy propounds two kinds of relationship between matter and properties. They are *Samyoga* and *Samavāyi*. The relationship between a table and the book on it is *Samyoga*. Even if we separate them, nothing is disturbed. The relationship between a material thing and its colour; between Gold and jewellery is *Samavāyi*. Both of them can't be separated. Nyaya philosophy is actually a theory of causation. It says that cause invariably precedes effect.

Vaiseshika philosophy espoused a theory of evolution. It envisages a gradual effect from a cause. In the end, explaining the relationship between cause and effect is problematic. It is this difficulty that gave rise to various theories and arguments. Buddhism regards the relationship between cause and effect as that which exists between *Pratyaya* and *Utpatti*. According to Buddhist *Pratitya Samutpada theory*, cause and effect eternally flow interdependently. As there exists a similarity between manifest events our common experience is not affected.

The fourth article is titled 'God'. Our causal thinking compels us to seek an ultimate cause of the world and makes us accept the existence of a Supreme Being. This eternal and undifferentiated Being is the subject of all religions and holy books. But philosophers like Charvakas deny the existence of a God. There are many other philosophies which do not accept God as the First Cause. Vedantins call the omnipresent, omnipotent and omniscient being as Brahman. Adi Shankara who envisaged a *Nirguna, Nirviśeṣa* and Blissful *Brahman* is also a theist. Prof. Murty declared that the cause of creation was not matter but spiritual Truth. Just like a magnet which remains unmoving yet moves iron, *Brahman* – the spiritual Truth is the force that moves the physical creation. Imagining an universe devoid of *Brahman* is simply illusory. Realising that *Brahman* and Creation are one and the same, enables us to grasp the Truth.

Holy Scriptures and all religions proclaim that God is the creator of the whole universe. Every atom here arises from the God who is the First Cause and Final Truth. The relationship between God and the Universe is like the one between fire and light. There are various interpretations and arguments regarding Him. One school of thought declares that God and his creation are different and separate. Others see no difference between the universe and Him. Still others deny His existence. Some people think that even if He is up there, proving His existence is impossible.

Some thinkers tried to deny God, by pointing out the wide-spread evil, sins and atrocities across the world and pose the question- if He is so omnipresent and omnipotent how come he is so silent? Here we have to bear in mind the fact that sins are temporary not permanent. They come and go. They are just a part, not the whole of life. For instance water can sink us, but it can also make us float. And we can't do away with it. Evil is also like that. We have to get a handle on that, not deny its existence. Otherwise life can't go on. It should be remembered that only in the face of evil that goodness and good deeds shine. That's why Believers of God assert that one can't disavow faith, Holy Scriptures and religion.

The last piece in this book is titled 'The Good'—which is generally deemed as an opposite to bad. We consider something as good when it fulfils our needs and interests. Everybody acts for his own interests. On the other hand God has everyone's interests in his mind. Hence *Kaṭhopaniṣad* prefers the word *Śreyas* instead of the Good and uses the word *Preya*s to denote that which is not good. Both are within man's reach. Morality is nothing but making the right choice between these two. Self-serving individuals can't hope to tread on the moral path. Only those things that benefit us personally are reckoned as good. It is by transcending the self-seeking path and by overcoming our petty desires, we will be able to understand the *Shreyas* or Common Good. It is Divine and can only be attained through meditation. In the light of this, Morality gives paramount importance to the Common and Highest Good or *Śreyas* over personal good.

The Highest Good is synonymous with *Sukha* or Happiness which is attained through God's Grace- so say Vedantins and Nyaya philosophers. *Sukha* is a longing, it is derived from and dependent on external things. It is largely personal. But when *Sukha* is experienced by one and all, it becomes Universal Happiness- which is the ultimate divine goal. All the moral teachings, holy scriptures and the science of Logic can only point out the path to it but can't help attain it. When all of us individually progress morally and meditate upon the highest Truth, the path to common good opens up before us. Just by living ethically we can't hope to attain it. It is only attainable through the unification of Universal and Individual Souls.

3. Thought and the Divine (1951)[3]

With the main discourse running into 104 pages, brief life-sketches of famous Western philosophers extending to 10 more pages with an additional page of references- this 115 page work contains a profound retrospection on the Western philosophical thought. But it was so complex that even those who are proficient in English language find it difficult to understand. Remembering Prof. Murty's caution that those who are good at English may not necessarily understand all the writings in English (same goes for Telugu also), readers should try to grasp the concepts enunciated in the book slowly and steadily. It critically examines Western philosophical concepts. It can be said that only those who acquired certain command over Western Philosophy will be able to make sense of the book. The current book is divided into five chapters. Refuting the arguments of atheist Western philosophers, supporting those who firmly believe in God, Prof. Murty sets out to praise the grace of Almighty. That's why, the Catholic Bishop of Guntur got the book printed at the St Michael Industrial Training School Press. The Bishop also wrote foreword to it.

The annals of Western Philosophy generally starts from Socrates period (5th century BC) and proceeds through Plato (427 BC) and Aristotle (384 BC). It makes us wonder whether there were no philosophers before them. The truth is that there was Thales who lived during the 7th century BC. He was hailed as the Father of Western philosophy. There was Anaxagorus (494 BC) who ridiculed the custom of imagining God in human form. Heraclitus (5th century BC) famously insisted on eternal change as the essence of the universe. Many other philosophers imagined the origins of the universe in four elements. The Idealism of our Upanishadic Seers can be seen among them also. But these ancient Greek philosophers did not aim at building a new world order. Plato and Aristotle did that. That's why they came to be recognized as the pioneers of Western philosophy which is being influenced by many other thinkers to this day.

These philosophers can be classified into three groups. Those who imagine a Creator fall into the first group. They propound Natural Theology. Plato regarded Natural Science as his God. It was Aristotle who coined the word Theology. He deemed God Almighty as the origin of everything. Theology found many adherents later on. Rene Descartes has been dubbed as the father of modern Western philosophy. He propounded that Truth should be arrived at through reasoning. This came to be known as Rationalism. It holds that which can't be experienced can never be Truth. This gradually led to the development of Idealism which regards Human Mind as the ultimate Truth. That which can't be grasped by the mind can never be true. Naturally God took a back seat in the Mediaeval philosophical thought.

Later on, there were renewed efforts to prove the existence of God rationally. As a result Rational Theology developed in the later mediaeval age. This was used as a validation of Christian thought. Western philosophy hovers between the Theologies of Natural and Rational varieties. Prof. Murty in the current book criticized those who rejected the idea of God and supported those in favour.

The substantiation of existence of God proceeds systematically in the four chapters of the book. The first chapter introduces us to the arguments proffered by Plato in favour of existence of Divinity. The second chapter consists explanation of four laws which proposes God's existence. They are Aristotle's Law of Identity, Law of Difference, Law of Contradiction, Law of Excluded Middle. Leibniz later added a fifth law—The Law of Sufficient

Reason. The first law comes from God's self-identity. The second law states that God and Creation are different. The Third law asserts that there is nothing self-contradictory in the Divine. The fourth one states that nothing should stand between Divine and non-divine. The last law states that there is sufficient reason to believe that there is a God.

Prof. Murty rejects Berkeley's Subjectiveness, Hume's Skepticism, Kant's Transcendentalism and agrees with Plato's ideas of Divine and Aristotle's proposition of the omniscient, omnipresent and omnipotent nature of God. He affirms that there is nothing that God can't do and there is nothing beyond God.

The third chapter recounts the views of Saint Augustine on God. Since creation should start from an original source, we can call the All-source as God. This contention is known as Ontology. According to Epistemology, God is forever beyond our limited comprehension. Aeschatology believes in the end of the world and reunion of humanity with the divine. Teleology contends that natural entities have intrinsic purposes and proposes that there is a final cause or God. St. Augustine reviewed all these viewpoints and averred that God is the moving force behind everything. The fourth chapter recounts Anselm's theory of Summum bonum which believed in the existence of an ultimate God. The fifth chapter contained an analysis of 24 laws of Thomas Aquinas in support of God's existence. Thus Prof. Murty reaffirms his faith in God by drawing from various ancient concepts, natural laws and rational thought.

4. Evolution of Philosophy in India (1952)[4]

Prof. Murty published this book in 1952. After several years , the book was republished as *Evolution of Indian Philosophy* by VVN Saibaba and P. George Victor, the professors of philosophy department, Andhra University as its second edition. I have taken up the original version for review here.

Remarkably, MN Roy, the great radical humanist wrote the introduction to this book. Roy was annoyed at the way philosophical systems and religion were mixed up in Indian tradition and commended Prof. Murty for striking an independent path by incorporating all the later day developments in philosophy. He declared that ignoring social and geographical developments, philosophy cannot hope to develop in abstract. 'One has to study and understand religion and philosophy separately. Untouched by emotions, patriotism and cultural commitments one has to objectively and scientifically evaluate the philosophical systems. All the arguments and counter-arguments have to be taken into account.' Prof. Murty affirmed that he will follow in the footsteps of Ganganath Jha, Bhandarkar, Vidya Bhushan, A.R. Wadia and Humayun Kabir in evaluating Indian philosophical and religious systems through Western methods of analysis. The 25 chapters in this book bear testimony to his sincere efforts. Satchidananda Murty was the first Indian to boldly analyze our religions and philosophical systems in the light of historical developments.

The first chapter in the book starts off with the review of the growth and influence of Sociology and Psychology and goes into the question how the thinking process generates and blossoms in humans. After analysing the geographical influences on Indian thought and culture, he sets out to describe how the local culture was intermingled with those who entered India over the course of history. He dedicated five chapters to retrospect on the background of the evolution of Indian philosophy and surveyed the later developments in the rest.

Just like an exact science, philosophy should also proceed by reconciling and harmonizing contradictory factors to develop into a consistent system—opines Prof. Murty. He adopted exactly such an angle of analysis. Refraining from mixing up religion and philosophy, one should discern various fundamental influences exerted upon philosophical thought over the course of time. Ancient religions everywhere including India, were unable to grasp the true nature of natural forces and imparted divinity to them. Indus Valley civilization and many other older ones displayed the same animistic trait. This gradually evolved into polytheism and ultimately into monotheistic thought.

By analyzing Vedās, Murty recounts the way this stream of thought crystallized into various schools of philosophy by 7th century BC. Then he looks into Lokayata School which stressed material world over the other. Later he goes into the development of Jaina tradition and then takes a deep look into Buddhism. Remarkably, Murty doesn't equate Buddhism with a rational school of thought. He reminds us the fact that Lord Buddha himself achieved *Prajñā* through meditation and attained *Nirvāṇa* through *Prajñā*—which is definitely not a rational process. Murty then proceeds to bring out various mystical and tantric beliefs and traditions which transformed Buddhism into a religion. As a result Buddhism can no longer be termed as a school of philosophical thought. But treating the so-called gods as simply higher beings, avoiding extremes and striking a middle path, accepting natural evolution and proposing *Pratītya Samutpada theory* of causality to deny the existence of God are the distinctive characteristics of Buddha's teachings.

Murty then proceeds to examine Samkhya philosophy which was basically materialistic but later got transformed into a theist philosophy. Significantly Murty considers Buddhism to be earlier than Samkhya philosophy.

Gradually Indian religious thought progressed from polytheism into monotheism. Murty makes a study of *Bhagavad Gītā* in this context.

Prof. Murty clearly established that all philosophies should be seen as systems or schools of thought which arose to meet the needs of the times and places in which they arose. When Brahmins indulged in excesses in the name of *Yagñas, Yagas* and other rituals, *Kṣatriyas* struck on a different path to emancipation giving rise to Buddhist and Jaina religions. While Jainism confined itself to a few areas, Buddhism, first under the patronage of Ajata Shatru and Bimbisara, later under Asoka spread to other countries as well. King Kanishka encouraged it further. Prof. Murty recounts the way Buddhism spread to China and describes the influence of Mahayana Buddhism which in turn is based on *Lankāvatara Sūtra*. He also details the contributions of Nagarjuna, Asanga and Vasubandhu in the development of Buddhist philosophical tradition.

It is truly amazing that before Murty, no other Indian commentator could analyze the evolution of Buddhist Thought so authoritatively. Likewise Murty also recounted the decline of Buddhism in an equally definitive manner. Thereafter he sets forth to examine how Buddhism influenced the development of Advaita philosophy and of its various offshoots.

The prominence he gave to Buddhism, defining Shankara as a monotheist, holding Ramanuja and Madhwa sects in high regard- all this shows Murty's way of thinking during his initial years as a Professor of Andhra University. By exploring the similarities between *Bhagavad Gītā* and Buddhist Lotus *Sadharma-Puṇḍarīka Sūtra* proceeding to analyze Sāmkhya and Vaiśeṣika schools right after Buddhism, Prof. Murty gave us reason to believe that he regarded all these streams as post-Buddhist. Such a line of reasoning is repellant to traditional thinkers.

With Sri N.T. Rama Rao, CM of AP and Prime Minister of India Sri Rajiv Gandhi on the occasion of Philosophy Congress at Hyderabad.

Contrary to what illustrious scholars like SN Dasgupta, S. Radhakrishnan, Jadunath Sinha delineated in their writings, Vivekananda, Aurobindo and some political leaders tried to put Advaita on a high pedestal. It was really gutsy on Murty's part to differ with such a politically correct view and declare that Advaita was not the only important Indian thought. Follow your own course and let people talk- so advised Dante. True to this axiom, Murty boldly set out to review Indian philosophical thought on the strength of his own study and understanding.

5. Ṣad-Darśana Samuccaya (1957)[5]

Murty had done a great service to the students and general readers by translating this complex Sanskrit work into simple English. Here he elucidates the background and development of six schools of Indian philosophical thought. Though interpretation of the Sanskrit ślokas was in English, the shlokas themselves were printed in Dev Nagari script. This gave access to the original word order in the Sanskrit shlokas. Modern scholars identify Nyāya, Vaiśeṣika, Sāṁkhya, Yoga, Mīmāmsā (Pūrva Mīmāmsā) and Vedanta (Uttara Mīmāmsā) as six Darśanas or systems of Hindu philosophy. But most of them don't know that many more systems were in existence in ancient India and the classification into six systems was effected only in 12th century. The way Murty enunciated the historical development of these systems was truly unmatched. He proved that the phrase *Ṣaḍ Darśanas* was coined much later. According to him there were only three *darśanas*-Nyāya, Mīmāmsā and Anvīkṣikī before Buddhism and Jainism which over time got classified as philosophical systems along with Cārvāka School. It was in 10th Century AD that Jayanta in his *Nyāya Mañjari* identified Nyāya, Mīmāmsā, Sāṁkhya, Buddha, Jaina and Chārvaka as six logics (*Ṣaṭ Tarki*). He classified Cārvāka as an atheistic school of thought and rest as theistic. Later Jaina and Buddha were also clubbed with Cārvāka as atheistic philosophies. And Nyāya, Vaiśeṣika, Sāṁkhya, Mīmāmsā, Yoga and Vedānta as six systems of theistic philosophy. They were recognized as *Ṣaḍ Darśanas*, for the first time in 12th century work *Viśwa Saara Tantra*. This was the historical background as such.

Hari Bhadra Suri, the 8th century Jaina commentator, while categorising Cārvāka as an atheist philosophy in his *Ṣaṭdarśana Samuchhaya*, also added Lokayata School into his work. So in effect he included a total of seven systems under *Ṣaḍ Darśanas*. Yet he was regarded as the very first commentator who presented us with a classification of *Darśanas*. Later, Sankara (8th century AD), Madhwa (14th Century) provided us with a vast spread of philosophies.

However Indian tradition didn't differentiate between religion and philosophy. Prof. Murty based his analysis on Hari Bhadra Suri's work. He gave out reasons for this: 'Though Suri's work is more complex than Madhavacharya's, it took up the theme of major darshanas. It stayed away from fringe schools like Pāśupata and Rasavāda. Moreover, Suri adopted an unbiased view and refrained from unnecessary criticism. Understandably he displayed special interest toward Jainism, but stayed away from glorifying it over others. Murty also explained that he used Hari Bhadra Suri's liberal commentary on *Shad Darśana Samucchaya* as a reference work for his book. He advised philosophy students to study such major works to broaden their understanding. The current book was first published by Tagore Publishing House, Tenali in 1957 which was republished by Eastern Book Links, New Delhi in 1986.

Chill mode activated after lectures.

6. Revelation and Reason in Advaita Vedanta (1959)[6]

This was a Ph.D. thesis by Satchidananda Murty. As he himself admitted in the foreword, it was entirely based on an original Sanskrit text and its commentaries. In his thesis Prof. Murty upended many longheld, traditional viewpoints on Indian systems of philosophy to come out with an entirely novel perspective. It was highly acclaimed by Indian scholars like Radhakrishnan, K. Raja, Kalidas Bhattacharya and foreign intellectuals like Karl Potter, Archie J. Balm et. al. Gaining an understanding of this complex work is no easy matter. Only those who have a certain mastery over Indian philosophy will be able to comprehend this work which analyzes Indian schools of thought from a Western perspective. Prof. Murty himself provided a brief note on his thesis. "My thesis is divided into two books and each is sub-divided into two sections. The first part is descriptive and the second contains comparative critique. The first section of the first book briefly sketches Advaita monotheism with an effective commentary. The second section explains the function of discretion in Advaita Vedanta."

"The first section of the second book discusses about the rest of the five systems in Ṣaḍ Darśanas and explains the authority of Holy Scriptures. It contains a critical appraisal of these Darśanas. It also presents briefly the arguments and counterarguments between Nyāya and Mīmāmsā adherents". Murty holds that "As I agree fully with Nyāya Darśana principles and conception of God, I gave them proper representation in my thesis. Contemporary writers failed to recognize that most of the criticisms regarding God hypotheses were countered by ancient Nyaya philosophers themselves. Nyaya philosophy tells us that by inferential reasoning one can prove the existence of God."

Prof. Murty continues: 'In the second section of the second book, I tried to analyze the metaphysics of Advaita Vedanta and Holy Scriptures and tried to derive satisfactory solutions to the philosophical questions. My views regarding revelations expressed here are almost similar to those of Jayanta. My opinions on God are not different from those proffered by Ramanuja. Study of Western philosophical systems greatly helped me in bringing out my thesis' (Introduction, pages XVIII-IX).

The *first chapter* in the first book tells us about God, Advaitic Brahman and four kinds of revelation. The second chapter details *Śabda Pramāṇa* (words of past and present reliable experts) and the eternal nature of Vedas. Third chapter provides a definition of Vedas and declares them as the ultimate Truth. The fourth chapter is on 'Language and Brahman'. It discusses the significance of the word Brahman, and the logical oddness of the world 'Brahman; Fifth chapter explains the meaning of the word *Brahman* and declares that one can't discern it by logic only. The sixth chapter explains Mahavākyās. Seventh chapter avers that the knowledge of Brahman attained through integral experience makes us realise Brahman is the ultimate and eternal Truth. But once Brahman and individual soul are united, even Vedas and Brahma Gyana turn out to be illusory. Eighth chapter declares that emancipation is nothing but merging of individual and universal (Brahman) souls.

In the first chapter of the second section of the first book declares that Brahman and Individual souls are eternal. They can't be experienced but can be perceived through Yogic insight. Through meditation one should eliminate *Rajo* and *Tamo* gunas and gain *Prajñā* or wisdom. Sankara revealed that knowledge of Veda confers various powers or *Siddhis*. Third chapter describes various *pramāṇas* (means of obtaining knowledge) and points out that Advaita accepts inferential knowledge or *anumāna pramāṇa*. But Advaita makes it clear that one can't attain Brahman just by *pramāṇās*. Among *pramāṇās,* inference is the process of reasoning i.e., logic. There are *Anvaya Vyatireka* and *Arthāpatti* (presumption) varieties of logic also which was initiated by Adi Sankara and developed by Sureswara. The fourth chapter introduces us to the perspectives of Gauda Pada and Sankara regarding discretion and revelation and looks into relationship between tarka (logic) and Āgama Gaudapada, after critically examining the viewpoints of Upaniṣads and Buddhism declared that the teachings of Holy Scriptures is non-differential and non-origination. Their exposition on the so called difference between individual and universal souls is only secondary. Gaudapada stressed the importance of discretion and suggested that teachings devoid of this quality can't be justified. While certain Upaniṣads agree that one can attain Brahma Gyana through logic others maintained silence over this. Observing this fact Sankaracharya made it clear that logic for logic sake has no place in Vedanta. He declared that only the logic displayed by ancient scriptures should be respected. Logic which doesn't conform itself to Vedas is imperfect. Satchidananda Murty explains that Sankara regarded the teachings of scriptures as beyond logic. The fifth chapter presents us with the Śrī Harsha's interpretation of Advaita Vedānta. According to Śrī Harsha the purpose of Advaita Vedānta is nothing but showing the way to understand the unity of Brahman and Atman.

The *sixth chapter* acquaints us with the logic adopted by Advaita. The Advaitic dictum- *Brahma Satyam Jaganmithyā Jīvo Brahmaiva nāparaḥ* was criticised by many scholars on cause-effect grounds. When everything is Brahman, there should invariably be a cause-effect relationship between Brahman and Creation—so they say. Some others posed the question, how can material world spring forth through non-material Brahman? Sankara countered these arguments through the property of modifications. Milk turning into curd and mistaking a rope for a snake are examples of modifications. While Brahman is as real as a rope, the creation is an illusion like the mistaken notion of a snake. No one can know the true nature of the world by experience alone. One needs to take the help of scriptures to understand it.

Thus in the first part of the text, Prof. Murty completely reviews the past and future of the advaitic evolution and begins to intically explaining the second part of the book. The first chapter of the first section of this book starts with the- non-advaitic- Hindu darshanas conception on the knowledge of God. Neither Vedas and Upaniṣads nor *Bhagavad Gītā* debate about the existence or non-existence of God. It was only after Buddhism, Jainism and Cārvakas questioned God's existence, that the need to justify arose. Even Mīmāṁsakas who accept the eternal nature of Vedas do not agree that they are the word of God. Nyaya philosophers countered by saying that they are indeed God's gift. Yoga school of thought declares the existence of an ultimate *Puruṣa*. Samkhya philosophy declared that proving the existence of God is impossible. Vaiśeṣika holds that God is the efficient cause and atoms are the material cause of the Universe. But this school does not accept the argument that God is the ultimate ruler of the universe. That's why Vaiśeṣika School is regarded as atheistic one by Sankara and others. According to Nyāya philosophy, God drives us in accordance with our karma. Most systems of Indian philosophy excepting Kapila's Samkhya, agreed that God can be attained through transcendental knowledge.

The second chapter discusses Mīmāṁsā darśana. Vedas declared that Rishis (Seers) were Mantra Drasṭas.

Through the technique of Prāṇāyāma they enter Hiranya Garbha (God). Upaniṣads aver that Vedas are God given which were seen by them in their visions. The view of Vedas were discussed by Mīmāṁsā and that of Upaniṣads was discussed by Nyāya philosophers. Though Advaita differs with Mīmāṁsā, all Indian systems of philosophy agreed that Vedas are self-evident i.e., they sprung from God. They declared that Vedas reveal many unknown things to us (Ajñāta Gñāpanam). But Mīmāṁsā which regards Vedas as the Source of all and unauthored doesn't recognise Rishis as the originators of Vedas. Kumarila Bhatta held that the actions enjoined in the Veda had definite results without an external interference. Vyasa held that Śrutis, Smṛtis and Epics prove the existence of the Absolute. Sāmkhya asserts that Vedas are unauthored and they are the word of God. Kaṇāda, founder of Vaiśeṣika School stated that it is by holy tradition that God's existence is proved. Nyāya philosophy doesn't agree Vedas are eternal. Mīmāṁsā contends eternal Vedas were bequeathed to us by sages. On the whole all theistic philosophies believe in the word of God.

The second section of the second book contains a total seven chapters. The first chapter looks at the relationship between word and thinking. Psychology confirms that there is a connection between the spoken word and stimuli in the brain. So it follows that the Vedic chants are also the product of our minds. That means, just like our words, Vedas are also non-eternal. But this runs contrary to the Mimamsaka view which holds Vedas to be eternal.

The second chapter begins with the question—What is God? This question gives rise to ambiguous answers. While Advaita declares the world as an illusion, Scriptures hold that duality ends through transcendental experience. Satchidananda Murty questions these assumptions by posing the question—when the world, the individual and his experiences are unreal, how can they lead us on the path of enlightenment? We are intrinsically aware of the existence of others, we also feel that the world runs through God's blessings. So accepting that the creation is God's handiwork, we have to recognize that God and beings are separate. While this view is acknowledged by *Bhagavad Gītā*, Ramanuja, Madhva and Shaiva sects, Advaita differs with it. All the believers concede that God and his creation are one. Prof. Murty states that we have to abide by this universal feeling and take that as the absolute Truth. In the third chapter he reminds that our language symbalises our thoughts. All our religions rely on symbolic language. Thus the symbol represents God- the fourth chapter declares.

The fifth chapter discusses the statement that God's word is final. The sixth chapter reviews the authority of various scriptures. The seventh and final chapter proceeds to establish the relationship between God's word and human discretion. Madhavacharya held that scriptures that run contrary to our experience cannot be deemed authoritative. Murty examines Western philosophers' opinions in this regard and goes into the nature of religions.

Western philosophers opined that religious dicta are unlike scientific statements. They classified Religious statements into four kinds. They are: 1. Expressions of perceptions 2. Statements aimed at encouraging good behaviour 3. Statements to be examined beyond faith 4. Psychological advice helpful in leading a worthy life. Prof. Murty differed with western philosophers in this regard. He held that religion is not merely a moral system. All the world religions are more theoretical than practical. Indian religions declare that it is only through Gyana that emancipation is attained. Buddhism also holds that in Prajñā lies the path to Nirvana. Islam and Christianity also express similar opinions. But Gyana is not rational knowledge, it is wisdom or understanding beyond reason. It is gained through one's own experiences. It is the relationship between experience and faith. It is unwise to regard religious faith as irrational. Even primitive humans harboured a rudimentary form of religious beliefs. The idea of God changes with times. Though the idea of God may not be grounded in reason it can't be out rightly denied. Prof. Murty holds that the word of God and human discretion are not contradictory but mutually reinforcing.

7. Studies in the Problems of Peace (Co-author) (1960)[7]

This book is divided between Dr. K. Satchidananda Murty and Dr. A.C. Bouquet, according to their respective occupations. Dr. Murty, as a philosopher deals with the theoretical aspects of the subject; while Dr. Bouquet has tried to give a historical account of the progress of movements towards peace. The book has thus three parts. Part one was written by Dr. Bouquet, Part two by Dr. Murty and Part Three consists of three chapters, the first by Dr. Murty and the last two by Dr. Bouquest. It is claimed by the authors that while they have "naturally helped each other, read and discussed each other's contributions, and no doubt influenced each other", each of them "is nevertheless only responsible for what he has written".

Applauding Dr. K.S. Murty and Dr. A.C. Bouquet, K.D.D. Henderson, the then Secretary, Spalding Trust, Oxford, wrote "I have just finished reading studies in the Problems of Peace and I wanted to let you know how very highly I regard it. Your review of the history of thought puts the book, to my mind, in the Toynbee class and it is about as sane and balanced a work as I have come across in a very long time".

8. Samakālika Bhāratīya Darśanam (Samakaleen Bharathiya Darshan- Hindi) (1962)[8]

This compilation was published by Akhil Bharatheeya Darshan Parishad, Faridkot in 1962 under the editorship of Prof. Murty. This compilation of articles by ten different modern philosophers starts with Prof. Murty's foreword which provides an overview of ancient Indian philosophical thought. Here is the list of articles in this work: 1.The basis of Indian Thought in 20th Century by Sampoornanand 2. Methods of Indian Philosophers—Narayana Shastri Dravid 3. Modern Hindu Spiritual and Dharmic philosophy—Brajgopal Tiwari 4. Contemporary Indian Pratyaya Vāda—Mangal Lal Pandeya 5. Tendencies of Anubhava Vaada in Contemporary Indian Philosophies—Rajendra Prasad 6. Aurobindo's philosophy—Tripathi 7. Gandhian Philosophy—SS Barlingay 8. Sarvepalli Radhakrishnan's philosophy—Narayana Murty (Rāma Murty's Hindi translation) 9. Contemporary Indian political philosophy—Chandrasekhara Rao (Hindi translation by Ajit Sinha) 10. Indian Muslim and Christian Philosophical Thought—Satchidananda Murty.

Murty's review stands as the highlight of the book. It is really awe-inspiring that a non-Muslim and a non-Christian could present the respective schools of thought in such an unbiased and inspiring manner. No other philosopher seems to have taken up such an uphill task before. It is a fact that Islam and Christianity exerted a deep and wide-ranging influence on the political and spiritual developments in India over the last 1000 years. While some emperors took an antagonist attitude towards Hinduism, others like Akbar adopted a syncretic attitude. Islamic thought was shaped by philosophers like Ibn Sina, Ibn Rushid and Al Ghazali. Mughal scion Dara Shikoh loved Upanishads. Many non-Muslims venerated Quranic verses. Many Muslims fought for India's Independence. There were educationists like Syed Ahmed Khan who established the Aligarh Muslim University. There were patriots like Iqbal among Muslims, statesmen like Abul Kalaam Azad who became part of the Indian mainstream. They influenced Indian religious and philosophical thought, way of life and strove to strengthen Hindu-Muslim unity. That's why one should stop regarding Muslims as foreigners and accept them as our own, asserted Prof. Murty. He also advocated that Muslim spiritual thought should be accorded a rightful place among Indian philosophies so as to achieve true integration.

Christianity entered India during Christ's time itself and gradually spread all over India. Those converted into Christianity were all Indians. So they shouldn't be branded as aliens. Christianity became one of the Indian religions. Christians are selflessly serving Christians and non-Christians alike. The invaluable, progressive policies followed by them in the fields of education and medicine have greatly influenced Hindu way of life and customs. Many Christian intellectuals made their mark in Indian politics and other fields and are enriching our culture. Christian missionaries are building harmonious relations between Hinduism and Christianity. In the light of this, it is wrong to accuse all Christians as serving foreign religious interests. Only by recognizing Islam and Christianity as Indian religions and by adopting a tolerant and egalitarian view can India stand as a truly secular democracy and uphold the spirit of Indian constitution- declares Satchidananda Murty. His novel visionary approach can provide a firm foundation for our democracy.

9. Metaphysics, Man and Freedom (1963)[9]

This book was already referred in chapter 6, as it was

translated into Telugu. However, a brief review of the book is done here. This a series of three lectures, delivered by Prof. Murty at the Annamalai University in 1960.

In the first lecture, he has given an explanation of the three-fold need for metaphysics- the intellectual, linguistic and psychological- and points out how metaphysics arises-from meditation on man's situation in this world and on his knowledge, or out of boredom, dread and "essential situations".

In the second lecture Prof. Murty formulates a conception of man by coordinating the results of reflective analysis on man's being with the findings of psychology and anthropology and goes on to develop a phenomenology of man.

In the third lecture he discusses freedom as an escape from finitude through the ways of *gnosis* and *askesis*, and of the possibility of freedom in the world on the basis of empirical experience and psychoanalysis.

Students of philosophy will find this book very interesting and informative for the scholarly treatment of the subject, as also the general reader for the simple and breezy style in which it has been written.

10. General Education Reconsidered (Ed.,) (1963)[10]

Through a grant made available by the Ministry of Education (under the Ford Foundation project) Government of India, four seminars were conducted and a number of discussion meetings were conducted during 1960s and papers presented in these seminars were published in this volume along with a few specially contributed papers.

Murty emphasizes the importance of general education to the degree and post-graduate students. He emphasizes the importance of General Education to the degree and post-graduate students. He observes that the course on General Education must teach about Man- his powers, limits and destiny. Man must know about himself (*atmanam viddhi*). This is the first thing to be taught in the course. Secondly, this course must emphasize on the outlook and scientific method. Thirdly, the course should have "universal curriculum". The syllabus must select themes, movements, and ideas from all the major cultures of the world. Quoting Prof. Humayun Kabir, Murty writes, the syllabi must foster international knowledge and understanding and evolve a "common culture". The course, says Murty, must seek "to find the golden mean between aimless education and an education of indoctrination". He adds that the course must develop "critical discrimination and nourishes a sense of the multi-facetedness of things. Its purpose would be achieved if it can keep the discussions constructive yet tentative, and inculcate in the students a desire to know more".

11. Indian Foreign Policy (1964)[11]

In this book an attempt is made to analyse and appraise Indian foreign policy. Part I of this book starts with a brief discussion of classical Indian theories, passes on to a consideration of Gandhism and ends up with an analytical exposition of independent India's foreign policy. For this last purpose it relies heavily on the writings and speeches of Jawaharlal Nehru, who is not only a great statesman, but also a "a philosopher with great distinction of mind". In part II are discussed three specific issues—Goa, Sino-Indian and Indo-Pakistan relations. Part III carries further the general discussion, reaching certain conclusions and ventures to make a few concrete suggestions "for improving the fundamental instrumentalities of foreign policy". An Annexure containing the following four sections throws more light on some of the points discussed in the text. (1) The sastras, Ashoka and Gandhi. (2) Ethics and Politics (3) The Blocs and Peaceful co-existence and (4) Russia, India and China.

In his Foreword to this book, Harold D. Lasswell, Professor of Law and Political Science, Yale University wrote: Professor Murty's timely volume comes at a period of tragic yet necessary transitions from the era of Nehru. .... I interpret Professor Murty's book as evidence of the emerging policy sciences of India and hence of the entire world community. These essays clarify the value goals of national policy, distinguishing long range from currently pressing objectives".

12. The Indian Spirit (1965)[12]

Western philosophers with their half-baked knowledge about Indian culture, history and philosophy propagated half-truths about this great country which were regurgitated by Indian writers. Prof. Murty in his book 'The Indian Spirit' strongly lashes out at this slavish behaviour. Andhra University Press published this book in 1965. It consists of 8 chapters: 1. The Indian Spirit in the past and present 2. Indian History: an Atavism 3. The Hindu Ethos 4. The Greek Image of Indian Philosophy 5. Experience, Reason and Transcendental Materialism in Indian Philosophy 6. Philosophical Thought in India 7. Religion and Ethical Practice: The Hindu view 8. Ethics and Politics in Hindu Culture. Satchidananda Murty briefly sketches the outline of the book in the preface. 'This book makes a study of certain important elements of the World and History; labour, property and wealth; Philosophy, Religion, Science, Social system, Morality and Politics. It seeks to understand Indian Culture with a humane perspective with the help of works delivered by Indian intellectuals and creative writers.' He evaluates original concepts of

Indian philosophy against the misconceptions harboured by Indians based on the hare-brained writings of Western writers. Five chapters of the book were reproductions of the talks delivered by Prof. Murty in various international seminars. The third & sixth chapters and the annexure to the sixth were new additions.

The book starts with a knock down of all the misconceptions propagated by Western intellectuals about India and Indian Thought. They branded Indians as prone to mysticism and resisting change; as servile and submitting to all the social injustices, oppression and poverty by mumbling philosophical mumbo-jumbo. They portrayed Indian history as nothing but a chronicle of Kings and their wars. The Orientalists and Christian missionaries who reached Indian shores first were instrumental in fabricating such nonsense. This pushed Indian intellectuals into taking defensive posture. As a response to the Western intellectual onslaught, our pundits began to depict Indians as superior to Westerners in matters of stoicism, spirituality and emancipation. But they had to accept Western dominance in politics, military affairs and industrialization. They were pushed into this pitiable condition because they were unable to fathom ancient Indian achievements in economics, astronomy, medicine, mathematics, chemistry and erotica. If only Indian thinkers shifted their attention awhile from Upanishads, Buddhism and Sankaracharya to Kautilya, Brahma Gupta, Varaha Mihira, Charaka and Vatsyayana, they would have avoided this self-defensive trap. Satchidananda Murty debunked all the Western misconceptions and re-established the greatness of Indian thought.

Spirituality was not monopolised by Indians. It is present in some form or other in all human beings and nations. Hindu texts did not solely dedicate themselves to otherworldly affairs. Renunciation and emancipation have no place in *Rigveda*. Even Hell has no mention in it. It only promises that those who fulfil their social duties fully will surely attain *Divya Lokas*. *Atharve Veda* stressed this world over the other. It also concerns itself with food production and meeting other earthly needs. Neither Hinduism, Jainism nor Buddhism never preached renunciation. They only advised it to a select few who are

Giving Spaulding Lecture at Oxford, UK.

really keen to strike out on that path. Caste system—the bane of Indian society had no place in *Rigveda*. Castes had their origin in *Brahmanas* and later crystallized in *Grihya Suthras* and *Smritis*. During the Vedic period Purohits did not wield undue authority. Every one including Sudras displayed a measure of independence. There were no single section which acted as the overlords. The caste and class discriminations found in Smritis, simply sprang up from the minds of Brahmins. Though Gautama declared that life is suffering, it should be understood in a proper way. What he actually taught was controlling the craving for material things lead to emancipation. Upanishads also stressed the same thing. Even Jainism never preached that all should give up the world to take *Sanyas*. We can observe many Jains occupying top positions in business. All these religions instructed us to lead life and prosper according to certain norms. Many cultures, religions and perspectives thrive in India. Under their influence newer objectives arise over time and people strive to achieve them. In no other country such great cultural traditions can be found- Prof. Murty declared.

In the second chapter Murty recounts the way Western scholars twisted Indian history. Western historian Reincourt's misinterpretation of Indian History as atavistic and as a pot of immoral politics was strongly condemned by Prof. Murty. He held that history can be analyzed from many angles. One shouldn't compare every other civilization to that of the West. Harappa and Mohenjodaro hold a mirror to the greatness of Indian civilization. Under the Mauryan rule, India witnessed an explosion of creativity, novelty and liberal outlook. Western misconception about Indians lacking a historical sense is utterly false. Our *Purāṇas* recount ancient geneologies and their glorious history. Kalhaṇa's *Raja Tarangini* and Buddhist work *Maha Vamsa* should be mentioned here.

Moola Kalpa of ManjuŚrī, *Pali Pithakas* and *Maha Bharata* depicted the societal conditions obtaining in those days. They may not merit as historical writings in the current sense, but such a great culture can be found in no other country of those times. One should not generalize the stray incidents described in ancient writings and blow them up out of proportions. Such unwanted incidents occur in modern America also- Prof. Murty explained.

The fundamental quality of Hinduism is neither stoicism nor reactionary. India served as a laboratory to many religions which proclaimed ever newer perspectives. One should refrain from comparing Indian culture and civilization with that of others. While there are certain variations between Indian and Western philosophies, similarities can also be detected. No philosophy springs out of a vacuum. National traditions, geographical conditions and historical developments shape up philosophical thought. Indian philosophy is no exception. Prof. Murty details the distinct traits and aims of Indian philosophy. Accepting the view that every individual has a soul, Indian philosophical thought encourages the blossoming of individual character. While it accepts the theory of rebirth, it doesn't say that life or karma is fixed. One can change his karma and character by doing good deeds. India upholds culture. Our philosophies strive for attaining emancipation. Yet they change according to the times.

Philosopher Oliver Lacomb opined that the essence of Indian philosophy is Advaita. Prof. Murty pointed out the existence of other philosophical trends to him. Betty Heimann in her work on Indian and Western philosophies commented that monotheism is absent in all Indian religions based on devotion. She argued that God and Soul are inanimate objects. No Indian intellectual cared to shoot down her senseless arguments. Only Prof. Murty effectively countered her arguments. Even famed Western philosopher like Karl Potter commented in his book *Presumptions of Indian Philosophies* that Vedanta, Buddhism and other Indian philosophies are aimed at making us jump from everyday life straight into a relentless endeavour to achieve emancipation. Satchidananda Murty debunked his assumptions by declaring that no Indian philosophy proposed such short cuts. He then moved on to examine the relations between religion and ethics in Indian culture. Even the atheistic philosophies gave prominence to ethics. *Puruṣa Sūkta* and *Bhagavad Gītā* unveiled an ideal social system suited to the olden times. Linking *Karma* with that system and rebirth gave shape to the present day varna system which is not a static one but changes with the times. Though the circumstances of birth, individual nature and behaviour give rise to Varna system, it is amenable to changes. But the static caste system prevailing today was artificially imposed by hegemonistic sections. One should bear in mind that change is the nature of the universe and human society. It is practically impossible to proclaim and apply unchanging laws at all times and places. Hinduism exhorts that we should do good to everybody. Prof. Murty states that man being a thinking being should consider ever changing times and conditions before taking decisions. All our Holy Scriptures and philosophical works teach that by controlling one's desires and maintaining self-restraint one can attain emancipation. Accordingly they advised three kinds of actions: 1. Fulfilling our daily duties 2. When we realise that just by doing karma one can't attain Mokṣa, we naturally turn towards *Gỹāna Yoga*. Karma done through that realization is *Niṣkāma karma* or action without seeking results 3.Certain texts advised against inaction. Whatever we do, it should benefit all.

Hindu culture gives importance to political consciousness also. Rigveda stresses morals and righteous behaviour as the bedrock of ethics. Our holy scriptures stipulated that upholding the law is the primary duty of the state system. Buddhist and Hindu texts averred that the ancient Indian republics (*Mahā Jana padas*) were ruled by Public Will. Decision-making was collective. But according to *Mahā Bhārata*, infighting of various ancient tribes led to the collapse of old republican system and invited invasions of external forces. Once they established their hold, these foreign rulers gave a short-shrift to public welfare and ruled dictatorially. Under their rule immoral behaviour proliferated. Hindu scriptures and Smritis came down heavily on sins and evil behaviour. But modern day twisted politicians indulge exactly in such evil deeds to perpetrate their misrule. Educated people can't hope to compete with them- Prof. Murty notes sadly.

13. Readings in Indian History, Politics and Philosophy (Ed.) (1967)[13]

This book contains Prof. Satchidananda Murty's selection of readings from the works of almost all modern major Indian historians, philosophers and political thinkers. It offers, in one volume, a historical, political and cultural conspectus hitherto available only from a wide variety of sources.

The work is divided into three parts. Part I provides a survey of ancient Indian historiography, the Hindu conception of history, varying interpretations of Indian history in particular and history in general, and gives an outline of historical methodology as well as a panorama of Indian history. Lastly it presents the essence of Indian culture from differing viewpoints. Part II expounds the nature and content of classical Indian political thought, discusses its relevance today, and brings together extracts from the theories of modern political thinkers. The possible approaches to ancient Indian philosophy are discussed in

Part III which covers Buddhism, Indian naturalism and several types of theistic and idealistic monistic Vedanta. Selections from four modern Indian Muslim thinkers and four modern Indian systematists are followed by an interpretation of the ethics of the *Dharmasastra*, the Vedanta and Bhakti schools.

This is a valuable source book which communicates to the reader something of the variety, profundity and significance of Indian thought and political and social tradition.

14. Nāgārjuna (1971)[14]

National Book Trust, New Delhi, asked Prof. Murty to deliver a biography of Buddhist philosopher Nagarjuna as part of their biography series which he promptly obliged. The book was published in 1971. Subsequently, Pullela Śrīramachandrudu translated this book into Telugu and this was published in 2010 by National Book Trust of India.

There are many tales extant about Nagarjuna in various countries. Fact and fiction were mixed up in those versions. Prof. Murty took it upon himself to depict Nagarjuna's life story in a historically truthful manner. Max Wallesser's article 'Nagarjuna from Chinese and Tibetan Sources' was helpful to some extent.

Prof. Murty's book was divided into two sections. The first section provides us with the background of Nagarjuna's life story. Renowned as the Father of Mahayana school of Buddhism, Nagarjuna's influence was far reaching. His teachings spread to China, Tibet, Korea, Vietnam, Japan, Central Asia and other Asian countries. But modern tales about Nagarjuna depict him either as a magician, Tantrik and a scientist or all combined. In the first section of his book Prof. Murty strove to properly establish the personality and role of historical Nagarjuna.

In the second section Prof. Murty examines the available biographies of the Buddhist philosopher. He categorized them as narratives of Siddhas, histories and literature. The *first category* contains the brief histories of 84 Sidhas, Lama Taranatha's Mystic stories, Nepali Sidhana Amnayam. These accounts describe Nagarjuna as having born in a South Indian Brahmin family who later turned to Tantricism and magic. He was also an alchemist. Nagarjuna was an advisor to a king on whose request he chose to live on Śrī Parvata. Nagarjuna reportedly received *Prajñāpāramita Sutras* from Naga loka and later revealed them to the world. But the authenticity of these stories cannot be verified. Buddha Charitras of Bu Stan (1290-1364 CE) and of Taranatha (1608 CE) and Crystal Mirror of 1947 fall into the *second category*. According to them Nagarjuna was born 400 years after Buddha in a South Indian Brahmin family who were told that the child will not live beyond 7 years. So his parents sent him away on a tour of the country accompanied by a female servant. His travels ended up at Nalanda University. After completing the study of *Sāma Veda* there, he attracted the attention of Saraaha who advised Nagarjuna to chant *Amita Ayu Sutras* which enabled him to achieve longevity. Nagarjuna was initially a protégé of Saraaha and Rahula Bhadra and later rose to be the Chancellor of Nalanda University. Later attaining the patronage and friendship of a king he shifted to Śrī Parvata and lived there till he breathed his last. But these accounts differed with each other in many ways. While Lama tradition deems Nagarjuna as an incarnation of Ananda. Bu Stan, Taranatha, Sanpa Khampo say that he initially studied *Sarvasti vada*. Certain Tibetan writings place Nagarjuna's time some 600 years after Buddha's Nirvāṇa. The authnticy of these works cannot be ascertained. The third was *Mahā Megha Sūtra* whose Tibetan and Chinese translations are available today. According to Chinese translations, 1200 years after Buddha's *Mahā Pari*

Nirvāṇa a Buddhist monk named Naga Raja renounced the world in the South Indian state of Sau Rashtra. They put his place of birth in a village called Kusumamala/ Samanamala on the banks of Supaya river in Satavahana kingdom. Contradicting with this version Tibetan sources say Nagarjuna was born as Naga Lichava 400 years after Buddha's Nirvāṇa in the village Maha Vakula on the banks of Sundarabhooti river in the Southern Rushila state during the rule of Vipathi Chikitsaka. Lichava later became Nagarjuna—the Buddhist monk and dedicated himself to Dharma Prachara. This discrepancy between Tibetan and Chinese translations of *Maha Megha Sutra* makes us doubt their authenticity. The Sagathaka chapter in *Lankavathara Sutra* states that a Buddhist monk named Nagahvaya had reconciled the differences between Satta and Astta to unveil Mahayana before attaining Heaven. Manjuśrī Moola Kalpa tells us about certain Nagahvaya who was born 400 after Buddha and over his 600 years of lifetime gained mastery over many arts and sciences including Mayuri Vidya and dedicated his life to Buddhism. Upon his death Nagahvaya reached Sukhavati heaven and finally attained Buddha Avatar. We may infer that both *Lankāvatāra Sutra* and *Manjuśrī Mūlakalpa* are referring to Nagarjuna. Though both of these were not regarded as part of Mahayana Buddhist canon, their narratives are considered as credible. What can be ascertained from these texts is that Nagarjuna was a South Indian, the originator of Madhyamika SunyaVada and was famous by 5th century CE.

Another source is Kumara Jeeva's Biography of Nagarjuna available as Chinese translation. Chinese traveler Sun Sa (596-694 CE) and Chinese *Tripiṭhakas* also give us information about Nagarjuna. Particularly *Dharma Piṭhaka Sutra* counts Kampila as 12th, Nagarjuna as 13th and Arya Deva as 14th Acharya. As this *sūtra* was derived from an ancient Indian text, it can be considered as reliable. Kuman Jiva's successor Huyan (334-416CE) had incorporated Nagarjuna's brief biography in the introduction to Prajñā Pāramita version. Father Sion's Sanskrit dictionary (1511 CE) also has an entry on Nagarjuna. We can deduce Nagarjuna's life story from these writings in the following manner:

Andhra Satavahanas ruled Deccan from 180 BC to 218 CE. They took up sea trade in a big way which helped spread Buddhism to other countries. Nagarjuna was born in Vedali village of South and lived in Dhanya Kataka (Amaravati) and Śrī Parvata for many years. We don't have precise information about his exact birth time or his parents. Only Nepali Amnayam names his parents as Trivikrama and Satali. Nagarjuna became famous during 170-200 CE. Having studied Vedas in childhood itself, Nagarjuna had become a renowned scholar by the age of 20 years. Seeking thrill he allegedly entered the royal palace with the help of Brahmajala trick to romance the princess but was caught by palace guards. Consequently he vowed that if released he will become a monk. But this seems to be a made up story. The fact is otherwise. As he grew up Nagarjuna gradually became discontented with worldly life. As he was unable to find solace in Hindu scriptures, Nagarjuna finally took up the study of *Tri Piṭakas* and led a simple life. He eventually became a Buddhist monk-wrote *Kumara Jeeva*. Nagarjuna's travels brought him into contact with an old monk in Himalayas who helped him with Mahayana studies, which he continued later. Pride got into his head. He entered into long and futile discussions with pundits and eventually realised that Mahayana texts lacked logic as their principles remained unproven. Having lost faith in Buddha and Mahāyāna teachings, he announced that he doesn't accept any Guru and set out to develop an association of monks all by himself. He even announced a date on which he was going to unveil a totally new, logical Dharma. Taking pity on his egoistic behaviour, Bodhisatva Maha Naga took Nagarjuna to Naga palace under the sea and showed him seven Dhatu Kalashas housed there. These Kalashas or metal pots contained supreme Dharma principles. Bodhisatva selected *Vaipulya principles* and presented them to Nagarjuna. He studied the principles for 90 days, gleaned their essence and returned to Buddha's path to become Bodhisatva. Maha Naga brought Nagarjuna to the South along with certain Sutras. Nagarjuna studied these principles ten times, defeated non- Buddhist philosophers in debates, attracted a large number of common folk and eventually spread Mahayana school far and wide.

We can infer from the above version of Kumara Jeeva, that the Vaipulya *principles* described by Kumara Jeeva are none other than *Prajñā Pāramita Sūtras*. In fact, these very sutras were prevalent in the Buddhist sects of those days. The mythical story of Maha Naga must be a later day addition. Jataka tales did mention Naga kings. Maha Naga might be a chief of a Naga tribe. The brisk sea trade under Satavahana rule, might have given rise to the story of sub-sea Naga palace. The name Nagarjuna Denotes Naga connection. Nobody knows the first name of Nagarjuna. *Laṅkavatāra Sutra* mentions it as Bouddha Śrīman.

Nagarjuna participated in the rituals of Buddha, Bodhisatva worship and circumambulation (pradakṣiṇa) of stupas. He built boundary walls to Bodh Gaya and Dhanya Kataka stupas. Worshipped Amitabha Buddha. Developed Madhyamika Darshana under the name of Bodhisatva ManjuŚrī.

Attained spiritual heights through meditation. Achieved fame through yogic powers like *Prajñā, Karuna*. He was a noted alchemist too. Śrī Parvata hill on which

Nagarjuna lived was later came to be known as Nagarjuna Konda. He had close relationship with a Satavahana king. Raja Pari Katha in *Ratnavali* mentions such a relationship. We are yet to ascertain the name of that king. Wallace suggested that he might be Yajnaśrī or Vijayaśrī who lived between 178-207 CE. But it still remains uncertain.

According to Tibetan tradition, Nagarjuna lived for 60 years. Others say he lived for 100 years. Mahayana texts state that he died upholding *Dhamma*. There were still other versions which claim that he died due to the conspiracy of a Brahmin or took his own life as per the request of a princess. But all these tales agree on one thing: that Nagarjuna died on Śrī Parvata. Kumara Jeeva says that temples were built for Nagarjuna after his death and people used to worship him. Two teeth found in a box excavated from Śrī Parvata were said to be of Nagarjuna.

There is no clarity regarding Nagarjuna's writings even. Tibetan sources say that he wrote a total of 116 texts. But it seems that anonymous authors wrote those books using his name. It is generally believed that only *Mādhyamika Śāstra, Mūla Mādhyamika Kārikā, Vigraha Vyavartani, Ratnāvalī* and *Suhṛllekha* were originally written by Nagarjuna. Also *Dvadasha Mukha Shastra* and *Maha Prajñā Paramitha Shastra* were believed to be penned by him. These two works wield enormous influence on Chinese and Japanese philosophical thought. Lamotte and Venkata Ramana provided us with an index of reference works. Arya Deva who was a direct disciple of Nagarjuna was waylaid and killed by rivals who were defeated in debates with him. *Chatuh, Shataka* and *Shatasaara* are reportedly Arya Deva's works. The Chinese list Nagarjuna as the 13th and Arya Deva as the 14th in a long line of Buddhist teachers. ManjuŚrī Mulakalpa names Nanda and Sangha as Nagarjuna's disciples. E Jinh mentions another disciple named Naga. A stone inscriptions says that Śrī Parvata

Maha Chaitya was repaired by one Naga Thera Ananda, a Buddhist monk from Nandigama, Krishna district. He was obviously another of Nagarjuna's disciples according to Subramanian.

Buddha Palitha of 5th century CE launched a Madhyamika branch in the name of Nagarjuna which was further developed by Chandra Keerthi. And Shanti Deva promoted worship of Bodhisatva stipulating that one should maintain good character and undergo spiritual training. *Shikṣā Samuchaya, Bodhi Charyāvatāra* were Shanti Deva's famous writings. During 6th century CE, Bhava Viveka Bhavya developed Svatantrya Madhyamika School. Simha Rashi, a teacher of Nalanda University termed Mādhyamika as a school of Skepticism. "Tipiṭaka", a Chinese scholar and Nalanda teacher opined that Madhyamika is an idealist school. It is to be noted that all of the famed Mādhyamika teachers like Chandra Keerthi, Bhava Viveka and Budhapalitha were South Indians.

Madhyamika School deeply influenced Tibet, China, Japan, Korea and Mongolia. This school rejects both Essentialism (or Eternalism) and Nihilism and proposes Sunyata (Emptiness). All phenomena are empty of essence or substance because they are dependently co-arisen. Sunyata is synonymous with saying that it is dependently originated. Not only Matter, the ever changing universe also lacks permanent existence. On the basis of the Buddha's view that all experienced phenomena (*dharma*) are "dependently arisen" (*pratītya-samutpanna*), Nagarjuna insisted that such phenomena are empty (*śūnya*). They are devoid of a permanent and eternal substance (*Svabhāva*). It is through *Prajñā* that one can attain absolute Truth. In that state all duality i.e., existence and non-existence; permanence and impermanence- cease to be and non-duality is realized. The perceived world is non-substantial. Everything is empty. There is no difference between worldly existence and Nirvana. *Mukti* means realization of Sūnyatā—so declares Madhyamika School.

Mahayana teaches that the rule of the state should be based on justice, character and compassion. Nagarjuna's *Suhṛllekha* and *Ratnāvali* elaborate on this concept. Mahayana gives prominence to Amitabha worship. It is believed in China, Tibet and other eastern nations that Nagarjuna was the originator of this form of worship. The Bodhisatva concept of Mahayana further encouraged this. Certain ancient texts preaching Amitabha worship were found in 150 CE.

Thus Prof. Murty helped us to view Nagarjuna's life history from a chronologically and philosophically correct perspective. He gave us extensive information regarding his works, his disciples, endeavours and the evolution of Mahayana Buddhism.

15. Current trends in Indian Philosophy (Ed.,) (1972)[15]

This compilation of essays by noted writers was jointly edited by Prof. Satchidananda Murty and Prof. K. Ramakrishna Rao and was published by Andhra University, Waltair in 1970. It came out 34 years after publishing of *Contemporary Indian Philosophy* by Radhakrishnan and Muirhead. The current book contains 38 pages of rather longish introductory essay 'Modern India and Philosophy', by Prof. Murty. There are a total of 23 essays in this compilation. The contributors were highly accomplished in their fields. Their articles serve as great reference works. It contains following articles: 'The Philosophical task in contemporary world' by former Chancellor of Andhra University VS Krishna; 'The Desired and the Good' by AN Ayub, a professor of Kolkata University; 'The Foundations of Advaita Vedanta' by SV Banerjee, another savant of the same university; 'The nature of Reflection in Metaphysics' by Professor Kalidas Bhattacharya; 'Scientific Humanism' by Prof. S. Chaturvedi, a student of Radhakrishnan and Surendranath Das Gupta; 'From Structuralism to Mystical Personalism' by Prof. C.T. Krishnamacharya of Madras Christian College; 'Conception of World Philosophy' by Prof. SC Chatterjee of Kolkata Varsity; 'Critical Philosophy' by JN Chub of Mumbai, Elphinstore College; 'Nature and Validity of Value statements' by Prof. N.K. Devaraja; 'The concept of Axionoctics' by A.G. Jayadevkar of Baroda MS University; 'Adventure into the Unknown' by D.D. Kosambi of Benares University; 'Appearance and Reality' by Prof. Daya Krishna of Delhi Hindu College; 'Truth and Error' by Prof. SK Mitra of Kolkata University; 'An Empirical Study of Theological Statements' by Yakub Masi of Bihar University; 'Phenomenology and Ontology' by J. Mohanty of Kolkata University; 'The Humanism of Roy' by GD Parikh; 'A Functional Analysis of Language' by Rajendra Prasad, Professor of philosophy in IIT, Kanpur; 'Practicalist Approach to Philosophy' by Prof. K. Ramakrishna Rao of Andhra University; 'Man and God' by Prof. Syed Wahiduddin of Osmania University; 'Search for Integral Philosophy' by KC Varadachari of Śrī Venkateswara University; 'The Vision of God in the Godly' by Jayachamaraj Wodeyar, Mysore Raja Pramukh and Governor.

Prof. Murty in his introductory essay 'Introduction-Modern India and Philosophy' provided a retrospective of Indian philosophical thought. It was distilled from Prof. Murty's extensive study and research spread over many decades. It looks into evolution of Independent India under five heads: Thought and Society; Modernization and National Liberation Movement; Social and Economic Development in Independent India; Renaissance and Reformation in 19th and 20th centuries; and Non- academic philosophy in 20th Century.

16. The Realm of Between (1973)[16]

Prof. Murty explains in the introduction how the title was fixed for this book. Man dreaming about Eternity and finding God is stuck in a twilight zone i.e., the realm of between. His mental processes in this state are described in this work. It took shape out of the lectures delivered by Murty in Manchester College, Oxford during November 1963. The concepts contained in those talks were further developed in May 1970 while delivering lectures as Visiting Professor at the Indian Institute of Advanced Studies, Shimla. Those talks were published by the institute in 1973 in a book form. It contains four chapters. The *first one* titled Suffering (Dukha) is divided into five sections giving prominence to Buddhist perspective. Lord Buddha's definition of suffering and the way out of it was described in the first section. The second section recounts the views of Kathopanishad and Chandogyopanishad on Dukha. The third section takes up a Western book which dealt with Buddhist concept of Dukha. The fourth section details the Bible's teaching about God and the importance of freeing oneself from sin through devotion and penance. The fifth section deals with the relationship between man and God and acquaints us with the Intellectuals' viewpoint that only a free human being can attain emancipation. Thus the first chapter concerns itself with explaining nature of suffering, God's role in helping man on his path to enlightenment and Man's duty in this regard and declares that ultimately Man strives for ending of all suffering.

The *second chapter* 'Salvation' is divided into three sections. In this Prof. Murty gives a short shrift to the categorization that West is materialistic and the East is spiritual. He argues that a country's geographical and cultural conditions influence its people's world view. Refraining from sticking solely to materialistic path, one should aim for spiritual awakening and free his soul from material desires. But before that mankind should definitely achieve material well-being which enables all of us to pursue emancipation. Those who are poor and lead a dependent life will not be able to think of higher ideals. But unless we control our desires, we can't hope for inner peace. Attaining riches should not be the sole aim of life. One can see this for himself just by looking at the way the West has become neurotic in its singular pursuit of physical desires.

By salvation, Prof. Murty means the freeing of not just individuals but entire mankind. Accepting that material life is full of suffering, all religions declare that life's ultimate aim should be liberating oneself from material desires. They taught us different ways to reach this goal. Some religions supported the theory of reincarnation. Other mythical theories were also propagated. Such baseless ideas and arguments coalesced into complex belief systems- explains Murty.

Prof. Murty analyzes Indian culture which proclaims that man has an ever-changing body and an everlasting soul and which are different from each other. Soul being trapped in an impermanent body is plunged into sorrow. Religious teachers averred that meditation and devotion to God will free the soul from countless rebirths. Some others taught that Gyana and Karma Yogas lead to salvation. Those who attain salvation while living are called *Jeevan Muktas*. Attaining *Mokṣa* after death is called *Videha Vimukti*. Buddhism defines *Nirvāna* as cessation of desires. *Nirvana* is not void. It is inexplicable. Each has to attain the state individually- so declares Buddhism.

Generally all religions agree that there is a Transcendental Truth but proclaim different and at times opposing paths to attain it. People are utterly confused about the correct path. Prof. Murty proposed seven ways out of this logjam. 1. We can scrutinize all the available paths and prove them as self-contradictory. 2. Declare that all ways are partial but collectively offer ultimate Truth. 3. Deriving general properties from them and synthesize the Final Truth. 4. Accepting one path as the true one and treating other paths as supportive to it. 5. Rejecting all the paths as meaningless. 6.Taking a path which is most appealing to one's own culture and traditions. 7. Picking the best path according to the personal choice.

The *third chapter* deals with the religious rituals. They are the practices followed by populace by accepting the sanctity of Religion. Rituals keep everything in its place. They help us find Truth through reminiscing about ancient *Prajñā* (Supreme Wisdom), through study, quest for knowledge and by inculcating good qualities. Hinduism imposes two kinds of rituals: Pooja and Yajña. Seeing the divinity in the forms one worships is Pooja. There are three kinds of relationships between God and his creation. God creates the world, He enters the world and finally he dies and offers himself to the animate and inanimate universe. This divine offering is celebrated through *Yajña*. In a way, by conducting *Yajña,* man offers himself to the world.

Rigvedic *ṛṣis* worshipped divinity in various forms. They offered their most valued resources like horse, bull, soma and ghee to the Almighty in the Yajñas hoping that their prayers will be answered. Those who helped with these rituals were classified as Brahmins. Conducting the *Yajña* in the stipulated way is termed as *Ritam* which causes every event to happen in a proper order. Thus *Yajña* serves as a bridge between God and Man. *Dhyāna* or Meditation is intrinsic to it. But those who conduct *Yajña* should be truthful. Participants of *Yajña* collectively consume the offerings and gain the fruits of *Yajña*. Rigvedic hymns do not contain the concept of God's death. Only *Puruṣa Sūkta* holds that the *Puruṣa* is divided and offered in the *Yajña*.

It also assures that offerings in a *Yajña* are surely partaken by gods in heaven.

The ancient texts of *Brāhmaṇās* display two different viewpoints. Holding the *yajña* mechanically and treating it as magical. According to the second view *yajña* is an earnest spiritual ritual. The person who is conducting the *yajña* should firmly believe that the gods who partake his offerings will fulfil his desire soon. In reality there are no gods. Only the strong beliefs of the *yajña* holders and the rituals followed produce desired results. *Satapatha Brāhmaṇā* is the most important among all Brāhmaṇās. Hymns in its last chapter are formed into *Bṛhadāraṇyaka Upaniṣad*. It replaces Rigvedic Purusha with Prajāpati who is the creator of animate and inanimate universe. In every *yajña*, Prajapathi dies and takes rebirth. *Yajña* embodies this endless process. The tenth canto of *Bṛhadāraṇyaka Upaniṣad* says that Prajāpati arose from sacred fire Agni. It sees no difference between Agni and Prajāpati and treats Man, Mind, Vaiśvānara and Prajāpati are nothing but the internal parts of the Great Prajāpati. Brahman is the inner soul. Meditating on Brahman is the highest form of worship. Brahman is omnipresent. He exists in everything and outside of it. The essence of *yajña* is unveiling of this ultimate Truth. The man who sacrifices his inner soul to the Great Soul—Brahman will be free of all sins and attain Heaven. In this manner *yajña* turns out to be a magnificent task.

In general there are five kinds of Yajñas: 1. Brahma Yajña 2. Deva Yajña 3. Pitru Yajña 4. Nṛ Yajña and 5. Bhootha Yajña. Doing Yajñas properly purifies one's inner self. This process need not be limited to a physical process. Through meditation also one can purify himself—so say Upanishads. Certain Upanishads even ridiculed *yajña* rituals. *Bhagavad Gītā* also terms *yajña* rituals as putting breaks on one's own self. Lord Krishna tells us that self-serving actions are futile. The highest form of *Yajña* is nothing but doing actions with outmost devotion to God. *Gÿāna yajña* is the highest form of yajña—declares the *Gītā*. *Yajña* is done for the benefit of the whole mankind.

Prof. Murty also discusses about the highest regard given to *yajña* by Mīmāṁsā and the views of Aurobindo and Heidegger in this regard. In the concluding part, he brings out the problems in self-sacrifice. Doing *yajña* to worship Para Brahman is also without problems. Prof. Murty points out to the Dravidian roots of the word *Pūja* and reveals that *Pūja* was an integral part of Tantricism. The third chapter of *Ananda Lahari* states that to worship the nameless and formless God, the worshipper has created myriad forms. This practice has been contested by many Tāntriks who said that *Gÿāna Yoga* is the only true way to worship God. Western philosophers—particularly supernaturalists went further to declare God is dead. When we believe that God is dead, ethical systems also die with it- cautions Prof. Murty. German philosopher Kant posed the questions: Is there a God? What is God? Though initially Kant believed that trying to solve such questions is the purpose of philosophy, but in the end he veered to the view that asking such questions is meaningless. Heidegger explained that the question of God entered metaphysics in three ways: 1. Mistaking one's own understanding of Being as Being 2. Fundamental unity of being is existence 3. Totality and Unity of being is existence. The first one is logical understanding, the second-theological understanding and the third is metaphysical understanding.

Rationalism which destroyed the collective ideal has replaced it with individualism. It also replaced the concept of orderly and evolutionary universe with infinite space. Thus Western philosophy destroyed the concepts of universe and the collective, making the existence of God irrelevant. Reason has taken the paramount position. With the individualistic rationalism and other materialistic philosophies refusing to accept transcendental Truth, they ended up directionless.

But not all Western philosophers adopted such views. Hegel suggested that we can understand the statement 'God is dead' in three ways.: 1.Rational arguments seeking to prove the existence of God ended up giving the opposite result. They made the existence of God meaningless and abstract. Theists and religious preachers isolated God from the universe. 2. After the act of dying, God has created human beings and through human consciousness he manifested himself. 3. In philosophy Being has replaced religious idea of God. Thus the difference between God and Man disappeared and God has lost his relevance. Ethics also met the same fate. In this manner God is dead in Western philosophy—Hegel opined. Another German philosopher Nietzsche also didn't accept an all independent God saying that such a concept created much moral and cultural chaos everywhere. French philosopher Jean Paul Sartre cautioned that removing God necessitates the elevation of moral values to take that place. This trend has become intrinsic to Western literature. In the Eastern countries morality is entwined with God. Though God has no place in Buddhism, Jainism, Confucianism and Taoism, ethics certainly are intrinsic to them.

Prof. Murty also felt that there need not be any link between spirituality and morals. He also discusses the questions regarding the existence or non-existence of God in the second chapter.

17. Far Eastern Philosophies (1976)[17]

This work introduces us to the philosophies of China and Japan. It starts with the three talks given by Prof. Murty during 1966 in Mysore University. His talks on Chinese religious beliefs in Viswa Bharati, Shanti Niketan were also added in this book. Mysore Varsity published them in 1976. Prior to Prof. Murty, no other foreign intellectuals took care to look deeply and comprehensively into Chinese and Japanese religions and philosophies. He was the first foreign scholar to do so. Highly commending his effort Chinese scholar Wing Chit Chan and Japanese philosopher Hajime Nakamura wrote introductions to this work.

It contains five chapters. The first three dwell on the Chinese and last two deal with the Japanese spiritual thought. In the first chapter entitled "Chinese Philosophy", Prof. Murty stresses that in history, progress and decline run in a cycle which is dependent on the rise and fall of dynasties. During the period of decline, saintly kings take up reforms in philosophical and spiritual thought. Good and Bad; Rise and fall naturally occur in every field.

Buddhism influenced six dynasties immediately after its entry into China. Kumara Jeeva introduced Buddhist metaphysics there. Others systematized *Śunya Vāda* concepts. *Madhyamika Vāda* developed as an important school of thought. Vasubandhu's commentaries helped the propagation of *Vijñāna Vāda*. All these influences continued till 7th century CE. After continuous decline of China under the previous six dynasties, the country witnessed cultural renaissance and unity again under Tang dynasty. While Confucianism moulded the moral and political thought of China, Buddhism and Taoism guided its religious and artistic life. Japan and Korea regarded China of those days as the land of Buddha.

Under Tang dynasty many Buddhist schools flourished. Based on *Saddharma Puṇḍarīka* (Lotus) *Sutra,* Tiantai school of Buddhism was developed by Zhiyi in China. Huayan School was based on Avatamsaka Sutra. Based on Sukhavati Vyooha Sutra, the Pureland Buddhism was developed. The Chan school of Mahayana Buddhism was initiated by Bodhidharma. *Vajrachhedaka Prajñā Pāramita Sutra* which teaches that Bodhi Chitha helps one attain Nirvana became a part of this school. But in later day China, Buddhism began to be viewed as a foreign religion. This led to the destruction of Buddhist monasteries and killing of Buddhist monks. Though later day rulers again patronaged Buddhism it could not fully recover. Confucianism reasserted itself in 12th century. Chan and Pure land schools became main streams of Buddhism. During the 16th century serious attempts were made to achieve cohesion between four Buddhist schools. Tiantai and Huayan schools dedicated themselves to the worship of Bodhisatva and meditation. Till 20th century, crores of Chinese regarded Buddhism as their principal religion which dominated Chinese thought, literature, language, arts and sciences. In this work, Prof. Murty details a total of six schools of Chinese philosophy: 1.Confucianism 2. Taoism 3. Legalism 4. Monism 5. Ming Chiya 6. Yin-Yang.

In the second chapter, Prof. Murty introduces us to the concepts of Confucianism, which was reputed to be an educated man's philosophy. He recounts the way Zisi, grandson of Confucius, further developed Confucianism. Prof. Murty also describes the efforts of other Confucianists like Mencius, Hsun-Tsu and Chu-Hsi. Their ideas helped the blossoming of Neo-Confucianism. Prof. Murty compares this school with the ideas of Western philosophical thought.

The Third chapter explains Taoism of Lao Tzu. Prof. Murty spells out the key concepts of Taoism saying that Tao means Truth which is ever changing and mystical. Tao is the source of everything, which contains consciousness and non-consciousness, change and eternity. All these dualities arise and end in Tao. Tao is formless but infinite. It can't be seen or heard. But it is limitless. Taoism, propounded by Lao Tzu, is understood by different people differently. Tao signifies the way or code of behavior. It applies not only to personal behavior but to conducting the government affairs also. It is the absolute principle underlying the universe. It is akin to the formless and nameless Brahman put forward by Upanishads. Thus it is eminently possible to understand Taoism from the perspective of Buddhism and other philosophies. Taoism gives prominence to Ethical values. It doesn't find much use for meaningless rituals, legacy problems, feudal rights and responsibilities. It advises that we should free ourselves from all those constraints. Taoists say that we should be free of all preconceptions and lead normal lives. The most important tenet of Taoism is *Wu Wei* which can be defined as effortless doing or action without action. It is purely natural way of behaving. Later day Chinese philosophers added ideas of emancipation and nirvana to Taoist thought.

The fourth and fifth chapters outline Japanese philosophy. Japan's ethical, religious and philosophical systems were influenced and shaped by Chinese Confucianism and Indian Buddhism. This gave rise to a misconception that Japan lacks an original religious and philosophical system. In fact Japan has assimilated the useful elements in other cultures and discarded the useless and finally developed a system of its own. The compilation of ancient Japanese mythologies was done during 8th Century CE. It gives us a broad understanding of Japanese Shintoism. Worshipping the forces of nature, the ancient Japanese regarded Sun as the lord of the pantheon. And Sun was reckoned as the progenitor of Japanes royalty. Shintoism is the ethnic Japanese religion, it is action-centred and focused on ritual practices and ethical behavior. Picturesque Japan has many village gods and goddesses. Devotees wake them up by clapping their hands on entering the temples. The important thing to note is that no temple hosts a statue of a god or goddess. Japnese worship various spirits, a practice which gradually gave rise to monotheism.

Japan, which is geographically isolated, has developed a distinct religion influenced by Indian, Chinese and Western philosophical thought. Aesthetically oriented Japanese culture finds its expression in a variety of art forms and reaches the pinnacle in Zen Buddhism which shaped up their simplicity, hospitality and moral courage. Neither hostility to the physical world nor anti-social behavior can be traced in Japanese mindset. As both Confucianism and Buddhism taught that man should behave according to his natural urges and qualities, quest for material comforts shaped up Japnese religious perspective- Nakamura explains. Japanese believe that as every man has an intrinsic Buddha nature, everybody should strive to attain it by following Dharmic path. They believe in *Saddharma Pundarika* tenet that one can achieve miraculous powers through meditation and Yoga. Saicho, founder of Tendai School propagated these principles of Esoteric Buddhism in Japan. Kukai, founder of Shingon School taught that one can attain *nirvana* by unifying the body and mind through tantric practices. According to another Buddhist monk Dogen, there is no gap between practice and enlightenment or Zazen and daily life. Buddha's nature can be attained only through integral experience. This was the teaching of Mahayana *Avatamsaka Sutra* too. Dogen often stressed the critical importance of zazen or sitting meditation as the central practice of Buddhism. Compassion, ethical living, sitting posture and breathing practice are the characteristics of Zazen. It is the simple and pleasant practice of Buddha under which the supreme law appear of itself and one will be free of delusion. Without terming the world a delusion, the Japanese achieved a sense of non-dualism.

Following the spirit of Zen, the Japanese Samurai (warrior) class developed a code of honour and ethics which is termed as the *Bushido* or the Way. It is regarded as the essence of life. Even while following Buddhist tenets, the Chinese and Japanese sages gave utmost importance to worldly life. The Japanese word *Kami* means The Way which is their fundamental religion. The ancient inscription dating back to 604 CE serves as the basis for Japanese governance system and creative thinking. The Chinese synchronized Buddhism and Confucianism and took them as guiding force. While the former guided their spiritual life, the latter moulded their political and social life. In Japan Emperor Shomu accepting Sun God as Maha Vairochana Buddha, commissioned a 53 feet high idol of him in a great temple.

In the middle ages, Hidoyoshi, a powerful Japanese Lord, harmonized Shintoism and Christianity. Believing that in India, Sun God was being worshipped as Buddha, he commissioned a great Buddha statue in the city of Kyoto. Ieyasu, the first Shogun (military commander) of Tokugawa Shogunate who unified Japan made an everlasting impression on Buddhists and Shinto followers.

In the fifth chapter, Prof. Murty describes the origins of Shintoism, ancient scriptures, traditions, concept of God, and their prominent role in Japanese culture. He compares Indian cultural development with that of Japanese to derive valuable insights. In Japan Tendai and Shingon Buddhist schools combined Buddhist thought with Shintoist teachings. Tendai is based on *Saddharma Pundarika Sutta* and Nagarjuna's philosophy. The Chinese Tiantai School has transformed itself as Tendai in Japan. There arose another school of thought professing Vairochana Buddha as the creator of the world with all living beings in it. All the gods and demons sprung up from him. The power of his word drives worldly life, movement, concepts, human thought and sounds. This school seems to be an offshoot of Shingon sect. It regards Vairochana Buddha as the ground of being itself and the matrix from which all phenomena emerge. Murty observed that some Japanese philosophers synthesized Shinto, Buddhist and Confucian thought and presented novel ethical and religious values.

18. Andhra Contribution to Buddhist Thought (1980)[18]

On the invitation of Telugu University, Hyderabad, Prof. Murty delivered Radhakrishnan Memorial lecture in 1975. The same talk was published in a booklet form in 1980. He started the talk with praising Radhakrishnan's efforts to develop Buddhist tradition. Radhakrishnan in his work *Indian Philosophy* discussed the origin and evolution of Hinayana and Mahayana schools of Buddhism. In 1988, he delivered the talk titled *The Master Mind- Gautama Buddha* in the British Academy. He had also translated into English the *Dhamma Padha*. After dwelling on these facts, Prof. Murty moves on to the development of Buddhism in Andhra Desha.

Buddhsim which entered Andhra during Gautama Buddha's time in 6th Century BCE, thrived here till 6th Century CE, i.e., for an uninterrupted period of 12 centuries. A huge amount of Buddhist artefacts were unearthed all over Andhra. Amaravati sculpture, Nagarjuna's philosophy emerged and spread out from here. Theories of Andhakas, Prajñā Paramita Sutras, Ratna Koota literature, Mantra Yana were developed on Andhra soil. According to *Sutta Nipata*, a Brahmin belonging to Bavari gotra lived on the banks of river Godavari flowing through Asmaka and Mulaka lands. He was a great scholar in Vedas, Epics and Puranas. On learning about the greatness of Buddha, he sent 16 of his 500 disciples to the city of Shravasti, where they met the Buddha, cleared their doubts and gained an understanding of Buddhism. Among them, only an old disciple called Pingiya returned to Asmaka Maha Janapada and reported his experiences to Bavari. Thus Buddhism entered Andhra Desha during Buddha's lifetime itself. Dhanya Kataka (Amaravati), Śrī Parvata (Nagarjuna Hill) and Vengi developed as major centres of Buddhism.

According to the 16th edict of Emperor Ashoka, Andhra Desha was part of his empire. Andhras worshipped Buddha's Dhatu Stupas. Ashoka helped to construct the Maha Chaitya in Dhanya Kataka. Nagarjuna built a boundary wall around it. Other Chaityas were built in Bhattiprolu, Jaggayya Pet, Guntupalli, Shali Hundam, Sankaram and Nagarjuna Konda. The rock edicts found in there describe Buddha's physical and spiritual characteristics. The copper inscriptions of Indrapala city depicted that Andhra Chaityas helped people's spiritual and moral upliftment.

After Buddha's Maha Pari Nirvana the First Buddhist Council was held in Rajgir, Bihar. The second Council was also held in the same city 116 years later during Kala Ashoka's reign. Two centuries after Buddha's death Maha Sangha was established. The Mathura inscription dating back to 120 BCE mentions Maha Sanghikas. Later Vaishali and Pataliputra emerged as Maha Sanghika centres. Kaushambi, Mathura, Avanti developed into centres of Traditional Theravadins. After some time Maha Sanghikas split into Chaityakas and Shailas. Those who worshipped Chaityas became Chaityakas. Poorva Shila, Apara Shaila and Uttara Shailas lived in Dhanya Kataka city. Inscriptions of Chaityakas and Shailas were found in Dhanya Kataka, Alluru, Ghantasala, Varthmana and Kanheri. Shaila inscriptions were found on Nagarjuna Konda. To sum up, by 3rd Century BCE Maha Sanghikas and Shailas settled in Andhra Desha and spread Buddhist teachings here. Bhikshus from Palanadu visited Śrī Lanka to participate in the erection of Suvarnamalaka Stupa in Anuradhapura.

Prof. Murty cautions us that not to assume Andhra Desha was home to only Maha Sanghikas. It should be noted that Śrī Lankan *Bhikshus* who spread Buddhism in China and Gandhara also lived here. Though Buddha's idols were not yet worshipped, images of the Holy Feet of Buddha began to receive adulation.

Prof. Murty moves on to the emergence of *Mahayana* and its principles. *Mahayana* which had its origins in the thought and practice of Nagas and Shailas during 1st century BCE was systematized by Nagarjuna into *Sunya Vāda*. It replaced logical understanding with intuitive one. It helped to propagate devotion to Buddha among the general populace. Prof. Murty then recounts the prominence of *Madhyamikas* in Andhra Desha and how Nagarjuna, Buddhapalitha, Bhava Viveka, ChandraKirti split into *Prasangika* and *Svatantrika* sub-schools of *Madhyamika*. He also describes the logical methods adopted by Dignaga and Dharma Kirti. He supports Subrahmanya Nainar's suggestion that Buddha Ghosha might have hailed from Kota Nemali Puri (Gundla Kamma). Buddhaghosa was reputedly responsible for an extensive project of synthesizing and translating a large body of *Sinhala* commentaries on the Pāli Canon.

Prof. Murty also elucidates the growth of Tantrayana in Andhra Desha. He points out that Mahayana is also known as Paaramita yaana and Matrayana. *Prajñā Paaramita Sutras* mentioned certain Dharani Pitaka of Maha Sanghikas. Tibetan Buddhists believe that the Buddha launched Mantrayana by holding Dharma Chakra pravartana in Dhanya Kataka which was also known as Dharani Kota which took its name from Dharani Pitaka of Maha Sanghikas. It was here that the Shaila subsect further developed Mantrayana, Vajrayana and Tantrayana. Shaila sect was instrumental in raising Buddha to Godhood and developed a cult around him.The Tantrik texts regarded the Sunyata (Void) as female principle- Bhagavathi and Upaya as the male principle. Tantrayana sees no difference between the Void and Compassion which combinedly give rise to Bodhi Chitha. Mantrayana originated in the Śrī Parvata- Dhanya Kataka region during 1 st century BCE. Śrī Parvata was mentioned as Vajra Parvata in Tibetan texts. 'Sarvadhishthana Tathagatha Vyuha' a Tantrik text belonging 5th and 6th centuries reveal that Buddha taught Tantra and Mantra yanas on the Pothalaka Hill. Chinese, Hindu and Buddhist texts describe Śrī Parvata as the dwelling of Tantriks and Siddhas. In this manner, Prof. Murty proves that Andhra Desha was the origin of Hinayana, Mahayana and Tantrayana which later spread to Tibet and Japan.

19. Indian Philosophy Since 1498 (1982)[19]

Professor Satchidananda Murty's talks during 1950-70 were collected and published by Sundara Ramaiah, professor of philosophy, Andhra University in the year 1982. He took up the task on behalf of the Varsity. Prior to Prof. Murty no other scholar seems to have dealt with the issues touched by him in these talks. There was a misconception that from 16th century till 1947, there were no worthwhile developments in Indian Philosophy. There were scholars who regarded the period which began from the year 1498 upto early 20th century as the Epoch of Vasco da Gama. It was the entry of Vasco da Gama onto Indian shores that eventually led to British colonial rule. Contrary to the view held by certain section of intellectuals, Prof. Murty saw many new developments in Indian philosophy during the 400 years of Vasco da Gama's Age.

This compilation was divided into five chapters. 1. Indian Philosophical Thought in the Vasco da Gama Epoch 2. Modern Indian Philosophy 3. The Philosophy of Gandhi 4. A critique of Satyagraha 5. Some aspects of Gandhian

Ideology 6. The Philosophy of Radhakrishnan 7. On some views of Ambedkar 8. Philosophical thinking of Indian Muslims 9. Indian Christians and Philosophy.

The Western domination over India, which began with the advent of Vasco da Gama weakened after Second World War and eventually ended with the country gaining Independence in 1947. Thus, western domination and eastern stagnation were the defining phenomena of this epoch. Here a question arises regarding the status of Sanskrit language and its influence on Indian thinkers during pre-modern and modern ages. The writings of Radhakrishnan and Hiriyanna give out the impression that after the systematization of three Vedantic schools- Advaita, Visistadvaita and Dvaita- no other creative philosophical thought had emerged on the Indian soil. Contrary to this view, Indian Philosophy during this period, did indeed break new ground. In the 16th century Navya (Logic) tradition was developed in Nava Dvipa (present day West Bengal). This Neo-Logical Darsana developed a sophisticated language and conceptual scheme that allowed it to raise, analyse, and solve problems in logic and epistemology. Abstract logic and Technical logic were part of its scheme. Other philosophers tried to integrate *Vedānta Darśanas*. A section of scholars revived Mīmāṁsā Darśana's Bhatta system. Inspired by Chaitanya, a line of six Goswamis developed Theological Metaphysics. Vallabha's sect also emerged during the period under review. As debates on Advaita and Dvaita schools intensified, the fame of Advaita spread far and wide. It came to be recognized as the paramount Indian philosophy. Francois Bernier, a Frenchman who travelled in Mughal India during 1658-1667 described the way Advaita had influenced Sufi saints and Persian scholars. *Alangir Nama* written in 1688 revealed Vedantic influence on Dara Shikoh, the eldest son of Emperor Shah Jahan.

On being appointed as prince of Varanasi in 1656, Dara used to discuss Vedanta with yogis, Sanyasis and Brahmin pundits. He himself translated 52 Upanishads into Persian and wrote introduction to it. Titled *Sir-E-Akbar,* this translation deeply influenced western thought. While 16th century witnessed intense philosophical activity, 17th century saw overblown emphasis on Bhakti, Tantra and rituals. Consequently, the intellectual effort in philosophy took a back seat.

The seeds laid for British dominance in the battle of Plassey in 1757, sprouted up in the battle of Panipat in 1761. During the rule of Governor-General Lord Wellesley (1798-1806), new streams of thought can be discerned in Indian social and economic fields. These trends necessitated a deep rethink on our ethical and Dharmic values. Gentoo Laws enacted by Warren Hastings (1773-75) led to the replacement of ancient legal code by new laws.

With the unearthing of ancient Maha Nirvana Tantra in 18th century, monotheism gained wide-spread acceptance. This Tantra supported widow remarriage, inter-caste dining and opposed food taboos, Sati Sahagamana and caste slavery. *Shukra Neeti Saara* the text advocated an equitable governance system. All these writings stressed that Hinduism should evolve in tune with the changing times. Deeply influenced by western thought and way of life, Raja Rāma Mohan Roy (1772-1833) acted as a catalyst of change in Indian society. In 1805, Henry Colebrook delivered a work titled 'On Vedas', in which he explained the Upanishadic concepts also. Rāma Mohan Roy translated Upanishads into English and successfully presented the Indian spiritual knowledge contained in them. Dayananda Saraswati (1824-1883) published 'Satyartha Prakashika' based on Rigveda. Theosophical Society established in 1875, entered India in 1882 and worked for religious tolerance. Narayana Guru (1857-1928) who was born in a backward caste in Kerala combined Advaita with an universal perspective and worked for social and religious reform. Swami Vivekananda (1863-1902) spread the essence of Advaita all over the world with his powerful talks. *Bhagavad Gītā,* which was translated into English in 1785 and into German in 1802, came to be regarded as the foremost Hindu holy text by the western world. Bal Gangadhar Tilak's (1856-1920) commentary on *Gītā* served as the bedrock for many social and political movements of the day. In the 20th century, Aurobindo's writings made him a world-renowned Indian philosopher. Many other Sanskrit pundits delivered valuable commentaries on ancient Indian texts winning recognition for Modern Indian Philosophy.

Human thought doesn't spring up from a vacuum. It is shaped up by the prevailing social, economic, political and cultural developments. So we have to understand modern Indian thought in the light of our Independence struggle. No society in the world remains unchanged during the course of time. Various times see various sections dominating the society. Even those thoughts springing up from the unconscious have old memories and experiences as their source. Some people try to overcome old habits of thinking and strike out into new directions. Modern Indian philosophical thought evolved under the influence of contemporary trends without ignoring national perspective. Indian freedom struggle gave rise to many bold, novel and subversive ideological, philosophical trends.

Under British colonial rule local industries were wiped out. Britain which was witnessing Industrial Revolution promoted its own industries here. Roads, railways and dams were built in India to serve British interests. This created connectivity between various parts of the country. Caste evolved into class. English education and foreign travels brought Indian intellectuals into contact with western values, perspectives and parliamentary democracy. Gradually the urge for achieving self-rule deepened among Indians. The First War of Indian Independence in 1857 saw local rulers fight against the British colonial dominance. Indian National Congress which was established in 1885 eventually led the self-rule movement. The movement gained momentum after Gandhiji joined Congress in 1920. By 1929 the Congress began to intensify the struggle for total independence. The Second World War pushed British into a crisis. They were forced to declare independence in 1947, but before granting it, the British stoked communal fires and divided the nation into India and Pakistan.

Independent India strove to achieve social and economic development for all its people. Science, technology, industrialization led to the development of modern social and economic structures. India under the Prime Minister Jawaharlal Nehru led the Non-aligned movement. Parallelly many intellectuals endeavoured to achieve progression from orthodox concepts and habits to modernity. Academics too played a key role in the revival of India.

Gandhiji achieving an excellent balance between tradition and modernity, leading an ideal life, helped to evolve new ethic for our society and emerged as the undisputed leader of our freedom struggle. He had heralded the concepts of Non-violence, Satyagraha and non-coperation and successfully united Indian people in the struggle against British rule. He worked to end caste discrimination and achieve social cohesion. Though a section of national leaders preferred armed struggle, eventually Gandhiji's path of non-violence prevailed and he is regarded as the Father of Indian Nation. Gandhian way is now accepted by the rest of the world also.

Prof. Murty later turns to Dr. S. Radhakrishnan's contributions to philosophy. 'A visionary or a sage is one who realized Truth. As I am merely a rational interpreter of philosophical Truth, I am no sage' declared Radhakrishnan. But Prof. Murty clarifies that Radhakrishnan is not only an interpreter but also a visionary with an independent viewpoint. According to Radhakrishnan, a philosopher is a visionary who endeavours to understand the working of the universe and tries to ascertain Truth in the light of contemporary national and cultural conditions. An ideal philosopher is distinguished by four characteristics: 1. He should not delude himself by believing everything he sees as truth; 2. Without giving into desires and selfishness, he should explore the nature of Truth which lies beyond Time; 3. His personality should shine with dignity, self-control, patience, mental poise and peace and above all Faith; 4. He should have a strong will to free himself from ignorance, selfishness and fear of death. Only with such characteristics, one will be able to gain Right Knowledge and the intuition necessary to attain emancipation. A philosophy which doesn't include in its ambit logic, physics, psychology, ethics and religion is no philosophy, said Radhakrishnan. Such a holistic philosophy should help us lead an ideal and progressive life. Philosophy should help us withstand the challenges that Life throws at us.

Radhakrishnan's viewpoint is clearly enunciated in his book *An Idealistic view of Life*. Philosophy is not just a collection of ideas, it is a way to gain inner knowledge. Radhakrishnan explains that knowledge gained through senses, debating with the Wise and through insights are three ways to understand Truth. This very understanding leads us to Right Knowledge which is holistic. It erases the sense of the other and helps us achieve Unity. The difference between the Knower and Known ceases to exist and only Knowledge remains. Radhakrishnan made a comparative study of Indian and Western philosophical systems and provided us with an integrated philosophical system.

There were many scholars who regarded Radhakrishnan not merely as a commentator but as an original philosopher. He belongs to the Idealistic school rather than the Materialistic one. It is mistakenly believed that the world springs forth from the Mind. Idealism sees this infinite universe as purposeful and invaluable. It puts human life on a high pedestal. It regards the consciousness as the driving force of the Universe. Ideals, Morals and Truth are interrelated. The spiritual Truth is self-sustaining, it is the essence of all and it is the Divine consciousness. The infinite universe springs up from it. It is not incomprehensible void. It is total freedom and boundless consciousness. In short it is God who is the Consciousness which in itself is Life. It is neither matter nor energy. It is self-existent. Human living permeated with wisdom is an enlightened one. Such a kind of living is *Satyam, Shivam* and *Sundaram*. Radhakrishnan terms this line of philosophical thinking as eternal and vibrant. Human living can be likened with the infinite Truth which can be attained by discipline and study. In this way Prof. Murty enlightens us with Radhakrishnan's philosophical outlook.

Later he briefly apprises us of Ambedkar's ideas on ending the caste system for which he suggested three ways: 1. Inter caste marriages 2.Imparting a democratic base for Hinduism. To achieve this we should abadon four-fold Varna system and destroying the belief that Vedas, Shritis and other scriptures are infallible and holy. 3. Changing the mindset of upper castes, pulling them out of the stupid thinking that untouchability is preordained. By imbibing the spirit of equality everyone should fight for the rights of the depressed classes. Ambedkar saw this struggle as inevitable.

But Prof. Murty expressed doubts about the success of caste-based reservations in achieving social equality. As long as elections are held on caste based quotas, caste system will keep on strengthening- he felt. If Scheduled castes and Adivasis launch violent struggles, it will push the society into crisis. That's why Prof. Murty suggested that we should strive to achieve economic equality which will go a long way in ending caste inequalities.

Prof. Murty then moves on to the analysis of Muslim philosophical viewpoints. In the Mediaeval India, Muslim society didnot display any notable independent philosophical thought, except for Akbar and Dara Shikoh who promoted a unique monotheistic religion. Dara who studied Upanishads found certain similarities with Quran and tried to synthesize them both. But it earned opposition from Muslims while Hindus did not support him either. Later Indian Islam witnessed the development of two streams- Firangi Mahal and Khairabad. Mullah Qutbuddin Shahid (d.1691), Mullah Nizamuddin (d.1747), Maulana Abdul Ali Bah-ul ulum (d.1819) were notable philosophers in Firangi Mahal School. Whereas Fazal Imam Khairabadi (d.1827), Fazal Haq Khairabadi (d.1827), Abdul Iluq Khairabadi (d.1898) were famous in Khairabadi school.

During the declining days of Mughal Empire, Shah Vali Ullah (1703-1762) led a campaign against Sufism and tried to strengthen orthodox Islam. His son Abdul Aziz and grandson Ismail (1781-1831) strove to build a social and political movement to revive Muslim society. Syed Ahmed Khan (1817-1898) endeavoured to pull Muslim society from despair with his liberal and rational views. He declared that all the people living in this land- whether Hindu, Muslim or Christian are Indians. Syed Chirag

Ali, Nawad Mohsinul Mulk stood by him. Syed Ahmed Khan who promoted english education among Muslims established Aligarh College which eventually developed into Aligarh Muslim University.

Mirza Ghulam Ahmed (1839-1908) formed Ahmediya sect to modernize Islam. Mohd. Iqbal (1873-1938) who was regarded as the Muslim philosophical thinker of modern times, assailed inaction among Muslims reminding them that human life should be always be active and overcoming the evil should be the life's aim. He gave a call for world Muslims to unite. Though Iqbal was initially a nationalist, he took to international Islamism and inspired Pakistan movement later.

Overzealous Hindu nationalism created a rift with Muslims during the Independence movement. As a consequence Iqbal demanded the creation of a separate Muslim state in 1930. While Maulana Abul Kalam Azad (1888-1958) enunciated basic concepts of Quran, Syed Abul Ala Moududi founded Jamat-i-Islam and strove to mould Quranic laws according to modern conditions. Zakir Hussain systematized Gandhian thought and designed a basic education format based on it. He became the vice-chancellor of Aligarh Muslim University and eventually became Bihar governor and later President of India. Prof. Humayun Kabir held independent views and worked for social progress. Satchidananda Murty laid focus on many other Muslim visionaries who served Independence movement by combining Hindu, Islamic and Western influences.

Prof. Murty in the last chapter briefly explains Christian philosophy. Christianity entered India much before the advent of the British. By 7th century Syrian Church was formed. It was the Portuguese who started religious conversions which later gained momentum under the British. Though Christianity was existing in India since many centuries, no notable philosophers emerged from that religion here. Murty opines that poverty, lack of access to higher education were the reasons for this backwardness. Moreover Christianity has inculcated a deep love for Western culture and thought which further distanced them from the Indian mainstream. Though a myriad of Catholic educational institutions mushroomed in India, they did not lay much stress on Philosophical studies. Yet Indian Christians did incorporate certain yogic practices and rituals into their religious practice.

Prof. Murty acquaints us with the integrative concepts of three of Indian Christian philosophers. The first among them was Keshub Chandra Sen (1843-1884). Though he did not convert to Christianity, Sen was highly receptive to the Christian religious concepts. He delivered many lectures and wrote many books on that religion. He regarded Jesus Christ as the pinnacle of humaneness. He reminded us that Christ was an Asian. He felt that by following the tenets of *New Testament*, India can get rid of Hindu-Muslim divide and caste discrimination. Sen endeavored to synthesize an universal religion. His concepts echoed in the ideas of Vivekananda, Tagore and Aurobindo.

Next Murty gives an account of Sadhu Sundar Singh who though born into a Sikh family, turned into a Protestant Christian in his youth. Singh gave a novel interpretation to Christianity. According to him, God is a fusion of Vedanta Brahman, un-manifest, incomprehensible and an infinite ocean of compassion. He saw the universe as an embodiment of God's boundless love. Singh regarded Christianity as the paramount religion.

The third Christian philosopher that Murty referred was Upadhyaya who exhorted the integration of Hinduism and Christianity. He declared that he was born as a Hindu and die as a Hindi. But he did not see this as an impediment to his love of Christianity.

20. Naihśreyasa Dharma (1984)[20]

When the Central Institute of Higher Tibetan Studies, Sarnath, Varanasi launched Prof. Lalmani Joshi's commemorative lecture series, it invited Professor Satchidananda Murty to deliver the inaugural address. His lecture was published in a book form in 1984 under the title—*Naihśreyasa Dharma*. Prof. Murty reminded us of Buddhist philosophers like Nagarjuna, Shanti Deva, Kamala Sheela and Shanta Rakshita who taught that relinquishing of Ego and attachments lead us to enlightenment. This path is termed Naihshreyasa Dharma. Prof. Murty analyzed the Dharma in an easily comprehensible way in his lecture. *Nagarjuna's Ratnavali described Dharma as progressive* and a way to attain eternal bliss and contentment (Nihshreyasa). Hence *Dharma* is an injunction to direct man to his all-round development and prosperity in the world and Nirvana beyond. The second one is *Anatta* (not-self). Vasubandhu reminds us that only Buddha put forward the idea of emancipation without the concept of soul (Anatta or Anatma). Yasomitra and Shanta Rakshita stressed this point. In Buddhism *Anatta* means not-self. One should abandon various views of self-such as "this is mine, this I am, this is my self", "I will be", "I will be this", "I will be otherwise" etc. The soul is intertwined with the ideas of I and ego which are caused by ignorance. Soul doesn't exist beyond the five skandas in man viz., form, feeling, perception, impulse and consciousness. But Karma continues which gives rise to birth-death-rebirth cycle. When the idea of I dies Karma and rebirth ceases. That state is neither existence nor non-existence. It is called *Nirvāṇa* which according to Nagarjuna is the cessation of discrimination between existence and non-existence. In that state the ideas of sins (*pāpa*) and blessings (*Puṇya*) have no place. Attainment of blissfull or hellish states is rendered meaningless. Nagarjuna explains that Buddha rejected the concepts of soul and non-soul. The compassionate womb of the Void becomes the instrument to gain perfect knowledge or consciousness. Those who have not freed themselves from the duality of existence and non-existence can't grasp it. Understanding the nature of the emptiness of phenomena is simply a means to an end, which is *nirvāṇa*.

Thus Nagarjuna explains that the middle way or right way lies between this polarity. Only those who transcend this duality can enter pure *Bodhichitta* which is a spontaneous wish to attain enlightenment motivated by great compassion for all sentient beings, accompanied by a falling away of the attachment to the illusion of an inherently existing self. Meditation, right conduct and *Prajñā* (great wisdom) help to attain *Bodhichitta*. Nagarjuna's *Mūla Madhyakarika* imparts exactly such *Prajñā*. In this world nothing is neither created nor destroyed, nothing is neither permanent nor temporary. This description applies to the teachings of Buddha, including the concept of Dependent Origination (*Pratītya Smutpāda*) also which declares that all things arise always dependently: not by their own power, but by depending on conditions leading to their coming into existence. According to Nagarjuna whatever arises dependently is explained as empty. For that reason there is nothing whatsoever that is not empty.

Nagarjuna's philosophy represents a watershed not only in the history of Indian philosophy but in the history of philosophy as a whole, because it calls into question certain philosophical assumptions viz., the existence of stable substances, the linear and one-directional movement of causation, the atomic individuality of a person, the belief in a fixed identity or selfhood, and the strict separations between good and bad conduct and the blessed and fettered life. All such assumptions are questioned by Nagarjuna's unique perspective which is grounded in the insight of emptiness (*sunyatā*), a concept which does not mean "non-existence" or "nihility" (*abhāva*), but rather the lack of autonomous existence (*nisvabhāva*). Denial of autonomy according to Nagarjuna does not leave us with a sense of metaphysical or existential privation, a loss of some hoped-for independence and freedom, but instead offers us a sense of liberation through demonstrating the interconnectedness of all things, including human beings and the manner in which human life unfolds in the natural and social worlds. Nagarjuna's central concept of the "emptiness (*sūnyatā*) of all things (*dharmas*)," pointed to the incessantly changing and so never fixed nature of all phenomena. The ultimate truth to Nagarjuna is the truth that everything is empty of essence and this includes emptiness itself ('the emptiness of emptiness'). The phenomenal world we experience arises from our imaginations (*Vikalpa*). This process sets up a false dualistic split that is imposed upon reality, and involves belief in the existence of a perceiving subject and perceived object. Professor Murty advises us to treat *Prajñā Pāramaitā* Sutras which propound non-duality, void and wisdom as Madhyamika Yogachara or Knowledge of Void.

Non-existence of self is the foundation for universal ethics which is beyond all differentiations and discriminations. It leads to equality of all. Attachment to selfhood or the idea of Me and Mine causes suffering. The path of no-self liberates us from this predicament. Kamala Sheela, a Buddhist scholar taught us that compassion frees us from selfishness and promotes equality. The Samādhirāja Sūtra is often cited as an important source for śamatha instructions. According to Prajnakaramati the Void, no- self and negation (*abhāva)* or one and the same. It is through no-self that the enlightened attain to the purity of void- Maitreya Natha explains. In the *Prajñāpāramitā* sutras, the early Buddhist notion of no-self (*anatta*) is extended to all objects, so that all things are emptiness (śūnyatā), without inherent existence (*svabhāva*). Prof. Murty stressed this concept very effectively in this book.

21. The Advaitic Notion (1985)[21]

This was the book-form of the talk, Prof. Murty delivered at the silver jubilee meeting of Shankara Kripa, a Telugu magazine published by Shringeri Sharada Peetham in 1985. The book titled 'Advaita Buddhi' was republished by the Peetham under a new title 'Advaitic Notion'. The title was again changed to 'Advaitic Vision' when Bharatiya Vidya Bhavan published it in 1990. This book which explains Advaita Vedanta was divided into five chapters. The first three chapters focused on elucidating awareness of consciousness. The fourth chapter interprets the Great teachings. The last chapter expounds the relationship between society and social duties in the light of Advaita concepts. It is generally believed that Advaita doesn't concern itself with the worldly life. Yet Prof. Murty effectively gave a social dimension to it. He also admitted that though he dedicated 40 years of his life to the study of Advaita, he was not a great fan of Advaitic non-duality. It was the magnificent way in which Śrī Harsha's *Naishadha* described Advaitic concepts that prodded him to deliver this talk.

Prof Murty begins his talk with interpretation of Vedāntic terminology. Upaniṣads taught us that we should aim at understanding the unity between Brahman and individual soul. This unity is called Advaita or non-dualism. This unity is infinite, knower and known distinction doesn't exist here. Brahman is eternal and it is the total understanding, bliss and true existence. Those who devotedly follow meditative path will be able to grasp the Truth. This path is self-evident, it is not dependent on anything else. Only Brahman is the ultimate Truth and it is unique.

Such an ultimate truth can never be proved through worldly means. Only Holy Scriptures can provide such proofs which can't be disproved by other means. This Truth can only be grasped subjectively i.e., through self-knowledge. Once we attain such self-knowledge, the need for scriptures falls away. That's why Sankara declared that *Brahma Vidyā* is gained through life experience.

Many Advaitic pundits believe that the world is an illusion. But Prof. Murty states that it is not true. The basic Advaitic concept holds that the world exists as long as *avidyā* (ignorance) exists. He reminds that Śankara explicitly stated that when *advidyā* is destroyed by the advent of the consciousness of Reality, the world becomes unreal. But just as the reality of the world is not absolute, so also its unreality is not total, like a barren woman's son or the horn of a rabbit. Brahman, the Existence-Conscious-Bliss Absolute (Sat-chit-ananda) is the one ultimate Truth. It is He who appears as the entire world owing to ignorance, just as a shell appears as silver. When the illusion gets dispelled, the silver dissolves into the substratum—the shell. Similarly, when ignorance is erased the whole world dissolves into its substratum Brahman, which is the same as *Ātman*. This is the supreme knowledge, as also *Mokṣa* (liberation from births and deaths); and the Upanishads are the authority for this proposition—particularly the sentences like *Tattvamasi* and *Aham Brahmāsmi*. Sankara also opined that epics, Puranas and *Bhagavad Gītā* too provide us with transcendal knowledge. Then how to ascertain that one has attained Brahman? Sankara says that it is through a person's behavior that we can know this. The relevant behavior rules are provided by the Upaniṣads.

As the Ultimate Truth is indivisible, self-existent and self-evident, it doesn't require any mundane validations. It does not need us or the rest of creation for anything. The world can't exist independent of it. This is what Advaita means when it describes the world as an illusion.

Many scholars try to find secular knowledge in *Śrutis*. But Prof. Satchidananda Murty differs with this view. Though Indian scriptures and other Eastern texts do contain certain historical and scientific elements, it should be clearly recognized that all these ancient texts are basically mystical. Yet unlike modern sciences, these religious scriptures show us the path to the Ultimate Truth. Prof. Murty reminds us that even modern scientists are finally veering to the view that what we see may not be real.

Debunking the view that the Knowledge of Brahman leads one to inaction, Prof. Murty explains how it helps us lead socially useful lives. *Bhagavad Gītā* also states that those who overcome duality will attain a balanced viewpoint and work for human welfare. Cessation of duality leads us to transcend the divisions of caste, class, money and power. Thus, Advaitic understanding helps to attain good will, fraternity, economic and social equality and peace—Prof. Murty affirms. All this goes to prove that Advaita is more a practical philosophy than an idealistic one. Sureswara Acharya teaches us that non-egoistic state and a mind free of hate and other negative emotions leads one to the knowledge of Brahman. Those who are free of ego and passions embody ethical behaviour. It is true that mind binds us to the world, yet it also can free us from worldly desires. That's why both *sanyasis* and householders need to be pure in mind and heart. Humans need food to survive which is supplied by house-holders. Modern Advaitins regard knowledge and practice as interconnected. That's why worldly activities are not impediments to the attainment of *Brahma Gÿāna*. Prof. Murty brings out these points by drawing from the writings of Sureswara, Padma Pada and from the book *Jñāna Deepa*.

Adi Sankara emphasized that the Universal Soul is beyond all dualities and divisions. Those who are free of the ideas of I and mine do not care for caste and creed. They dedicate themselves for the greater good. Sankara's *Daṣa Ślokī* holds that *Brahma Gÿānis* will attain emancipation whether they die in Varanasi or in a dog house. Prof. Murty hopes that everybody will heed Hastamalaka hymn: "I am neither a god, yaksha, brahmin, kshatriya, vyshya, sudra nor a sannyasi, householder nor a forest-dweller. I am the True Self."

22. Philosophy in India—Traditions, Teaching and Research (1985)[22]

The work of Prof. K. Satchidananda Murty "Philosophy in India—Traditions, Teaching and Research" is a useful publication. It offers to the reader a remarkably synthetizing view on one complete sphere of human thinking, on a stage of development of philosophizing.

This book is a result of a UNESCO project commissioned in 1982 on the teaching and research in the field of philosophy in India. It bears witness also to the unbroken continuity of Indian philosophy over thousands of years and also discusses the active philosophical life in India today. In the process of dealing with problems, interesting facts about the history of Indian philosophy and plenty of information about contemporary philosophical teaching and research in India is provided. The book gives an example of bourgeois - humanistic, rationalistic reception of heredity which differs such from the customary.

This book surveys philosophical thinking in India from antiquity to the mid-eighties of this century, which proceeds in the following sequence: (a) elucidation of the classical conceptions of philosophy and the views of Indian thinkers on the problems of philosophical diversity (b) brief sketches of the rise and development of philosophical ideas and various Hindu, Jaina, Lokayata and Buddhist schools and systems from the earliest period till the eighteenth century AD; (c) short accounts of philosophical insights and ideas in the religio-philosophical literatures of Indian languages, including those of the Sikh Gurus and the Shaikhs and Ulemas of India; (d) summaries of select modern Indian thinkers ; (e) discussion of the present philosophical situation in India; (f) an attempt to focus on the problems of professional philosophers, rectification of Indian philosophy and ideological autonomy and (g) an analysis and examination of the issues involved in philosophical teaching and research.

23. Quest For Peace (1986)[23]

The introduction and the following chapters and epilogue of this book by Prof. K. Satchidananda Murty were published in 1960 as part of Two and as the first chapter of Part Three of a book entitled *Studies in the Problems of Peace*, by him and Dr. AC Bouquet of Cambridge. Dr. Bouquet wrote Part One and the last two chapters of Part Three of that book. The Prologue of this book was newly written by Dr. Murty.

The first two chapters of this work, described by *John O' Londons Weekly* as "A Comprehensive Peace classic", are essays in historical society which attempt to expound and criticise the Hindu ideology. The third chapter is concerned with the philosophies of *Ahimsa* and their relevance to the contemporary world. The next two chapters contain "a Toynbee-esque historical review of the development of Western thought". Of these the first deals with the sociology of political conflict as it developed in the West; while the second is devoted to a discussion of the philosophies of revolution. The sixth chapter examines the psychological and anthropological theories about war. The seventh chapter attempts to explain in a way how and why there came to be some periods of peace in human history, especially with reference to the Roman Empire and to some extent with reference to Ashoka's empire, and why they did not last; and from this it proceeds to give an account of the development of the concepts which could serve as foundations for peace and their metaphysical bases.

The epilogue advocates promotion of inter-relationships among scientists and scholars leading to a new level of organization, transcending national, racial, religious and cultural boundaries; and urges that an attempt may be made to persuade some countries to formulate a world-conscience, and express its judgments.

24. Radhakrishnan: His Life and Ideas (1990)[24]

The Publications division of Government India as part of its biographical series assaigned the task of writing such a book on Dr. S. Radhakrishnan to Professor Satchidananda Murty. Though he was busy with other important activities, Prof. Murty could deliver the book in 1989 with the collaboration of Ashok Vora. Gathering information from Radhakrishnan's works, his friends and family and his students, Prof. Murty effectively recounted the great philosopher's life and ideas. Stretching into 17 chapters, the book recounts various stages of Radhakrishnan's life right from his student days to his attaining highest office in India.

Radhakrishnan was born in a poor Telugu brahmin family in Tiruttani on 5th September 1888. He was the second of six children born to Veera Swamy and Sitamma.

After completing elementary education in a local school, high school education at Luthern's and FA at Nellore's Voorh's college, Radhakrishnan finally did BA and MA at Madras Christian College. He married his 10 year old cross cousin when he was 15 years old. At Madras Christian College he was deeply influenced by Prof. Hogg who was trying to integrate Hinduism and Christianity. This experience helped him later to expound Indian philosophy, particularly Vedanta to the Westerners.

After getting LT certification in Teacher's Training, Radhakrishnan took up teaching position at Madras Presidency College. Later he attained a senior position in Mental and Moral sciences. It was during this time that his papers were published in many national and international journals. Radhakrishnan met Gandhiji when the latter came to Madras in 1915. He was later promoted and posted to the Government College at Rajamundry where he stayed till 1918. It was in Rajamundry that Radhakrishnan published *The Philosophy of Rabindranath Tagore*. He also met Tagore and got his blessings.

Radhakrishnan's depth of understanding, his teaching style and eloquence became widely known and his fame spread rapidly. This led to Mysore University, established in 1916, to invite him for a faculty position. He took up teaching at Maharani College, an affiliate of Mysore University. Great scholars like C.R. Reddy and S.S. Subba Rao were already serving on its faculty. The academic environment prevailing there vastly helped his study, research and understanding. Radhakrishnan published his work *Reign of Religion in Contemporary Philosophy* in 1970 which earned much acclaim from Indian, British and American academics. Once Radhakrishnan took up writing in a big way he largely delegated the teaching responsibilities to his associate Hiriyanna and he himself concentrated on other themes. Radhakrishnan's simple living, high thinking, depth of understanding and humility endeared him to the faculty and student community.

The 1904 Indian Universities Act which transformed our universities from examining bodies to teaching bodies led to setting up of Calcutta University. Ashutosh Mukherjee, who was appointed as the Vice-chancellor was determined to enrich the varsity with famed professors. Accordingly he invited the then 30 year old Radhakrishnan to Calcutta University. Though he was hesitant to join the veterans, his colleague CR Reddy persuaded and literally pushed him to Calcutta. After reaching the university, Radhakrishnan was soon promoted as the professor of mental and moral sciences. Though it led to much heart-burn among the senior faculty belonging to Bengal and Bihar, Radhakrishnan shrugged off their remarks and concentrated on his work. He brought out the first part of *Indian Philosophy* in 1923. This book with its excellent English was a rage in the West. Though Jadunath Sinha went to court accusing him of plagiarism, Radhakrishnan went on with his endeavours.He played key roles in many committees and panels; delivered lectures at many western universities. Radhakrishnan established that the concepts now proposed by Western philosophers were much earlier expounded in India i.e centuries ago. His book 'An Idealist view of Life' was much popular.

CR Reddy took charge as the vice-chancellor of Andhra University when it was established in 1926. The University College of Arts and Science was launched in 1931. Honors and PG courses were launched in Philosophy, Maths, Economics, Politics and Foreign Languages in 1932. Radhakrishnan felt a strong urge to work for the development of Telugu people in Andhra region. At 43 years of age he became the vice-chancellor of Andhra University. Adopting Asuthosh Mukherjee's policy of appointing famed professors in the faculty,

Radhakrishnan also invited noted intellectuals to Andhra University. While discharging the duties of vice-chancellor he continued teaching philosophy.

Meanwhile Radhakrishnan's talks delivered in 1929 at Manchester University and in 1930 at London University gained in popularity. HN Spaulding was notable among those deeply influenced by his lectures. He was instrumental in establishing a Chair on Oriental Philosophies and sending an invitation to Radhakrishnan following which he went to UK in 1936. There he was greatly honoured by All Souls College. He took classes on Philosophy of Religion every Wednesday at 5 pm. He regularly helped reseach scholars. Radhakrishnan was much impressed by the academic environment prevailing there and wished such an educational institution should flourish on Indian soil too.

Radhakrishnan published *Eastern Religions and Western Thought* in 1939. As Second World War broke out in the same year he returned to India from Britain. Radhakrishnan held Gandhiji and Nehru in high regard and published an essay on the duo in *Calcutta Review* in 1921 itself. He gave a talk praising Gandhiji under the title 'Revolution through Suffering' in 1930 at Manchester University. Delivering a lecture at Allahabad University convocation, he described Gandhiji as religious reformer and his word as the voice of humanity. When Radhakrishnan met Gandhi at Sevagram in 1938, he suggested that Netaji Subhash Chandra Bose be made the president of Tripura Congress session to which the Father of Nation readily agreed. Radhakrishnan took the editorship of a special issue on Gandhi focusing on the period between 1936-39. The compilation titled *Introduction to Mahatma Gandhi:Essays and Reflections* was presented to him as a birthday gift on 2nd October 1939.

When Madan Mohan Malaviya quit the VC post of Benares Hindu University (BHU) due to ill-health,

Radhakrishnan was invited to take charge. But as he was working at both Oxford and Calcutta University, it was agreed that Radhakrishnan will limit his Oxford teaching assignment from January to June and work honorarily at Benares Varsity. He took over as Honorary VC of BHU in September 1939. He intensively worked for the development of BHU, without taking any pay. When Maharaja Gaekwad came to know about this, he arranged payment from his government's coffers. Following this, Radhakrishnan left the VC post of Calcutta University in 1941 and moved to BHU. In those days, Independence movement was in full swing under the leadership of Gandhi. Its influence naturally reached college and university campuses. Consequently the British colonial rulers deployed police in educational institutions. Though Radhakrishnan strongly objected to the police presence on

With Sri PV Narasimha Rao, Former Prime Minister of India at Central Institute of Higher Tibetan Studies, Sarnath as Chancellor (Chairman) of the Deemed University.

the campus, the colonial government refused to budge. As a protest he closed BHU. Radhakrishnan invited national leaders, academics and rulers of princely states to the 1942 BHU silver jubilee celebrations. Gandhiji, Nehru, Gobind Vallabh Pant, Syam Prasad Mukherjee, Vijaya Lakshmi Pundit graced the occasion. Nehru and Rajendra Prasad were awarded honorary doctorates.

Due to Malaviya's insistence Radhakrishnan continued as VC for two more terms. With the Second world war coming to an end, he once again took up teaching assignment at the Oxford from January to June each year. On Malaviya's death, differences arose among BHU governing body. This led to Radhakrishnan's resignation and he refused to change his decision even after appeals from various quarters.

In December 1947, Radhakrishnan met Gandhiji in Birla House and got his approval to dedicate his English translation of *Bhagavad Gītā* to the Father of Nation. The ideas of Vivekananda, Gandhiji, Tagore and Aurobindo moulded Radhakrishnan as a nationalist. These relations eventually led to his political entry. Under Radhakrishnan's chairmanship a sub-committee was formed at the Non-party conference held in 1943 at Pune under the leadership of Tej Bahadur Sapru. The sub-committee looked into the conditions of Scheduled Castes and Tribes and submitted a report on the action to be taken. His political views which were expressed in that report were much appreciated. Later he was appointed as a member of the Constituent Assembly. There too his opinions found wide acclaim. As a member of University Education Commission, Radhakrishnan helped to devise guidelines for varsity development.

Soon after he was appointed as Indian Ambassador to Russia, Radhakrishnan's fame spread far and wide. Eventually he became the Vice-President of

India. Radhakrishnan was recognized as the Spiritual Ambassador of India in the whole world.

In 1956 Radhakrishnan's wife died. In 1957 he was once again elected as the vice-president of India and in 1962 he became the President of India. The same year border war broke out with China in which India faced humiliating defeat. In that difficult moment, Radhakrishnan stoically provided solace to the Nation. After his term as the President of India came to an end, his health began to deteriorate. He suffered his first heart attack in 1968. Though he recovered from it, repeated heart attacks occurred from April 6 to 16th in 1975. He breathed his last on 16th.

The world paid rich tributes to a man though born in a poor family, attained great intellectual heights and eventually rose to be the President of India. He stood as the embodiment of Plato's Philosopher- King.

25. Ethics, Education, Indian Unity and Culture (1991)[25]

This contains selections from some of the addresses that Prof. Murty delivered in the 80s in universities all over India: e.g. from Kasi to Kashmir, Madhyadesa (Agra) to Kongunadu (Coimbatore) and Vanga to Maharashtra.

In the preface of the book Murty wrote: "between September 1980 and September 1989 I had the opportunity to visit, by invitation, a number of Indian Universities and deliver in them several lectures, convocation addresses etc. Portions from some of them are brought together in this small book. Much of what is contained in the following pages is concerned with these: the good life, values and virtue; universities and studies in them; higher education in India; Indian culture and unity; the problems of diversity of cultures and plurality of religions and the issue of possible exclusive superiority of any one of them; political, institutional and personal autonomy and freedom; and Tradition: its perennial importance and contemporary relevance. The analytical table of contents will give a synoptic idea of what has been said in these addresses/lectures".

26. Gītā Bhāṣyatraya Vivecana (1992)[26]

This was the paper that Prof. Murty submitted at an international symposium held in Bologna, Italy on Sankara, Ramanuja and Madhva. It starts out with a brief review of *Bhagavad Gītā* which was a compilation of important aspects of *Sramana, Brahmana, Shaiva, Vaishnava* philosophies prevalent at that time. Prof. Murty places the period of *Gītā* at about 4th century BCE i.e two centuries after Buddha and two centuries prior to Jesus Christ. On the whole Murty's paper confines itself to the introductions (*Praveshikas*) of three great teachers to *Gītā*. Sankara in his *Gītā Bhashya Pravesika* details that there are two ways- *Pravritti* and *Nivritti* margas- to attain *Brahma Gyana*. *Gītā* holds that God created this world through the power of his *Maya*. He originated the four-fold varna system. Out of compassion towards mankind, the Great Lord Krishna revealed *Pravritti* and *Nivritti* ways of life to Arjuna. *Pravritti* is *Sakama Karma*/doing action with the desired fruits and *Nivritti* is the *Nishkama Karma*/ doing action without having any personal desire of its results. This two-fold vedic *Dharma* was compiled into 700 ślokas by Veda Vyasa. *Gītā* helps us overcome birth-rebirth cycle. *Brahma Gyana* is attained by dedicating ourselves to God and doing actions without seeking results. Prof. Murty analyses the ślokas from *Gītā* and *Anu Gītā* enunciated by Sankara.

Sankara's *Gītā Praveshika* or commentary contains two aspects: 1. *Gītā* provides us with two ways to attain emancipation 2. Vasudeva is the ultimate *Brahman*.

Mankind can find fulfilment through *Gītā* and *Vasudeva*. Prof. Murty's analysis proceeds in five parts. 1. Though following from *Gītā* interpretation, Lord Krishna becomes the resurrector of *Vedic Dharma*, this reading may be erroneous. Because Vedas themselves ask us to attain *Nirveda* meaning 'going beyond Veda.' Lord Krishna himself declared that he is teaching unheard of *Dharmas* to Arjuna. On examining carefully one finds not only *Vedic Dharmas* but *non-vedic Dharmas* also in Vedas. So doubt arises as to whether Vedic spirituality is confined only to two *Dharmas* expounded by Sankara.

2. The argument that four-fold varna system was passed on to us by Vedas is not supported by history. Ancient scriptures did not accept varna system. *Gītā* accepts one's own Karma, natural Karma and one's own *Dharma* only. No mention of *Ashramas* is found in *Gītā*. Prof. Murty disagrees with Sankara treating Lord Krishna as simply a mythical incarnation. Sankara equating Vasudeva with Paramartha Brahma is simply an effort to correlate Chandogya and Brihadaranyaka Upanishads. In the end Incarnationism, varna system are not supported by neither Vedas nor epics and puranas.

Later Murty moves on to evaluate Ramanuja's commentary on *Gītā* and applies the same critique as above. Madhvacharya regards *Maha Bharata* as providing Vedic and non-vedic knowledge. Ultimately one is led to conclude that as the four vedas could not convey God's teachings fully, a fifth Veda viz., *Maha Bharata* was necessitated. Significantly Madhva asserted that *Maha Bharata* is accessible even to women and Shudras. This goes to prove, opines Murty that Madhva displayed liberal thought and reformist outlook.

27. Vedic Hermeneutics (1993)[27]

Shruti means divine revelation. It is none other than

Veda. We should not interpret Vedas according to our own whims and fancies, but should understand it in the way established by ancient traditions. To help the seekers and scholars 'Vedic Hermeneutics' was published by Lal Bahadur Shastri Rashtriya Sanskrit Vidya Pith, Delhi. It was printed and distributed by Motilal Banarsidas Publishers, Delhi in 1993. Though it was not for ordinary readers, Prof. Satchidananda Murty tried to convey the Vedic essence to one and all. He explained how the Vedas should be studied and their meaning be grasped. The book contains three chapters: 1. A Right Approach to Sacred Lore, 2. The Content of Sacred Lore, 3. The Essence of Vedas. In fact these chapters were written forms of his earlier talks. His talk delivered in 1976 was published by *Triveni* magazine in a revised form in the year 1978. It was further expanded into the first chapter of this book. The talk delivered in Los Angeles, USA in 1992 was incorporated as the second chapter. His research paper presented in 1988 to the Gurukul University in Hardwar became the third chapter. Thus Vedic Hermeneutics was encapsulated knowledge.

Vedas were interpreted by different scholars in different ways. Sayanacharya's definition of Vedas as being a collection of sounds of the *Mantras* was widely accepted. But there was no clarity as to the meaning of *Mantra*. A scholar called Koutsa even went to the extent of terming *Mantras* as lacking in meaning (*Anarthakah Mantra*). Likewise Brahmanas were also left undefined. They were treated as non-mantric part of Vedas. Sayana declared that Vedas help one attain *Dharma* and *Brahman*. He also made it clear that Vedas can't be understood in a worldly way. That's why Mimamsa and Vedanta declared Vedas to be eternal and infallible. Brahman can't be attained through subjective experience and inference. Only Upanishads can show the way. History and Sciences can't be expected to be found in the Vedas.

It is said that Vedas sprang up from the meditative minds of ancient sages. But modern viewpoint may not accept this. Prof. Murty says that even if we do not accept ancient views, we may still gainfully study *Bhagavad Gītā* and *Bhagavatha*. The study of Vedas doesn't involve rote-learning. One has to grasp their true meaning. Offerings by rote-learners of Vedas will not be received by the gods.

Brāhmaṇas, Āraṇyakas and *Mahābharata* treat gods as mystical and *yajñas* as symbolic. Sāyana saw high and low in Vedas. So Prof. Murty opines that Vedas should not be regarded as holiest of the holy. He pointed out that caste, gender and racial differences had no place in Vedas. Yet, in later ages, women and low castes were prohibited from studying Vedas. In an earlier period, there were many instances of Śūdras, Dāsas and their children propagating Vedas. Even women like Lopa Mudra and Apaala took up this responsibility. Kakshavan who propagated Rigvedic hymns was born of a servant-maid of the King of Anga country. His father Dirgha Tamas was also of questionable birth. Yet both the father and son became famous sages. Satya Kama Jabali was the son of a prostitute but was able to gain supreme wisdom. Instances of women teaching the essence of Vedas can also be found in *Bṛhadāraṇyaka Upaniṣad* and *Patañjali Mahā Bhāṣya*.Though no scripture expressly prohibited women and Shudras from learning Vedas and wearing the sacred thread, the reactionary practice was forcefully imposed on Hindu society in later days. But Adi Sankara agreed that even low-borns like Vidura and Dharma Vyadha attained *Brahma Gyāna* due to the good deeds done in previous births. He also stated that all the four castes can attain Supreme Knowledge through listening to epics and puranas.

Though no Veda forbade Śūdras from learning four vedas, the Taittirīya Samhita declared that Śūdras should not perform *Yajña* even. But Patanjali differed. One thing is sure. It was in middle ages that Śūdras were denied the right to study Vedas and perform *Yajñas.* In the modern era, Arya Samaj opposed this interpretation by pointing it out that sages like Jaimini and Badari had long ago confirmed that all the four castes including women can study Vedas and perform *Yajñas.* Certain *Smṛtis* went to the extent of declaring that study of Vedas is imperative for women. Thus everyone who is interested in studying the Vedas or their translations can perfectly do so. When Western pundits can freely study Vedas, how can we deny that right to the sons of soil?—asks Satchidananda Murty.

In the second chapter, Prof. Murty acquaints us with the methods to be followed to understand Vedic literature. Various interpreters of Vedas followed various ways. There might be no unanimity. The best method is to understand the direct and indirect meaning of Vedic hymns. The Shastra enables us to know many unknown things. We should be able to find connections between the contents revealed by Vedas and other ancient Shastras. Six procedures help us to gain such an understanding: 1. Realizing the unity between opening and end sentences 2. Continuation of contents 3. The conclusions intended to be drawn 4. The utility of those conclusions 5. The general acclaim or criticism and 6. The generally prevalent arguments. Taking great care one has to properly understand Vedas.

Prof. Murty later examines the methods adopted by Western scholars to fathom Vedas and pointed out that they largely followed Sāyaṇa's interpretations which led them to non-traditional understanding. While adopting the good points from Westerners, we have to continue life-long efforts to grasp the meaning of Vedas. It should be realized that logic is a tool to derive meaning of Mantras. The logical interpretations given by ancient scholars help us fully comprehend Vedas. Mīmāṁsā philosophy, says

Prof. Murty, is such a highly logical tool. Both Vedānta and Mīmāṁsā contain exegesis, apologetics, epistemology, metaphysics and ethics. Mīmāṁsā primarily concerns itself with *Dharma* and man's duties. Vedanta enquires into the nature of the Ultimate Truth. Both of them hold Vedas as impersonal and authorless. They are not the handiwork of man. The Founders of three religions—Advaita, Viśiṣṭādvaita and Dvaita differently interpreted Vedas which should be fully understood with all their nuances. Prof. Murty later moves to interpretations given by Sāṁkhya, Yoga, *Manu Smṛti, Mahābharata, Rāmāyana* and *Bhagavd Gītā*. He also analyzes the viewpoints of various visionaries and ancient logic and grammatical texts. All these interpretations can be classified into four groups. 1. Terming Vedas as meaningless by focusing only on the twisted words found therein. 2. Arguing that Vedic dos and don't do not bestow ethical results. Treating them as being true only in certain conditions. 3. Denying the authority of Vedas, as their meaning can't be derived through direct perception or indirect inference. 4. Regarding Vedas as omniscient and accepting their authority. On the whole the various viewpoints enumerated so far prove that Vedic literature is a logical inquiry in the nature of the Ultimate Truth.

In the third chapter Prof. Murty deals with the division of Vedas. According to *Śrīmad Bhagavad Gītā,* in the beginning there was only one Veda, one Nada 'OM', one deity 'Narayana', one fire and only one caste. The son of Satyavati who divided the one Veda into three was named as Vyasa. Puranas and epics explain the reasons for the four-fold division of Vedas: 1. Most of the hymns in Rigveda are concerned with exploration of *Sat* (fundamental Truth). 2. Next comes *Karma* or *Yajña karma*. Yajur Veda details the Yajña karmas. 3. The third Veda constitutes melodies and chants. 4. Atharva Veda teaches the unity of Brahman and individual soul. That's why Sayana declares that this particular Veda give us the essence of all Vedas. He declares that all four vedas bear testimony to the existence of Brahman. All schools of Indian philosophy assert these very points. They declare that Brahman can't be experienced physically. The knowledge of Brahman can be gleaned from Shrutis. While a section of philosophers hold that *Brahma Gÿāna* is the only way to emancipation, another section deems devotion (Bhakti) as the surefire way to it. Vedas imparts us the *Brahma* and *Dharma Gÿāna*.

Professor Murty doesn't regard Vedas as non-human in origin, but concurs with the view that they are an effective tool to *Brahma Gÿāna*. That's why he doesn't agree that Vedas contain worldly knowledge. Vedic religion is generally regarded as ritualistic. *Karma* is taken as Yajnik action. Vedas treat Yajña as the bond between gods and mankind. Because it is performed to achieve common good, it is a social programme. Creation means God sacrificing himself in *Yajña*. In this manner Prof. Murty explains the meaning of five Yajñas—Brahma, Deva, Pitru, Manushya and Bhooth Yajñas. He also reminds us that Upanishads regarded meditation and practice as the *true Yajña*. They opine that Yajñas and rituals can't lead to spiritual advancement. Even *Bhagavad Gītā* considers *Yajnic life* as sheer waste.

In the end, Ṛgveda declares that Truth is one, but the learned describe it in various ways. That ultimate Truth is equated with infinite existence. Atharva Veda assures that those who attained the ultimate Truth become immortal. Thus all Vedas preach Unity of God and his creation. Prof. Murty while agreeing with the view that Vedic teachings lead us to Truth, he also differed with certain traditional positions.

28. The Divine Peacock: Understanding Contemporary India (Ed.) (1995)[28]

The book is a curtain raiser to the International Symposium on India Studies, with contributory articles from eminent scholars on different subjects on India like science and technology, human rights, international relations, philosophy, sociology etc.

The book gives a glimpse of India. It is a journey towards unravelling a magical mystery. It introduces to the symposium participants different aspects and developments in modern India and help thereby in the projection and perception of a holistic image of this great, vibrant, dynamic and pluralistic democracy.

29. The Perennial Tree (Co-editor) (1996)[29]

It puts select papers presented at the International Symposium on India Studies (ISIS) organized by Indian Council for Cultural Relations (ICCR) and promises to be one of the most important books about India. It is edited by Prof. K. Satchidananda Murty and Amit Dasgupta. This volume contains 24 papers selected from among those contributed to the symposium, and the inaugural address was delivered by Śrī P.V. Narasimha Rao, the then Prime Minister of India. The volume ends with a report on the proceedings of the symposium.

The symposium was intended to review India studies in the world, consider the methodologies in vogue and the results obtained, identify neglected areas as well as new ones, stress the equal importance of the present and the past, suggest possible, new ways of research and promote a holistic understanding of India.

30. History, Culture and Truth (Co-editor) (1999)[30]

This book was edited by Daya Krishna and Prof. K. Satchidananda Murty, published by Bhuvan Chandel for Kalki Prakash, New Delhi.

This festschrift is presented to Prof. D.P. Chattopadhyaya on the occasion of his sixty-fifth birthday. It consists of 25 contributions centering around his thought and works of eminent scholars from India and abroad. These essays, ranging from philosophy to science, history, culture, social and political studies, are concerned with issues that have engaged Chattopadhya's attention throughout his work.

31. Be a Lamp unto Yourself (Attadipa Viharatha) (2000)[31]

In 1987 Prof. Murty gave a talk at the International Conference of Theosophical Society which was published as a book the same year. *Ehipassiko* - this was the advice Buddha reportedly gave to the seekers. It means to see for yourself, to not believe the Buddha's teachings without trying them out for yourself. When *Bhikshus* enquired him about *Dharma,* Buddha instructed them to be islands unto themselves –*Attadipa Viharatha*. It means that those who wish to walk on the path of Buddha should so by their own effort– through looking inward, without reliance on externalities. Pali canon attributes both these instructions- *Ehi Passiko* and *Attadipa Viharatha* solely to Lord Buddha. But, Prof. Murty points out that these two teachings exist even before in Hindu and Jain scriptures also. In the end, we shouldn't be fixated on a single Guru but should examine for ourselves the truth or lack of it in their teachings.

Maha Pari Nirvana Sutra recounts that the last words spoken by Buddha to Ananda were: *Attadipa Viharatha,*

Atta Sarana, Anajna sarana. He made it clear that whatever he had to say was said already. And the seekers had to strive for *Nirvana* on their own. They should not depend on any Guru or his teachings including Buddha's. Every seeker has to discern the truth and make his own way to the Truth. Though Prof. Murty points out that such teachings pre-date Buddha, commentators of Śrī Lanka, Myanmar and Thailand argue that these teachings were delivered by Buddha only. He stressed that the power of discernment is attained by following *Ashtanga Marga*.

Uttara Adhyana Sutra of Jainas also states that everybody has to attain *Gyana* by his own efforts. People fall prey to endless suffering due to *Avidya* or ignorance. *Gyana* sets them free. It is *Gyana* which differentiates the living from non-living and lead to good of all.

Brihadaranyaka Upanishad declares that *Atman* (Soul) is the embodiment of *Gyana*, it is the inner light. Everybody has to experience its glory on his own. Without the knowledge of Upanishad one can't fathom *Gyana*. Sankaracharya instructs that Holy Scriptures and experiential knowledge lead us to *Gyana*. Vachaspati says that both Vedanta and Logic are necessary to attain *Brahma Gyana*. He tried to project Sankara as purely a logician. But Prof. Murty differed with his view. A Guru can only show the way. Students should walk that path and achieve what he has set out to do. Lord Krishna said the same thing to Arjuna in *Bhagavad Gītā*. In the end we all should seek such a supreme teacher- Prof. Murty suggests.

32. Life, Thought and Culture in India (C. AD 300 - 1000) (Ed.) (2002)[32]

This is a volume of the Project on "The History of Science, Philosophy, and Culture in Indian Civilization" which aims at discovering the main aspects of India's heritage and present them in an interrelated way. It is the Presentation of Centre for Studies in Civilization.

So far we have reviewed Prof. Murty's books, authored/ edited by him during his life-time. After his death, some of his writings were posthumously published by Routledge. Prof. Ashok Vohra, former Professor of Philosophy, Delhi University, Delhi and Prof. Kotta Ramesh, Former Professor of Human Resource Management, Andhra University, Andhra Pradesh are the editors of these volumes. These volumes are reviewed briefly in the following pages.

33. Buddhism, Taoism, Confucianism and Shintoism (2024)[33]

This book is analyzed into ten chapters.

In the first chapter, "Nihsreyasa Dharma: The Doctrine Leading to Salvation," Murty explains the Madhyamika Buddhist views of Nagãrjuna, Santaraksita and Kamalastla regarding the supreme good. The distinction here is between *abhyudaya dharma* and *nihsreyasa dharma*- what is conducive to a happy life in this world and what is conducive to happiness in the other world, i.e., salvation.

In the second chapter "Attadipo Bhava: Be a Lamp unto Yourself", Murty comments on this well-known last utterance of the Buddha, taking into consideration various commentators like Buddhaghosa.

In the third chapter, "Buddhism: An Integrated Interpretation," Murty explicates that Buddha's noble quest was to find the good and the "Unsurpassed state of Peace."

The history of the growth and development of the text Praiñaparamita in Andhra is elaborated by Murty in the fourth chapter, "Praiñaparamita: Perfect Wisdom." In this chapter, he also explains the exclusive technique of teaching the text as developed by the Andhraites.

In the fifth chapter, "Buddhism and National Culture," Murty considers the origins of Buddhism and its interactions with the cultures of India.

The sixth chapter, "Andhra's Contribution to Buddhist Thought," is a historical essay delineating the history of Buddhism in Andhra. Murty upholds that Buddhism was introduced in Andhra even during Buddha's time. It flourished in Andhra until the sixth century AD.

In the seventh chapter, "Buddhism-Taoism Coalescence under Confucian Auspices", Murty portrays how Buddhism coalesced with the Chinese culture to produce Chan Buddhism and Neo-Confucianism, without ever losing its cultural identity or becoming other-worldly, as is claimed by some Western intellectuals.

In the eighth chapter, "Shinto: the Japanese Way of the Numinous," Murty traces the history of Shinto in Japan and its importance in the Japanese way of life and thought.

In the ninth chapter, "The Chinese Worldview," Murty defends the Chinese worldview against such of its criticisms that regard it as primitive. Murty claims that Chinese thinking was no more primitive than that of the ancient Greeks and Indians.

In the tenth chapter, "Major Asian Intellectual Traditions: Their Philosophy and Creativity", Murty discusses and compares the traditions of India, China and Japan.

34. Hinduism, Yoga and Indian Culture (2024)[34]

This book is a ten chapter exercise. In the first chapter, "The Classical Indian Conception of Dharma and Its Contemporary Relevance", Murty traces the etymological origins of the term "dharma" and points to the necessity of acting according to one's dharma: to satisfy one's conscience.

In the second chapter, titled "Contemporary Spiritual Situation in India", Murty cites various Indian classic texts to show that in the Indian tradition it is upheld that politics cannot be severed from ethics and spirituality.

In the third chapter, "The Hindu Creed for the Next Millennium", Murty says that there are two bases for Hindu metaphysics, Brahman and Ananda from which all beings are born and return. The knower of Brahman attains the Brahman.

In the fourth chapter, "Yoga: The Path to Freedom", Murty evaluates Mircea Eliade's thesis that there are similarities and differences between Yoga and psychoanalysis, between Yogic insight and other types of intuition, between samadhi and hypnosis, Hatha Yoga and athletics, and Yoga and Shamanism.

In the fifth chapter, "Indian Spirit: Past and Present", Murty observes that human nature is the same all over the world, whether Eastern or Western and the metaphysical and mystical experiences are the same the world over.

In the sixth chapter, "The Indian Character", Murty discusses Amaury de Reincourt's *The Soul of India*.

In the seventh chapter, "The Concept of the Unity of India and Its Development", Murty argues that the ideal of a unified India was never fully realised till recent Indian independence from British rule. He asserts that in contemporary times, true unity in India can be achieved only by a commitment to law and democracy.

In the eighth chapter, "Philosophy in Indian Culture", Murty traces the conception of philosophy in Indian culture during various periods.

In the ninth chapter, "Philosophy, Development, and National Crises", Murty reminds us that Philosophy should not be severed from social and political issues facing India.

Philosophers must work with social scientists, scientists and experts in technology to develop a "clear concept" of development. It is not enough to point to the good life; philosophers must provide the necessary means to achieve it.

In the tenth chapter, "Some Tasks for Philosophers", Murty states that Vedãnta is "metaphysical knowledge that leads to liberation" and requires prior acquaintance with the meaning of science and technology. It must relate to actual living. We need to renew our goals toward realising the values of national unity, integration and self-reliance.

35. On Education and the Philosophy of Education (2024)

Prof. Murty was known for his philosophical insights and expertise in comparative philosophy and education theory. His views on philosophy of education, advocating for aspects like free universal education and higher studies in science and technology, may have influenced policy discussions during this period, particularly through his writings, some of which are now collected in books like "On Education and the Philosophy of Education", the posthumous publication of Prof. K. Satchidananda Murty.

This book contains ten chapters. In the first chapter, "Education and Purpose of Life," Murty examines the claim that young men and women in our educational institutions lack a purpose in life. He is of the view that young people must have high ideals and live creatively and adventurously.

In the second chapter "Universities and Good Citizenship", Murty examines Plato's idea of education, namely that it should have as its goal of training for citizenship and leadership which is valid even today. The training should include the inculcation of a questioning and critical spirit.

In the third chapter, "Asian Studies", Murty asks that if no major European or American university has in its curriculum any course in Eastern thought, could Asian countries do the same? He contends that unfortunately, the historical situation in the Eastern countries would not allow them to ignore the West.

In the fourth chapter, "Education and Building Socialism", Murty advocates free universal education.

In the fifth chapter, "Education Policy-Some Reflections and Reactions", Murty argues that education must promote democracy, socialism, secularism, justice equality, individual dignity, freedom, national unity, and integrity. It should also adopt a way of life conducive to the realization of these sociopolitical goals.

In the sixth chapter, "Education of the Child", Murty argues that the aim of primary education of children must be to develop young people to become responsible adults who can carry out their civic duties in a democratic society. Both purely vocational education and bookish education fall short of real education.

In the seventh chapter, "General Education and European Universities", Murty divides general education into three categories, namely (1) integrated education, (2) encyclopedic culture and (3) liberal education. This classification is present in Hellenistic schools, schools of the Roman Empire, the medieval universities, and the post-Renaissance universities of Europe.

In the eighth chapter, "Teacher and Student Mobility", Murty defines "mobility" as the free movement of teachers, students, and other personnel within a country and across national borders, Murty traces the history of student and teacher mobility in Europe. He mentions problems facing Indian universities regarding such mobility, such as regional preferential treatment, except for the IITs.

In the ninth chapter, "Reflections on Administering Specialized Study Centers/Departments", Murty argues that the prevalent study centers for ideologies or systems such as Vedänta, Buddhism, Marxism, or Gandhism must not degenerate into unquestioning acceptance of these ideologies, which is how they differ from institutions run by religious organizations or political parties. They should rather be concerned with historical, analytical, critical, and objective studies of them.

In the tenth chapter, "Teacher-Student Relationship, Moral Education and Discipline", Murty argues that self-study, listening, meditation, and contemplation formed the core of the Indian system of teaching. He argues that the blind faith in teacher is responsible for the degradation of the "guru" concept. It has resulted in preaching to everyone that we should hold the teacher in high esteem and treat him like God. The consequence of treating a teacher like God, worshipping him, and meditating on him has made our society authoritarian, non-questioning, and noncritical.

36. Towards A New Philosophy (2024)[36]

This book comprises of eleven chapters. In Chapter One, "The Problem of God," Murty agrees with Albert Schweitzer in saying that "every profound religion is mystical." Then he enquires into the nature of religious experience.

In the second chapter, "An Exercise in Mystical Ontology" Murty asserts that all experience involves an awareness of God. Everyone knows God but is not aware of the fact that he knows Him.

In the third chapter, "Globalization of Philosophy" Murty argues that there is no single Western or Eastern culture or civilization. There are Chinese and Japanese cultures, as are Spanish, French, German, Iranian and Arabic cultures. Similarly, there is no single Western philosophy or even European philosophy.

In the fourth chapter, "Andhraites' Contribution to Philosophy" Murty refers to Andhra philosophers like Apastamba, Nagarjuna, Dharmakirti, Buddhaghosa, Kumarila, Nimbarka, Appayya Diksita, Annambhatta and expounded their contributions to different schools of philosophy.

In the fifth chapter, "Philosophy of Language", Murty argues that there cannot be any philosophizing in general based on the analysis and description of the structure of any particular language. He asserts that a philosophy of language should be based on the structures of different types of language, the psychology and physiology of human speech, the physics of sound, semiotics and anthropology.

In the sixth chapter, "History, Historical Consciousness and Freedom," Murty argues that history gives meaning to man's present life and shapes his will for the future. He asserts that historical consciousness liberates us from history and enables us to formulate new possibilities and goals and strive toward them.

In the seventh chapter, "Contemporary Trends of Thought in Europe" Murty, summarizes his discussions on the current trends such as theistic and atheistic Existentialism, Marxism, Empiricism and Catholic Realism.

In the eighth chapter, "Man and Nature", Murty proposes an ontology of man. According to him, we can understand man either through the empirical sciences or through reflective analysis. Man is a significant manifestation of Nature, and his thoughts and actions play a role in nature. An adequate conception of Nature is formed only when it is not understood in purely human terms or purely non-human terms.

In the ninth chapter, "The True Self" Murty claims that the idea of the "true self" appeared in Indian literature between the eighth- or ninth-century BC to the seventh- or eighth-century AD. In this chapter, Murty discusses this doctrine commenting on passages from the Brhadaranyaka Upanisad and Chandogya Upanisad.

In the tenth chapter, "Vindication of Atmavada", Murty chiefly examines Vinit Haksar's thesis that the ethical consequences are the outcome of the "assumptions of men in any society."

In the eleventh chapter, "Toward a New Philosophy", Murty argues that considerations of reality cannot be excluded from philosophy and that the business of philosophy is not merely linguistic analysis.

37. Vedãnta and Bhagavadgitã (2024)[37]

This is a compendium of nine chapters. In the first chapter, "Some Thoughts on the Veda and Its Study," Murty states that Veda is "what makes known the transcendental means of obtaining the desirable and avoiding the undesirable." He adds that the Vedas concern themselves with *dharma* and *moksa* and that they are universal in the sense that studying them and practicing the rituals prescribed in them are not restricted to any particular group.

In the second chapter, "The Vedãntic Vision," taking a cue from Sankarãcãrya, Murty focuses on a passage from the Brhadãranyaka Upanisad to elucidate the vision of Vedânta: 'So, the self alone is to be meditated upon, for there all become one, this Self alone is to be realized, for one knows all these through it.'

In the third chapter, "Reason in Vedãnta," Murty argues, based on textual passages, that although the Self transcends reason, it is only seen by "subtle and refined" reason. In grasping the Self, reason has to be transcended by its own help. The preparation of Brahma vicāra (discussion or reflection on Brahman) is necessary for the knowledge of Brahman.

In the fourth chapter, "The Advaitic Vision," Murty elucidates the basic tenets of Advaita Vedanta.

In the fifth chapter, "Sankarācārya's Conception of God," Murty expounds the Advaitic doctrine of the relationships between Brahman and God, Brahman and the individual self, Brahman and the world, as well as between God and the world and between God and the individual self, utilizing the key notions of *maya* and *avidya*.

In the sixth chapter "Sankarācārya—Some Observations," Murty discusses the authenticity of the claims of authorship of Sankaracārya regarding the many works attributed to him, especially because of the short span of Sankaracārya's life. It also examines the socio-political circumstances in both South and North India around the times of Sankaracarya.

In the seventh chapter, "Sankaracārya's views on Religious Life," Murty discusses how Sankarācārya attempts to reconcile his Advaitic ideas of Brahman alone being real with the various traditional means such as jñana, bhakti and meditation. He shows how Sankaracārya assimilates bhakti to jnana.

In the eighth chapter, titled "Reflections on the Three Bhasyas of *Gītā*" Murty compares the commentaries of the three great Vedānta teachers, Sankaracārya, Ramānuja and Madhva, concerning their views on the means of liberation, the three yogas, their views on varnasrama dharma and different interpretations of the final verse of the *Gītā*: "Abandoning all dharmas, come to me alone for refuge."

In the ninth chapter, "Here' (Iha) and 'There' (Amutra): 'The Excellent' (Sreya) and 'The Pleasant' (Preya)," Murty contrasts empirical knowledge with transcendental wisdom and surveys the history of Indian science and scientific views in ancient times. While ancient scientists utilized empirical and rational methods in their investigations, Murty asserts, they never ignored the role of spiritual pursuits or the sastras in human life.

In the next chapter, we will study the awards and honours received by Prof.Murty and the testimonials from distinguished scholars upon him.

Endnotes

1. Murty, K.S., *Hinduism and Its Development*, Tenali: Sundaram and Sons, 1947.
2. Murty, K.S., *The Rhythm of the Real*, Rajahmundry: Saraswathi Power Press, 1951.
3. Murty, K.S., *Thought and Divine*, Guntur: St.Michael's School Press, 1951.
4. Murty, K.S., *Evolution of the Philosophy in India* (A Brief Sketch) , Guntur: Michael's Industrial School Press, 1952.
5. Murty, K.S., (Trans.), *Sad Darshana Samuccya* by Haribhadra (A Compendium of Six Philosophers), New Delhi: Eastern book Linkers, 1986 , originally Printed in 1957, Tagore Publishing House, Tenali.
6. Murty, K.S., *Revelation and Reason in Advaita Vedanta*, Waltair: Andhra University Press, 1959.
7. Murty, K.S., *Studies in the Problems of Peace*, Co-author with AC Bouquet, Calcutta: Asia Publishing House, 1960.
8. Murty, K.S., *Samakalina Bharatiya Darsan* (Ed.) Akhila Bharatiya Darshan Parishad, Faridkot, Punjab. 1962.
9. Murty, K.S., *Metaphysics, Man and Freedom*, Bombay: Asia Publishing House, 1963.
10. Murty, K.S., *General Education Reconsidered* (Ed.) Bombay: Asia Publishing House, 1963.

11. Murty, K.S., *Indian Foreign Policy*, Calcutta: Scientific Book Agency, 1964.
12. Murty, K.S., *The Indian Spirit*, Waltair: Andhra University Press, 1965.
13. Murty, K.S., *Readings in Indian History, Politics and Philosophy* (Ed.), London: George Allen and Unwin, 1967 and Bombay: Allied Publishers.
14. Murty, K.S., *Nagarjuna*, Delhi: National Book Trust, 1971.
15. Murty, K.S., *Current Trends in Indian Philosophy* (Ed.), with K. Ramakrishna Rao, Bombay: Asia Publishing House, 1972.
16. Murty, K.S., *The Realm of Between*, Simla: Indian Institute of Advance studies, 1973.
17. Murty, K.S., *Far Eastern Philosophies*, Mysore: University of Mysore, 1976.
18. Murty, K.S., *Andhra Contribution to Buddhist Thought*, Hyderabad: International Telugu Institute, 1980.
19. Murty, K.S., *Indian Philosophy Since 1498*, Waltair: Andhra University Press, 1982.
20. Murty, K.S., *Naihsreyasa Dharma*, Varanasi: Central Institute of Higher Tibetan Studies, 1984.
21. Murty, K.S., *The Advaitic Notion*, Sringeri; Sringeri Sarada Pitham , 1985.
22. Murty, K.S., *Philosophy in India; Traditions, Teaching and Research*, Delhi: Motilal Banarsidass, 1985.
23. Murty, K.S., *The Quest for Peace*, Delhi: Ajanta Publications; 1986.
24. Murty, K.S., *Radhakrishnan: His Life and Ideas*. Coauthor with Ashok Vohra, New York: State University of New York, 1990.
25. Murty, K.S., *Ethics, Education, Indian Unity and Culture*. Delhi: Ajanta Publications, 1991.
26. Murty, K.S., *Gita Bhasya Traya Vivechana*, Bologna Nations Symposium, 1992.
27. Murty, K.S., *Vedic Hermeneutics*, New Delhi: Shri Lal Bahadur Shastri Rashtriya Sanskrit Vidyapeetha, and Motilal Banarsidass, 1993.

28. Murty, K.S., *The Divine Peacock: Understanding Contemporary India* (Ed.) , Delhi: Indian Council for Cultural Relations and Wiley Eastern Limited, 1995.

29. Murty, K.S., *The Perennial Tree* (Ed.), New Delhi: Indian Council For Cultural Relations and New Age International (P) Ltd., 1996.

30. Murty, K.S., *History, Culture and Truth,* New Delhi: Kalki Prakash, 1999.

31. Murty, K.S., *Be A Lamp Unto Yourself.* Chennai: The Theosophical Pub., House, 2000.

32. Murty, K.S., *Life, Thought and Culture in India* (Ed.), New Delhi: Center for Studies in Civilization, 2002.

33. Murty, K.S., *Buddhism, Taoism, Confucianism and Shintoism,* New York: Routledge, 2024.

34. Murty, K.S., *Hinduism, Yoga and Indian Culture,* New York: Routledge, 2024.

35. Murty, K.S., *On Education and Philosophy of Education,* New York: Routledge, 2024.

36. Murty, K.S., *Towards A New Philosophy,* New York: Routledge, 2024.

37. Murty, K.S., *Vedanta and Bhagavadgita,* New York: Routledge, 2024.

8

A Vision for Equality

This chapter recounts various honors conferred on Murty by Governments, Universities and admirers. It also includes the details of various books dedicated by him to his deities, friends and great men. Prof. Murty began to receive appreciations from his childhood itself.

I. Letters of Appreciation

1. **1934:** Yarlagadda Shivarama Prasad, Raja of Challapally sent a letter of appreciation to 10 year old Satchidananda Murty on 27-12-1934 in which he expressed amazement at the erudition displayed by Sachidananda Murty in Telugu, Sanskrit, English and Hindi. The Raja was wonder-struck at the achievements of this Child Prodigy.
2. **1936:** The sole Telugu daily of the day- *Andhra Patrika* reported the news of Kotta Satchidananda Murty passing Visharada examination at a tender age of 12 years.
3. **1940:** In an appreciation letter, M. Venkataramayya, the maths teacher of Hindu High School, Guntur, marveled at the commentary to *Gītā* written by Satchidananda Murty.

   In the same year, Palle Poorna Prajnacharya, the Sanskrit pundit of Hindu College, Guntur dedicated a poem to the intellect displayed by Murty in his commentary to *Gītā*. Kasi Krishnamacharya, the first court poet of Andhra Pradesh, wrote a poem in appreciation.

4. **1940-1944:** Appreciation letters poured in from notable personalities for the erudition displayed by Murty in his commentary to *Gītā*. These letters were written by: Ranga Nayakulu , Maths lecturer of Hindu College; Prajnananda Swamy of Chidananda Ashram, Guntur; Anubhavananda Swamy of Śrī Ramakrishna Bhakta Samaj, Bapatla; Chid Ghananda Saraswati, Guntur; Sahaja Kavi Mummalaneni Shivalinga Murty Chowdary; the editor of Manjuvani Press, Eluru; Bharathi magazine's laudatory review; Vijayananda Gajapathi, the Raja Bahaddur of Vijayanagaram and MLA; Raja Rangayya Appa Rao Bahaddur, Zamindar of Nuzvidu and Vuyyoor who conferred Vedanta Ratna title on Satchidananda Murty; Śrī Krishna Printing Press, Hospet, Ballary district; Jampala Venkata Narasimham, Senior Telugu Pandit, Board High School, Duggirala; Maha Rajadhiraja Virbhadra Singhji, Maharaja of Lonavala state, Bombay Presidency.

5. **1986:** Satchidananda Murty's former student MS Prabhakar Rao presented rich tributes to him under the title 'Guru Puja Kusumanjali' when Kala Prapoorna title was conferred on Prof. Murty on the occasion of 59th convocation ceremony of Andhra University.

II. National and International honours for Professor Satchidananda Murty

1980: Honorary D.Litt, Sanskrit University, Benaras.

1982: Honorary D.Litt, Andhra University, Waltair.

1983: Honorary D.Litt, Acharya Nagarjuna University, Guntur. 1985- Honorary D.Litt, Śrī Venkateswara University, Tirupati. 1959- Visiting Professor, Princeton Universtiy, USA.

1963: Spaulding Lectures, Oxford, UK.

1970: Visiting Professor, Indian Institute of Advanced Studies, Simla.

1973-75: National Fellow- UGC.

1978: National Lecturer in Philosophy, UGC.

1980: Meritorious Teacher's Award, Govt. of Andhra Pradesh.

1982- Dr. BC Roy Award- (The only award available for Achievement in Philosophy-KS Murty was the first awardee).

1982: Rajalakshmi Foundation Award.

1983: Swami Pranavananda Philosophy National Award.

1984: Padma Bhushan Award by the President of India.

1984-86: National Fellow, Indian Council of Philosophical Research.

2001: Padma Vibhushan Award by the President of India.

2010: Lifetime Achievement Award by the Indian Council of Philosophical Research, New Delhi.

Receiving the Padma Bhushan Award the Third National Highest Award

Receiving the Padma Vibhushan Award
the Second Highest National Award.

III. Books Dedicated To Professor K. Satchidananda Murty

1. Dinakar: Vaicharik Kranti ke Parivesh mein (Hindi).
2. Professor P. Adeswar Rao, Vani Prakashan, New Delhi, 1971; Bharat ke Suprasidh Darshanik, Vicharak Evam Lekhak Professor Sachidananda Murty ko saadar samarpith.
3. *Selected verses of Vemana,* Translated by JSR Narayana Murty & Elliot Roberts, Indian classic series, Sahitya Academy, Delhi, 1995
4. *Vishwa Darshanam: Bharatiya Chintana* by Nanduri Rāma Mohana Rao, Editor, Andhra Jyothi, Vijayawada, 1997.
5. *Gautama Buddhuni Charitra* by M. Rajagopala Rao, Bouddha Sahiti publications, Guntur, 2007.
6. *Visuddhamagga: A study* by M. Rajagopala Rao, Bouddha Sahiti publications, Guntur, 2012.

IV. Books Dedicated by Prof. K.Satchidananda Murty

1. At a tender age of 7/8 years itself, Satchidananda Murty wrote a Sanskrit ode to Harihara (Vishnu and Shiva).
2. When he was 13 years old, Sachidananda Murty translated Prabhudatta Brahmachari's Hindi talk into Telugu under the title 'Nama Sankeertana Mahima' and dedicated it to Chamarlapuri Sangameswara Swamy.
3. His independent work 'Hanumad Vijayam' was devoted to Anjaneya.
4. Devoted his work 'Śrīmad Bhagavad Gītā' to Venugopala swamy.

5. Dedicated his "Saptasloki Bhagavad Gītā" also to the same deity.
6. He dedicated 'Ishopanishad' to Lord Shiva in 1946.
7. In 1959 his talk on 'Pramana Padhati' was dedicated to Simhachala Varaaha Narasimha Swamy.
8. He dedicated his 'Revelation and Reason in Advaita Vedanta' to Lord Venkateswara in 1959.

V. Books Dedicated To Near And Dear

1. Sachidananda Murty dedicated his English translation of 'Shad Darshana Samucchayam' to his cousins Mr & Mrs Kotha Raghuramayya with love.
2. Dedicated 'Realm of Between' to his wife Mrs. Vedavati Devi. He wrote: "I married in 1942. Since then, like my father earlier, my wife enabled me to be free from familial and domestic chores, cares and responsibilities. So I have always been like a happy guest in our house, with all the time needed for reading, thinking and writing."
3. Dedicated "Indian Spirit" to his father with love and reverence. In this context, Prof. Murty wrote: " I dedicate the book "Indian Spirit" with devotion, I offer salutations to the feet of my father Śrī Kotta Veerabhadraiah Mahodaya, by whose kindness from childhood my spiritual practices accomplished".

VI. Dedications To Scholars

1. His work "Divya Jivitamu' was dedicated to Monsignore M. Ignatius, DD Bishop of Guntur.

2. His 1951 work 'Thought and Divine' was dedicated to Jacques Manitain, "Philosopher of Philosophy, Princeton University, Erudite Savant, Stimulating thinker and Charming writer."
3. "Rhythm of the Real" published in 1951 was dedicated to Sir Cattamanchi Ramalinga Reddy, the first Vice-chancellor of Andhra University with an eulogy: "I may also herein recall with gratitude the interest which that great educationist of South India, Dr. CR Reddy-used to evince in my work and the warm encouragement and high appreciation which he gave."
4. The 1952 work "Evolution of Philosophy in India" was dedicated to Professor VS Krishna BA (Oxon), Ph.D (Vienna), Vice-Chancellor of Andhra University, Great Savant and Perfect Gentleman "with admiration and affection."
5. Dedicated his 1963 work "Metaphysics, Man and Freedom" to Humayun Kabir who was "the symbol of cultural synthesis, creative thinking and Intellectual Independence".
6. Dedicated 1962 work "Darshanamulu-Mathamulu" to Dr. Sarvepalli Radhakrishnan, former Prime Minister of India.
7. Dedicated his 1993 work "Vedic Hermeneutics" to Śrī P.V. Narasimha Rao

VII. His Colleagues And Friends On Prof. K.Satchidananda Murty

Several commendations upon Prof. Murty were expressed by his friends and colleagues. Some such are:

1. "I am glad to receive the three booklets that you so kindly sent to me. I am happy to glance through the pages and I am impressed to see

that your acquaintance with European thought is channeling itself in a definite direction".

Prof. S.N.Dasgupta,
Author of *History of Indian Philosophy*,
5 Vols., 1952.

2. "His Publication record alone puts him on the forefront of contemporary Indian Philosophers and scholars..... One of Murty's strengths is a genuine facility in writing English prose: particularly in his commentary on Haribhadra's *Compendium* he writes with ease and even charm at times. Further more, he is well-versed in the *Darsana* literature".

Prof. Karl H. Potter,
(University of Minnesota) Philosophy
East and West, Hanolulu, 1961.

3. "I had been requested to suggest the names of some important Indian thinkers ... Naturally I suggested your name along with Professor Kalida Bhattacharya' in the field of philosophy as I regard you two as our best philosophers today.

Prof. Abu Sayeed Ayyub,
Editor, Quest, formerly Head,
Indian Studies Department,
University of Melbourne,1962.

4. "One among the outstanding Philosophers of the younger generation."

Prof. Humayun Kabir,
Former Minister,
Scientific Research & Cultural Affairs,
India, 1963.

5. "It seems that the mantle of Dr. Radhakrishnan has fallen worthily upon your shoulders and I

notice in your writings the same international outlook and perhaps you have gone into certain matters much more profoundly"

Dr. Sunil Kumar Chatterji,
National Professor of India in Humanities,
President, Sahitya Academy, 1970.

6. "No other Indian academic philosopher has attempted to discuss in such detail problems which belong to so many fields of study...Hindu scriptural exegesis, metaphysics, philosophy of religion, interpretation of Indian culture and history, social and political thought, International relations, Sino-Japanese philosophies." Preface to *Collected Criticism of K. Sachidananda Murty* (Eds. of the book)

Prof. K. Ramakrishna Rao,
Prof. K. Venkateswarlu and
Prof. B.V. Kishan, 1974.

7. "Sachidananda Murty is one of the foremost creative philosophers and prolific writer on a wide range of subjects with equal competence. He has combined in his thought the classical wisdom of Indian culture. What makes his works intellectually engaging is his philosophical catholicism organised and oriented by a definite point of view. Going through his stimulating works one feels that only a philosopher of his competence can enable us to properly understand other disciplines like religion, history, political thought and International relations."

(In his foreword to *Collected criticism of K. Sachidananda Murty)*

Prof. D.P. Chattopadhyaya,
(Educator and Former Minister of Commerce
in India), 1974.

8. "There is no doubt at all that today he is one of India's top-ranking Philosophers whose voice is heard with respect in the councils of the world. His books have been a force to be reckoned with, wherever people meet to discuss the affairs of the mind."

Prof. S.P. Adinarayana,
(Former Vice-Chancellor, Annamalai University),
Chidambaram, 1975.

9. "I have known Prof. K. Satchidnanda Murty for a number of years. He is one of our boy prodigies. While quite young almost in his childhood, he distinguished himself as a scholar in Saṇskrit and lectured on themes connected with Hindu Philosophy. Bhagavad Gītā and other sacred books seem to have been in him almost from his birth. At that stage he was a boy prodigy; scholar, no doubt, but also curiosity".

Dr. C.R. Reddy,
Vice-Chancellor,
Andhra University, 1947.

10. "I am glad to find that at this early age you have achieved such a poise in personal behaviour, and stature in your scholarship"

Prof. N.G. Ranga,
Father of the Indian Peasant Movement, 1963.

11. "Your sovereign detachment and openness, and the freedom from bliss and prepossessions in matters philosophical, make encounters with you an exhilarating event".

Dr. J.L., Mehta,
Professor,
Centre for Advanced Study in Philosophy,
Banaras Hindu University, 1967.

12. ".... I hope that I can benefit greatly from your studies which are wonderful syntheses of Eastern and Western Philosophy...."

Prof. Hajime Nakamura,
Professor Emeritus & Rtd., Dean of Faculty,
Tokyo University,
Director, The Eastern Institute, Tokyo, 1967.

13. "You have not only been a teacher but also a thinker and writer of outstanding eminence",

Justice A. Sambasiva Rao,
High Court of Andhra Pradesh, 1973.

14. "One may be a scholar and not a thinker. It is also possible for one to be a thinker, and not a scholar. In the case of Murty we find him to be both",

Prof. R. Balasubramanian,
Former Professor of Philosophy,
University of Madras, Chennai &
Former Chairman, Indian Council of
Philosophical Research, 1995.

15. "Prof. Satchidananda Murty is a prolific writer. Moreover, the scope of his philosophy is vast. His books and papers containing, as they do, his deep philosophical insights and penetrating analysis of complex concepts, are not easy reading",

Prof. Sibajiban Bhattacharyya,
Acharya BN
Seal Professor of Mental and
Moral Philosophy (Retd.,) and
Former National Fellow,
Indian Council of Philosophical Research, 1995.

16. "K. Satchidananda Murty is one of the very few scholar-thinkers in contemporary Indian actively engaged in exploring and cultivating the fields of

philosophy, religion and culture in their varied forms and expressions".

Prof. N.K. Devaraja,
Former Professor of Philosophy,
Banaras Hindu University, Banaras, 1995.

17. "K. Satchidananda Murty's place in the 20th Century philosophic world of India is unique. He has not only written on different subjects but has also pointed out the philosophical inter-links amongst them. This is perhaps due to his inter-disciplinary training. His scholarship in history is as profound as his understanding of Western Logic and Nyaya. His basic interest is, of course, in metaphysics which he uses for integrating different spheres of knowledge. He downs not brush aside tradition but rather makes use of it skillfully and with open mind",

Prof. S.S. Barlingay,
Former Professor of Philosophy,
Pune University, Pune, 1995.

18. "K. Satchidananda Murty lived an ideal life, a true exemplar of the authentic life. He lived what he preached; he taught what he believed in. He was an ideal man; an ideal scholar, an ideal colleague and an ideal friend. He believed, preached and practiced that 'daily there would be occasions which "let-down" and "let-up" one and it is wise to preserve equanimity without being depressed or elated'. These qualities make him tower over his peers. It will be difficult to fill the vacuum created by his passing away".

Prof. Ashok Vohra,
Former Professor of Philosophy,
University of Delhi,

19. "In the good sense of the term, I would say he was Rajasic, he was dynamic, and wanted to do more than he need have done. Even when Prof. Murty was but a lecturer, he assumed the responsibilities of a leader of his discipline".

Prof. K.R. Śrīnivasa Iyengar,
Formerly Professor of English and
Vice-Chancellor of Andhra University, 1984.

20. "Professor Kotta Satchidananda Murty is among our outstanding thinkers in the tradition of Dr. Sarvepalli Radhakrishnan. His writings are extensive and his influence is felt widely. His influence goes beyond academic philosophers and his long line of students. Prof. K.S. Murty was my teacher, guide, colleague and friend. We had a very close personal and professional relationship for over sixty years".

Prof. K. Ramakrishna Rao,
(Doctoral Student of Prof. K. Satchidananda Murty)
Former Vice-Chancellor,
Andhra University & Chairman ICPR,
New Delhi, 2020.

21. ".....Prof. Murty was a teacher who injected his students with his own enthusiasm. He tried to draw them out to build their character, build their intellect and build their future. By his innumerable seminars he tried to inculcate a spirit of enquiry, a spirit of criticism and the power of analysis in all those whom he taught and who came into contact with him"

Justice Jaganmohan Reddy,
Former Justice, Supreme Court of India &
Former Vice-Chancellor,
Osmania University, Hyderabad.

22. "There may be some who are great scholars in different Sastras and there may be others who are efficient as administrators. No one can stand comparison with you, who have mastered many Sastras while at the same time being a great administrator."

Padam Shri Prof. Pullela Śrī Ramachandrudu
Former Professor of Sanskrit,
Osmania University, Hyderabad

23. "Prof.Murty always appeared to me to be an aristocrat. I am not referring merely to his family background or upbringing, but his temperament, his relations with people and the world, as well as his quest for knowledge, especially of the spiritual sort."

Dr. J.S.R.L. Narayana Moorty,
(Student of Prof. K. Satchidananda Murty)
Professor Emeritus of Philosophy,
Monterey Peninsula College, CA, USA.

24. "I had known Prof.Murty for more than twenty years. I interacted with him several times. When I once asked him where he stood philosophically, he was candid enough to say that he 'oscillates between Sankar and Ramanuja'."

Padma Shri Prof.Arvind Sharma,
Professor of Comparative Studies,
McGill University, Montreal, Canada.

25. "Prof. K.S. Murty mastered the discipline of Philosophy. His writings are an ample proof for the encyclopedic learning and critical scholarship of Philosophic schools, doctrines and theories. He surveyed the gamut of Indian philosophical wisdom, knowledge, and tradition from the ancient to contemporary times. He cultivated

a wholesome and critical vision of Indian Philosophical heritage in respect of philosophical love of wisdom and philosophical love of knowledge".

Prof. K. Venkateswarlu,
(Doctoral Student of
Prof. K. Satchidananda Murty)
Dept. of Politics & Public Administration,
Andhra University, Visakhapatnam.

The above testimonials collectively demonstrate Prof.Murty's significant contributions to philosophy, his reputation as a leading scholar, and his lasting impact on the academic world.

With His Highness Sri Dalai Lama at Central Institute of Higher Tibetan Studies, Sarnath as Chancellor.

9

A Life of Integrity

Śrīmad Bhagavad Gītā, the most revered book for Prof. Satchidananda Murty, declared that a true Pundit is one who maintains equanimity in all things (*Panditah Sama Darshana*). It further says that one who perfectly realized and perfected in Yoga perceives the realized self in all and all in his self (*Yoga Yuktaah Sama Darshana*). And Yoga is nothing but to fulfill his Dharma with skill and efficiency. (*Yogah karmasu Kaushalam*). So a pundit who fulfills his duties and responsibilities properly is called *Sama Darshana* (the one who attained equanimity). Prof. Murty fits perfectly into this description. He not only fulfilled his duties well, but also viewed and understood all the world religions and philosophies with equal regard.

Having born in a Hindu family Satchidananda Murty dutifully followed Hindu traditions and imbibed the true spirit of Hindu cultural legacy. Yet this did not prevent him from receiving and ingesting important concepts from world philosophical thought and teachings of other religions. His impartial analysis of these perceptions and forming of novel concepts is matchless. Prof. Murty not only made a deep and comparative study of ancient Indian religions like Hinduism, Jainism, Buddhism, Charvaka and Vedanta but also Parsi, Sikh, Kabirpanthis, Islam and Christianity. Asian and Arab philosophies, Confucianism, Taoism and Chinese Buddhism, Japanese Shintoism and the evolution of Buddhism in that country- were all his subjects of study and objective analysis. Later he turned his attention to Western Thought. All of this enabled him to write "Mathamulu-Darshanamulu" (Religions and Philosophies) in Telugu, "Samakaleena Bharathiya Darshan" in Hindi and 'Current Trends in Indian Philosophy" in English.

There were two prevalent misconceptions regarding the study of Indian and Western Philosophies all over the world: 1. Philosophies can't be understood by common people. Those who are unacquainted with philosophies won't be able to grasp them. In fact they need not take trouble to do so. 2. Philosophies do not concern themselves with temporal issues. They do not relate themselves to this world. They are mostly concerned with other-worldly matters only. They expend time and energies to grasp mystical and timeless concepts. Prof. Satchidananda Murty is among the few who debunked such arguments.

Except for a few dense minds, every one displays at least some spiritual leanings. Even those who were in the pursuit of riches may also ponder over other-worldly things someday. They may wonder what was the source for all and where it will all end? Brahman- both Saguna and Nirguna- is the one supreme, universal Spirit that is the origin and support of the phenomenal universe. Man is the focus of each and every philosophy or ideology. Based on our intellectual capacity, we will be able to grasp the philosophical truths. Though these capacities differ among individuals, ultimately spiritual thinking is common and open to all. Brahman or the Absolute or Godhead is perceived by different cultures differently. He is called Rāma, Krishna, Jesus, Buddha and Saguna or Nirguna Brahman. Whatever the name, he is the One and only. All religions strive to protect faith in God and ethical values and take up service for the betterment of mankind and continue ritualistic tradition. Without this continuous effort, religions may become extinct. The same thing applies to spiritual thought and practice also. Ultimately man has to see his self in all and all in himself. Great souls did exactly the same thing. That's why Prof. Murty debunked the argument that philosophical and spiritual thinking is meaningless.

But he believes that we should not concentrate on other-worldliness to the exclusion of everything else. That's why he came out with prolific writings on international relations, human welfare and world peace also. We can discern a common thread running through all the religions, rituals, traditions and thought processes all over the world. An underlying unity binds us in all things. It is abstract and universal.

There is another fallacy among scientists and philosophers that faith and reason are incompatible and mutually contradictory. Disagreeing with this view, Prof. Murty explains how religions evolve rationally and how faith can help science grow. To describe Religion as having sprung up from the fear of natural forces is totally wrong. Ancient humans in a bid to fulfill their needs held *Yajñas* which were seen as an instrument to please the gods and natural forces. *Yajñas* were thought to bestow worldly boons. They are a social action aimed at achieving social good. Even sciences proceed from experience and rational analysis. No scientist believes that something emerges out of nothing. They try to get to the source of all phenomena. All sciences advance based on certain postulates. Great scientists like Sir Issac Newton, philosophers like Bertrand Russell believed that there is certain incomprehensible Truth (Nous) beyond observable phenomena. In fact many Western scientists never completely abandoned their religious beliefs in favour of rational thought. So we can not separate faith from reason. Even atheists who debunk faith take reason as the ultimate.

Belief in God is intrinsic to mankind. Man in the search for his origins formed the concept of God. Different cultures view God or the Absolute differently. Some people held that God can be reached through mystical experience and meditation. Many others declared that God can't be seen through direct perception. All over the world, theologists made a rational study of concepts of God. They held that the First Cause (*Moola Sattha*) is God. He is the source of *Gyana*. He causes the evolution of the Universe. One should rationally support these concepts. Rigveda held that *Rta* is the principle of natural order which regulates and coordinates the operation of the universe and everything contained within it. *Dharma* and *Karma* flow from it. Nyaya philosophy accepts four out of six *Pramanas* as reliable means of gaining *Gyana* and thus God. They are: *Pratyakṣa* (perception), *Anumāṇa* (inference), *Upamāṇa* (comparison and analogy) and Śabda (word, testimony of past or present reliable experts). Except Charvaka, all the other Indian schools of philosophy accepted the concept of God.

Here it will be appropriate to investigate certain misconceptions prevailing about Satchidananda Murty. I have personally known people who described him variously as a theist, atheist and as a scholar difficult to understand. It will be interesting to know that the same criticism was levelled at Buddha also. Satchidananda Murty simply recited Buddha's advice that the seeker should not believe anything simply because it was stated by some individual authority or holy texts. Everybody has to personally make a deep study, gain an understanding and come to valid conclusions.

Prof. Murty held that it is inadvisable to dump ancient Indian philosophical traditions and try to grasp the essence of Indian culture purely from the Western viewpoint. It is better to learn Sanskrit and study ancient texts along with commentaries to gain a proper understanding. Indian Muslims and Christians should also try this. Otherwise, they will be prone to misconceptions regarding Indian culture and philosophical concepts.

By dedicating so many of books to various deities Prof. Murty showed himself as a Believer in God (*Saguna Brahman*). But later on he came to regard God as *Nirguna Brahman*- An Absolute- without name and form. Prof. Murty while declaring himself as a Visishtadvaitin opposed ritualistic worship of idols. Such pronouncements led to a confusion regarding his religious viewpoints. It is clear that Prof. Murty never cared for outer rituals but concentrated on and continued the inner quest. The orthodox people prefer outer symbols and ostentation over the true essence. They do not bother to study vedas and upanishads. But believe that reciting *Gītā* as a daily ritual will get them closer to God. They hold *Manu Smriti* as the ultimate standard and four-fold Varna system as sacrosanct.

Prof. Murty is no adherent to such an obscurantist view. He endeavoured to understand traditions in the light of contemporary conditions. Prof. Murty amply made it clear that he doesn't regard Vedas as self-evident and not created by man. But he accepts their historical significance and authority. The four fold Varna system doesn't find mention in the Vedas and Upanishads. *Bhagavad Gītā* proposed that *Varnas* are based on inherent qualities and actions (*Guna and Karma*). The caste system proposed by *Manu Smriti* was a conspiracy to maintain the dominance of a few over many. Prior to Manu this system never existed. Moreover there are lakhs of people beyond the pale of caste system. Confining the study of Vedas only to men, that too those belonging to higher castes and forbidding it to women and Shudras did immeasurable harm to Indian society by stunting its intellectual development. Upanishads, *Maha Bharata* and Atharva Veda did not impose any such restrictions on women and Shudras. Thus Prof. Murty vehemently opposed *Manu Smriti*.

He did not deny that at times others may find him incomprehensible. He explained that unless we acquire certain measure of knowledge no art, science or language can be understood properly. One has to make a deep study, that too with curiosity and enthusiasm to gain insights into any subject. While some of Murty's writings like commentary on *Śrīmad Bhagavad Gītā*, *Kaaru Mabbulu* (Dark Clouds) and *Hinduism and its Development* can be easily understood by common readers, his major works on Philosophers, academics, national and international scholars are only comprehensible to the learned.

It is generally believed that while Indian culture and thought are basically spiritual, the Western thought

With his wife Smt. K. Vedavati Devi.

is materialistic. But Prof. Murty did not subscribe to this view blindly. He said we have to examine this supposition critically. The onset of science and technology and liberal outlook into India during the British rule subjected Indian intellectual class to deep trauma. The spiritual Vs materialistic discourse started just at that time. Many Indian scholars mistakenly believed that cultural renaissance to a West was completely absent in India. In those days Kautilya's *Artha Shastra*, Ayurveda, ancient Indian astronomy, Alchemy and *Kama Sutra* were not deeply studied. If it was done, they would have realized that our ancients were well-versed in Maths, Physics and Chemistry. And spirituality is not a prerogative of Indians only. All the world cultures display spiritual leanings in ample measure. Those who could not see this fact were responsible for propagating the myth that Indian ethos is entirely spiritual and materialistic viewpoint has no place here.

Satchidananda Murty focused on the then conflicting systems of Capitalism and Communism. He opined that while people who toil hard do get enough bread in Soviet Union, there is enormous technical progress and unbridled freedom in the United States of America. Indians should not blindly follow any one of these systems. They should adopt a system suited to the ethos and conditions of this land. Living only to earn bread and basic necessities is as bad as leading a life of unconstrained life. There should be enough freedom to work and earn according to one's ability. Those who have no goals in life and prefer to idle away can't be rescued.

The Colonial British rulers destroyed handicrafts and cottage industries in India only to replace them with heavy industry. We have to shed the colonial legacy and diversify our economy. Rousseau and Karl Marx idealized an egalitarian society. Gandhiji proposed that our natural, rural democratic society should be reinvigorated. Prof. Murty considered that Currency transactions are the root cause of all evil. He proposed that we should abandon this artificial system and resurrect natural social relations where everybody helps everybody and lives in a cooperative spirit and in peaceful harmony.

Prof. Murty visualized a world of equality, goodwill and peaceful coexistence. It should be the goal of our economic, political, and philosophical systems. Aiming for world domination, provoking hatred and wars will lead us to destruction. By understanding the evolution of human society and drawing the best out of it and by disowning the evil we will be able to build a better world.

One may wonder, how this dream can be realized in the present-day conflict-ridden world? Such doubts did occur even to the great visionaries of the world. But they shrugged them off and put their shoulders to the wheel of change. Prof. Murty followed this hallowed tradition.

Prof. Murty's thinking was novel. His analysis was objective. By investigating and making a comparative study of the world religions and philosophies, he found a middle ground. That's why he neither seems to support nor oppose any particular viewpoint. He stimulates doubts among us and encourages us to find solutions on our own- just like Buddha. That's why Murty liked Buddha's *Atta Deepa Viharatha*. The same spirit can be found in Upanishads and Jainism also.

In 1996, the Tamil Nadu Government took a remarkable step by introducing Prof. K. Satchidananda Murty's biography as a lesson for IX Standard students in Telugu, featured in both the Reader and Supplementary Reader. The biography was penned by Dr. M. Surya Kameswara Rao, a student of Prof. Murty. What's truly commendable is that the state government, despite Prof. Murty not being from Tamil Nadu, recognized his significance and included his biography in the school curriculum, making it a notable and appreciable achievement.

Having studied philosophy extensively, Prof. Murty toyed with the idea of writing a great book called 'World Philosophy'. But his wish did not seem to have translated into action. Anyway, after the year 2000, he seems to have retired from active research and writing.

Satchidananda Murty always led a simple and spotless life. Money-making was never on his mind. He just preserved and left his ancestral property to his successors. Not a single cot or table was acquired by him on his own. After the death of his wife Vedavati Devi, he lived alone in a palatial ancestral home. He did not show much inclination to mingle and chat with others. Writers, young and old, used to send him books seeking forewords and blessings from him. He did not show much enthusiasm to oblige them. He used to eat an egg, a banana and a little amount of curd rice daily.

Parents and his wife enabled Prof. Satchidananda Murty to lead a life of peace. He utilized this comfortable living to make a deep study into philosophy. His life was tranquil to the end. His ideal was Lord Śrī Rāma. The way the Lord was described by Valmiki's *Ramayana*, Kalidas' *Raghuvamsha, Rāma Charita Manas* of Tulsi Das made a deep impact on him since a tender age. Great poets prayed that the stoic nature of Lord Rāma be bestowed on them. Prof. Murty mentioned so in his writings. He led such a peaceful, stoic and composed life. Leaving a great intellectual legacy to us, Prof. Satchidananda Murty breathed his last on 24 January, 2011. We feel the deep loss forever.

Conclusions

Prof. K. Satchidananda Murty's remarkable life and work

have left an indelible mark on the world of philosophy, inspiring future generations of scholars and thinkers. Through his groundbreaking work and tireless dedication, Prof. Murty has cemented his place as one of the most influential philosophers of our time, leaving behind a legacy that will continue to shape the world of ideas. As we reflect on Prof. Murty's life and achievements, we are reminded of the transformative power of philosophy and the importance of pursuing knowledge, wisdom, and understanding. As we look to the future, Prof. K. Satchidananda Murty's work will undoubtedly continue to be a source of inspiration, guidance, and insight for scholars, philosophers, and thinkers around the world.

ANNEXURE-I

AUTOBIOGRAPHY (1924- 1976)

Prof. K.Satchidananda Murty

(Written by Prof. Murty in 1977)

I was born on 25 September 1924 in a peasant family of Andhra (South India). But in their way of life my grandfather and father had become what in England are known as "gentlemen farmers", though the tract of land they owned was small (at that time). My siblings, all born before me, died in early infancy; so I was the only child of my parents. My father lavished great care and affection in bringing me up and having me educated. Although he did not finish high school, he developed himself intellectually and spiritually through his own effort. Getting interested in culture and religion, he read deeply and extensively the literature on these subjects available in Telugu, a language of over 44 million people, and collected the Telugu translations of the Hindu religio- philosophical classics, of the *Bible* and the *Quran*, and the writings of modern Indian religious personalities. My parents were both devotees of God; but while my father knew wisdom, my mother had simple and sincere inherited faith. Neither adhered to any exclusive creed or ritual. Openness to Parātpara, the Supreme Ultimate, in multifarious ways, prevailed in our home.

Peasants in the part of Andhra to which I belong have been, like the yeomen of England, independent owners and cultivators of whatever land they have. Our village

His statue in front of Andhra University, Arts College

had no kulaks, serfs or moneylenders. For our families agriculture was a way of life, and not for business and profit. Accumulation of money for its own sake and investing it in any way other than in buying gold and more land was unusual with them. Not to lend for interest and not to be indebted was a virtue. To be covetous and not be satisfied with what one has: both these were not right. They had affection and concern for land, plants and animals; and considered agriculture, government service and the learned professions good. Valuing intellectual and productive work, they led lives characterized by prudence and piety. Attempting to practice sobriety, decency and decorum, they avoided adventure, passion and violence. Till I was over 20 years old I lived with my parents. So to some extent all this has coloured my axiology.

I married in 1942. Since then, like my father earlier, my wife enabled me to be free from familial and domestic chores, cares and responsibilities. So, I have always been like a happy guest in our house, with all the time I needed for reading, thinking and writing.

From the time I was five years old, for about 10 years, I was taught by Sanskrit pandits trained in the traditional way, while simultaneously receiving education preparatory to admission to high school and in high school. Then I joined a college and after that a university, receiving in due course the degrees of M.A. and Ph.D. In short, my education was at the same time both classical and modern. At home I had access to my father's small but sufficient library, and made full use of it in my teens and twenties. My pandit teachers were specialists in grammar and logic: the first was a Smarta Brahmin (follower of non-dualism), and the second a Dvaiti Brahmin (follower of dualism) who was also a quite well-known poet. One of my university teachers (a student of Faddegon) was the Indian pioneer in the comparative study of Navya Nyāya and modern logic, who later translated a great Advaita classic; another (a student of Radhakrishnan) was a scholar in Sanskrit, well-versed in Vedantic and Hegelian epistemology and dialectic, who later became an authority on comparative philosophy.

For my philosophy Honours degree I chose Advaita Vedanta as my special subject, besides the required courses on histories of Western and Indian Philosophy, logic and theory of knowledge, psychology, and contemporary Western philosophy with reference to a prescribed text.

For the last subject, I was taught Whitehead, and later as a teacher for the same course I had to lecture on Whitehead, Dewey and Jaspers, for 2 or 3 years on each at different times. Immediately after getting my degree when I worked in a college for about a year, I had to teach Descartes 'Meditations.

In 1954-55 as a young teacher, I went on a sort of peregrinatio academica of Europe, during which I had the privilege of meetings and talks with some leading thinkers, and of visiting a few universities. In subsequent years I would go to Europe, USA, USSR and other countries again and again, and meet many philosophers and visit many institutions. Over the years, I was fortunate in becoming intimate with not only the best among the Indian philosophers of my generation, but also with some of the most eminent of the preceding as well as some of the most promising of the succeeding ones. From 1949 to 1984 I was a teacher of philosophy at Andhra University.

My intellectual life has been stimulated, shaped and developed by my father, my home life, my teachers, the thinkers and scholars I came into contact with, as well as by my wide travels and diversified reading. While philosophy is my profession, my passion is for belles—letters. I am an addict of fiction; and I have roamed afar in the fields of religion, history, political science, sociology, cultural anthropology and international relations. Abhorring narrow specialization and parochialism, in philosophy too I deliberately acquainted myself with Chinese, Japanese and West Asian philosophies, in addition to Indian and Western. My mind has thus become a hybrid of many influences. But, I am neither a disciple of anyone, nor a follower of any school or system.

I do not think of myself as an original philosopher, but only as one testifying to the manifestations of philosophy in different forms in the same as well as in different cultures at different times, and as one who has been and is endeavouring to emphasize the capacity of one type of philosophical thinking to: (i) lead to an awareness of That or Such ness which Suchness which is inaccessible to common sense and science and illumines the meaning of our existing, (ii) suggest modifications and reformulations – or may be abandonment or substitution – of our ideas, beliefs and values, after subjecting them to discriminating judgment and careful appraisal, (iii) give rise to the perception of the Same in all through the correction that as all others are like oneself they must be treated as one treats oneself, and (iv) lead to an integration of rationality and feeling, belief and behavior, in individual and collective life.

In 1939-40, I wrote in Telugu a translation and detailed explanation of the *Bhagavad Gītā*, which was published in 1941. It contained also an English translation of the verses. It maintained that while the metaphysics of this scripture was non-dualism of the sort later elaborated by Sankara, its ethics was positive and works-oriented. Non-dual knowledge leads to salvation, but it arises only in a mind: (i) purified by long performance of duty for its own sake in a disinterested way, or with the fruits of all actions offered as worship to God, and (ii) exposed to scriptural teaching understood in the right way. After attainment of wisdom one ought to continue to discharge his duties and work for the welfare of the world as long as one lives, making all one's action worship of the Supreme, because (a) while no one can remain even for a moment without doing anything at all, (b) working for the good of all without attachment and desire is real action-lessness. In the explanation of the relevant verses it was also shown that the message of the *Gītā* was universal and that it did not approve of rights and privileges based on birth. The specialty of this book was that for the first time in clear and simple Telugu prose this kind of interpretation of the great classic was given by so young an author who had knowledge of and respect for tradition, but did not accept what was unjust and regressive in it (in tradition).

My exposition in Telugu of the Īśa Upaniṣad appeared in the late Forties. In this the metaphysical position adopted was that ultimate reality was neither just an ineffable Absolute, devoid of all attributes, nor just the divine or the spiritual immanent and exhausted in the world or identical with it. It is the Absolute as well as the transcendent Lord (Īśa), who encompasses the universe and also dwells in it and yet is not limited to it. The world is his creation; it is not an illusion. Wisdom transcends empirical knowledge, but does not negate it. Withdrawal from action is not necessary; a happy life on earth is a value to be realized. The Upanishad only enjoins enjoyment through (i) relinquishing the fruits of actions and (ii) freedom from covetousness; and exhorts one to wish for an active life of a hundred years. An elucidation in Telugu of the meaning of this great, profound and the shortest Upanishad in this way did not appear before.

In 1962, was brought out in Telugu a one volume *Encyclopedia of Philosophies and Religions*, edited by me. It was released by Jawaharlal Nehru in July 1963. It consists of long, historical and systematic surveys of both philosophy and religion, written by me, followed by essays in alphabetical order by scholars from all over the world. There seem to be no such scientific surveys of these subjects in any Indian language by someone who has consciously avoided adopting some standpoint, say, of Vedanta or Buddhism, Marxism or linguistic analysis. All the essays were written by internationally known authorities who had empathy for the subjects they dealt with. The volume covered in its surveys and articles the philosophies and religions of both East and West.

Deeply impressed by Descartes *Discourse on Method*, 'the greatest manifesto of modern man', which depicts him courageously and unreservedly advancing towards conquest of truth, asserts the comprehensibility of nature and the possibility of mastery over it, and prophesies much that science and technology later achieved, I translated it into Telugu in co-operation with a Telugu scholar Dr. K.V.R. Narasimham, and wrote an introduction elaborating Descartes life story and thought and setting forth his importance in the world history of ideas. This was published in 1960. Such has been my contribution to philosophical literature in Telugu, a language of over 44 million people.

My work *Evolution of Philosophy in India: A Brief Sketch* was published in 1952. Under the influence of the psychology and sociology of knowledge, it attempted to briefly trace the development of philosophy in India in relation to socio-political conditions. It held that while, on the one hand, every thinker and philosophy are the products of their social milieu, and every man's theories and beliefs are also influenced by his character, upbringing, personality and unconscious motives, on the other hand, thinking and knowledge influence and shape social organization and economic conditions. It also made it clear that psychological and sociological conditioning of thinking and knowledge, while not irrelevant to their validity, does not determine it. It considered a clear distinction between philosophy and religion as the necessary point of departure for a history of philosophy. This work remains the first and only one of its kind by an Indian university teacher.

A collection of essays by me under the title *Indian Philosophy since 1498* appeared in 1982. The view found in many writings in English is that there has been either an absence or eclipse of philosophical thinking in India from the beginning of the 16th to the second decade of the 19th century. The first essay in this book shows that the period from 1498 to 1945 was no less creative than the one preceding it or the one succeeding it. Its second essay, which places modern Indian philosophy in its socio-political setting, has been described as "a model piece of writing"... "from a really newpoint of view", which "covers a vast area with wide learning and deep understanding". In three other essays it presents a critique of Gandhian thought, may be the only such thing by an Indian academic philosopher. It has an essay on Ambedkar (born a pariah), the principal architect of the Indian Constitution. It deals with some other objects also.

My *Philosophy in India*, 1986, was favourably reviewed by Indian, Soviet, German, Czech, Yugoslav and U.S. journals. For example, the leading Indian philosophical journal commented on it as follows: 'The present work from the pen of one of our most eminent philosophers and educationists is a veritable gem. Within a short compass it succeeds not only in lucidly presenting Indian philosophy, past and present, but also discusses at the same time some of the urgent problems aGītāting Indian philosophers today.... It is brief, unambiguous, quintessential, and comprehensive, a tribute to the author's vast and accurate scholarship, critical judgment and catholic taste".

My *Revelation and Reason in Advaita Vedanta* was first out in 1954 and reprinted in 1974. Part I of its Book I contains a fairly exhaustive study of the problem of scriptural authority in the Advaita school, after giving a summary of its conception of God and revelation; whereas its Part II deals with the function of reason in it. Part I of Book II critically studies (a) knowledge of God and (b) the nature of scriptural authority, expounded by the other five Hindu systems. In the last part, an independent criticismof Advaita metaphysics, theology and "Vedic revelation" is attempted and the possibility of more satisfactory solutions to these problems suggested. *The Philosophical Quarterly* (India) in its review remarked that this book "has for the first time... thrown a challenge to some of the philosophical doctrines maintained in Advaita Vedanta....A bold step A very lucid and comprehensive presentation of the problems... in a very impartial way, based on authoritative texts.... The author's own views are contained in Book II ... He applies strict logic to substantiate his position". The Hindu, described it as "the outcome of a deep scholarship in Indian and Western thought... encyclopedic in the treatment of these topics (revelation and reason) in all the religions and philosophies of the world". Radhakrishnan hailed it as "interesting and valuable" and "a very learned book" in which views had been stated "in a bold and unfettered way". Metaphysics, Man and Freedom, published in 1963 and reprinted in 1974, embodies three lectures. In the first is given an explanation of a threefold need for metaphysics -- intellectual, linguistic and psychological -- and an account of how metaphysics arises. In the second is formulated a conception of man by coordinating the results of reflective analysis on man's being with the findings of psychology and anthropology, and a phenomenology of man is sketched. In the third is discussed freedom as an escape from finitude through gnosis and askes is, and the possibility of freedom in the world on the basis of empirical experience and psycho-analysis is indicated.

The *Realm of Between*, 1973, consists of four chapters and two annexes. The book is mainly about the realm between the transience of things and the Truth of things, the middle state between what is and the Holy. Its first chapter deals with man's condition: suffering, evanescence and finitude;

and the second considers possible ways of escaping this condition. A good deal of suffering could be eradicated by radically transforming society through concerned rational human action. Salvation is the experience with certitude of peace, security, and contentment. We are saved by the meaning of our thought and acts and by the sympathy and compassion we feel and evoke. Its third chapter is concerned with two basic forms of religious action -- sacrifice and worship. Sacrifice is giving up of what one has leading to transformation of life, while worship is taking refuge in God with the prayerful thought that one is sinful, naught, and helpless and that He is the only means of salvation. The fourth chapter grapples with the questions of God's existence, His non-appearance, silence, absence and of one's own death; and with the dialectic of atheism and the relation between religion and ethics. A few arrive at an awareness of Being, while to some others it is revealed as a Person; but most of us have to be satisfied with believing what cannot be proved, and it is a glorious risk – a great wager – to have faith in the Unconditioned Being or the Supreme Person. But atheism does not necessarily lead to the deification of man or history, or to immorality; nor is it true that "there is no virtue if there is no immortality". Without a belief in God or immortality some can live, endure, find meaning, and engage themselves in ethical endeavours of the highest type.

In 1960 was published *Studies in the Problems of Peace* which I and A.C. Bouquet authored. He did the first part of it, while I wrote the second part entitled "Phenomenology of Peace" and the first chapter of the third part. In 1986, all that I wrote then has been republished with a 25-page prologue explaining the Hindu, Buddhist and Jain approaches to peace, and alluding to the views of Whitehead, Jaspers, Teilhard de Chardin and Russell. This new publication has the title: *The Quest for Peace*. It has seven chapters and an epilogue. The chapters are: The Hindu Philosophy of Force and Social Equilibrium; Critical Reflections on Hindu Philosophy; The Philosophies of Ahimsa and Forgiveness; The Philosophies of Violence and Terror; The Philosophies of Liberty and Revolution; The Causes of War; and Bases of Peace. John O 'London's weekly described the first two chapters as "a comprehensive peace classic"; while the third is "a Toynbee-esque historical review of the development of Western thought, both masterly and illuminating." The Journal of Asian Studies considered it "a competent philosophical examination of the phenomenology of peace"; and Justice dans le Monde said it was "not merely a work of scholarship, but of civil courage".

Part I of my *Indian Foreign Policy*, 1964, begins with a brief discussion of classical Indian theories, passes on to a consideration of Gandhism, and ends up with an analytical exposition of an independent India's foreign policy. Part II discusses some specific issues and the last Part, after a review of some problems of international, offers some suggestions for policy reorientation. The Annex has, among others, sections dealing with the Śāstras, Aśoka and Gandhi and Ethics and Politics. Harold D. Lasswell wrote of this work thus: "These essays clarify the value goals of national policy... A problem-oriented approach of this kind is too mature for fanaticism, too empirical for undisciplined fantasy, too responsible for self-indulgent passivity or despair. The most striking contribution of these essays is to locate the challenges of today in the perspective of the enduring conflicts of Indian tradition. (They) contain important suggestions for improving the fundamental instrumentalities of foreign policy ... proposals of a scholar who truly lives in his epoch "

The Indian Spirit, 1965, has these chapters: The Indian Spirit: Past and Present; India; History and Atavism; The Hindu Ethos; the Greek Image of Indian Philosophy;

Philosophical Thought in India; Experience, Reason and 'Transcendental Materialism, in Indian Philosophy; Religion and Ethical Practices; and Ethics and Politics in Hindu Culture. Among a number of unusual and non-stereotyped positions this book seeks to establish are the following: India is not especially spiritual. Basic Hindu scriptures are not opposed to progress and prosperity. Indian culture and civilization are only as much coherent and non-hybrid as the European. India was never totally indifferent to history, nor was it atavistic. No other culture was more concerned with this world, with material prosperity and sensual pleasure than Indian culture. Socialism and socialistic society only would be in tune with the Hindu ethic and attitudes to money, work and State. Classical Indian philosophy has these characteristics: Sense of Infinity, Sense of Human dignity, faith in Moral freedom, and a Tragic sense. Its ideal is an integral man. It is traditional. Philosophy is a power and privilege. It is approached through faith. It is a force for preservation of culture. It is largely interpretative. It is a science of salvation, and of review. It is a point of view, a quest for truth, and organicist. On the relationships among religion, ethics and politics in Indian Culture also the book brings to light facts not widely known, and expresses ideas and evaluations not perhaps found in other books on these. *The Philosophical Quarterly* (India) in its long review described it as "instructive, penetrating and well-documented... one of the most thought–provoking and formative of recent publications." The first chapter of *Far Eastern Philosophies*, 1976, has these sections: The Cycles of Cathay; Chinese History and Society -- Some Myths; Science in China; Philosophy in China; The Chinese 'Bildung', Chapters II and III are on Ju Chia (The School-of the Literati) and Tao Chia (The School of the Way). Chapters IV and V are entitled Japanese Philosophy and Shinto (The Way of the Numinous). Hajime Nakamura evaluated this work thus:

"This work is the first attempt to understand the intrinsic values of Japanese philosophy in the international scope by way of comparative study.... It will make a great contribution to further progress of philosophical thinking in the global setting in the years to come." Wing-Tsit Chan commented on it as follows: "Now we have for the first time a book length discussion of Far Eastern Philosophy written by an Indian philosopher. I rejoice in its publication. The significance is not merely its own merits—its high level of scholarship, its strictly philosophical approach without sentimentality, its freedom from misunderstandings or the usual clichés, and its many insights.... The far greater significance is that it may serve as a starting point of a renaissance of intellectual interchange between India and China."

Just before he was to be coroneted, Rāma was informed that he would have to go into exile in the forest for 14 years and that his younger brother would be coroneted in his place. People noted with surprise that the colour and luster of Rāma's face was the same while he was clad in auspicious silk robes before coronation and when he wore bark-garments before going to the forest."He exemplified the ideal of equanimity in prosperity and adversity. To be unruffled in happiness and sorrow: this is the ideal that appeals to me most.

(From *Philosophers on Their Own Work,* Peter Lang, Indiana University, USA , 1977).

ANNEXURE-II

Andhra University: Some Reminiscences

Prof. K. Satchidananda Murty

I joined the honours class in philosophy in Andhra University in 1943 and took my degree in 1946. We had only three teachers in the Philosophy Department then : Professor Sailesvar Sen, Dr. P. T. Raju and Dr. D. Ramakrishnaiah. Educated at Calcutta and Amsterdam, Prof. Sen was the pioneer in the comparative studies of Navya-Naya and Symbolic Logic and a profound scholar in Advaita Vedanta. He was an affectionate teacher very much interested in each student as an individual person, and his method of teaching was simple and slow such that even those without any previous knowledge of philosophy could understand the subject. He used to teach Greek and Indian Philosophies and Advaita Vedanta. Prof. Sen was a student of Urquhart, Faddegon and others in India and Holland, and he also attended lectures of Dawes Hicks and other British Philosophers. He was a contemporary or classmate in college of Netaji Subhas Chandra Bose and Ambassador Sen. He was a man of wide learning and insistent on meticulous, and precise expression of ideas. Dr. Raju used to teach Logic and Theory of Knowledge and Contemporary Western Philosophy. While he was a Sanskrit scholar who studied Indian Philosophy in the traditional way, he was also a deep student of European Philosophies, specially idealistic systems. He was a very hard-working and productive savant, and he remains so till today. In the classes he adopted the expository lecture method through his many works Dr. Raju became one of the fore-most philosophers of India. Dr. Rāma Krishnaiah gave us courses on Modern European Philosophy and Psychology. There used to be fraternal relations among philosophy; students and a rapport between teachers and students.

Prof. S. Bhagavantam was our Principal and Professor; G.V. Rao was then assistant to the Principal. As a younger collaborator of Dr. C.V. Raman and as one of the most distinguished younger scientists of India, Dr. Bhagavantam enjoyed a fine reputation among students though he used to be aloof and inaccessible at that time. I remember Prof. G. V. Rao as a conscientious teacher and educational administrator. Among other teachers who were then much respected were Dr. V.S. Krishna (Economics), and Prof. M. Venkataraingaiya (History) who retired in the year I joined as a student. Students used to consider Prof. Venkatarangaiya as a learned, lucid and analytical teacher, sincerely interested in their welfare. Śrī K.V. Goplaswamy was the Registrar, who due to; his guidance and organisation of cultural activities came into close contact with a number of students. He contributed a good deal to cultural life in the campus as long as he served, the University. Dr. C. R. Reddy was our Vice-Chancellor. One of the great Indian intellectuals of his time, students and teachers saw very little of him; he was a sort of live legend in the campus. Everyone was awed by his scintillating brilliance and afraid of his sarcasm. He used to make himself visible to the students arid: teachers once a year by delivering in his inimitable way either the inaugural or the valedictory address of the students' union or the HEPA (History, Economics & Politics Association).

In July 1949 when Dr. P.T. Raju left Andhra for the professorship at Jaipur, on the recommendation of Prof. S. Sen, Dr. C. R. Reddy appointed me as a lecturer. When I joined as a teacher, Dr. Reddy was the Vice-Chancellor, and Prof. V.S. Krishna was the Principal. I was teaching Logic and Theory of Knowledge and Contemporary Western Philosophy till 1954; from then on till the late sixties Advaita Vedanta, Early Indian Philosophy and Contemporary Western Philosophy, substituting the latter with Systems of Indian Philosophy-occasionally ; and in the seventies Buddhist Philosophy and Advaita Vedanta. Within about an year after I joined, Dr. C.R. Reddy left the University and Prof. Krishna was elected the Vice-Chancellor, and Prof. Rangadhama Rao appointed the Principal.

In 1954 Professor Sen suddenly passed away and I was put in charge of the philosophy department as its head, being the senior teacher available, in the department. In due course by 1960 I became a professor. Till 1967 I continued in that capacity and from 1967 till 1971 I was in charge of the postgraduate centre at Guntur as its principal and special officer. In 1971 I returned back to the philosophy department as its professor and head and remained so till 1973, when I was offered a National Fellowship free from administrative and regular teaching duties. In 1975, I came to Tirupati as Vice-Chancellor of Śrī Venkateswara University.

What I found most characteristic of Andhra University during 1949-1960 was the academic freedom which teachers enjoyed, the respect in which the professors was held, the absence of politics or groups among teachers, the Vice- Chancellor's acquaintance with most of the teachers and their work, and the keen interest he took in some of the teachers who impressed him. Among such, I recall Professors S. Meenakshisundarm (Mathematics),

B. Sarveswara Rao (Economics), B. Ramachandra Rao (Physics), myself, and others (Dr. Rao [now Vice-Chairman, U. G. C.) narrated in a public meeting at Tirupati that it was on Dr. Krishna's suggestion he took up space research. He was one of the first in India to do this].

Dr. Krishna's incessant encouragement, his ready accessibility, informality and kindness enabled us to achieve the best that we were capable of Dr. Krishna used to attend office for two hours every afternoon from three to five, after visiting the library. He used to spend the rest of his time in reading books on philosophy, education and history of science and in chatting with friends and listening to classical music. He had the vision to establish new departments like Sanskrit, Nuclear Physics, Anthropology, and Rural Studies. Due to the impetus Dr. Krishna gave, some of us- e.g., myself, Drs. B. Ramachandra Rao, D.V. Ramana (Economics) - developed an interest in the History and Philosophy of Science and also worked out a syllabus for an obligatory course in this area for all honours students, which we and some others gave for some years. Recently Dr. Ramachandra Rao told me that he still had with him the notes and bibliographies of his lectures of this course, which I hope he will publish. Later that type of honours course was abolished. Dr. V. S. Krishna was responsible for the formation of the Research Forum, which used to meet once a month or so, and in its meetings teachers and research scholars used to give an account of their current investigations and their wider significance and implications. Dr. Ramanadham and Dr. D.V. Ramana did an excellent job as the secretaries of the Forum. On Dr. Krishna's suggestion we also started the Saturday Club, of which I was the secretary. It used to meet over snacks and coffee every Saturday evening at six; one of the members gave a prepared talk followed by an informal discussion and both used to be at a high level, if I remember right, the first talk was given by Shri K.V. Gopalaswamy and the second by Dr. B. Ramachandra Rao, both at my request. The Forum and the club proved useful in bridging the gap between what Lord Snow called, the Two Cultures and promoting inter-disciplinary understanding. When Dr. Krishna left the university, unfortunately they ceased to exist. Among the persons with whom I came into quite close contact in Andhra University were the following: the late Professor Swami Jnanananda (Nuclear Physics) who was a great adept in Yoga and practised tapas for many years in the Himalayas and later worked in famous laboratories at Prague, Liverpool and Michigan and became one of the earliest leading nuclear scientists of India; the late Prof. C. Kunhan Raja (Sanskrit), educated at Madras and Oxford, after undergoing Sanskritic studies in the traditional way in India, he taught in the universities of Madras, Tehran and Andhra. Again, the late Prof. S. Minakshisundaram, a brilliant mathematician, and Prof. K. V. R. Narasimham, with erudition in Telugu and Sanskrit, became two of my best friends. I enjoyed the fellowship of Pandits, Śrī D. Venkataramana Sastry, Śrī Kolluru Somasekhara Sastri, and Śrī K. Ramanujacharya, who were respectively authorities on Telugu Vyakarna, Advaita Vedanta, and Sanskrit Vyakarna, Professors K. Rangadhama Rao (Physics), G.V. Rao (History), G.J. Somayaji (Telugu), C. Mahadevan (Geology), K.R. Śrīnivasa Iyengar (English), J. Venkateswarlu (Botany), S. Venkataraman (Law), and late D. Sitapati Rao (Engineering), were my well-wishers and uniformly nice to me. Of these Professors G. V. Rao, Venkateswarlu, Somayaji, Venkataraman and Śrīnivasa Iyengar are still happily with us.

During my early years at Andhra, Professors G. Sundara Reddi (Hindi) and O. Ramachandraiah (History), became my good friends. During the late fifties Prof., B. Ramachandra Rao and myself and in the sixties Prof. B. Sarveswara Rao and myself came close to each other. Prof.

B.R. Rao's genius, devotion to research and achievement, and Prof. B.S. Rao's razor-sharp mind deeply impressed me ever since I came into contact with them. In the seventies when I returned to Waltair from Guntur A. Śrīramadas (Geology) and V. Ramakrishna Rao (Applied Physics) used to meet with me on most evenings, for fruitful discussions on the sociology of science and research in India. Under Prof. Śrīramadas' leadership the Geology Department is making notable contributions. I used to have cordial relations with Professors R. Ramanadham (Meteorology), M.S. Raju (Electrical Engineering), T. Venugopala Rao Rao (Mechanical Engineering), K. Sivayya (Commerce), N. Subba Reddy (Anthropology), K. V. Ramana (Economics), K. Viswanatham (English), B. Prasada Rao (Applied Economics), B.S. Murti (Law), T. V. Avadhani (Statistics), G.J.V.J. Raju, N. Sastri, G. Parthasarathy (Applied Economics), Subrahmanyam (Mathematics), and a number of others. My relations with all the heads of departments at the Guntur Postgraduate Centre were also most happy. Some other scientists and scholars whom I have not been able to mention in this account have also been my good friends.

Outside Andhra University also I had the good fortune of being a friend of several intellectuals who attained eminence in diverse fields. My friendship or acquaintance and association with those mentioned above and others not mentioned has enriched me intellectually and socially and has broadened my interests and vision. I profited a great deal from my contacts with them and will always remain indebted to them. Some familiarity on my part with humanistic, social and natural sciences and a multidisciplinary way of looking at any problem, were partly the result of my intellectual fellowship with these scholars and scientists. My own inclinations and aptitudes as well as the academic environment at Andhra created by Vice-Chancellors Reddy, Radhakrishnan, and Krishna, and my contacts with scholars and scientists were responsible for my writing books like *Studies in the Problem of Peace, Indian Foreign Policy, The Indian Spirit, Far Eastern Philosophies*, etc., which a mere Indian philosopher confined to his own discipline would not have ventured to undertake.

Of the many students who studied with me perhaps the most brilliant and one who became my intimate friend is Prof. K.Ramakrishna Rao (Psychology),who now heads the famous parapsychology laboratory founded by J.B. Rhine. It would be difficult to mention all those old students of mine who are now; working in affiliated colleges or are indifferent walks of life, as well as others, who worked for their doctorates with me. I cherish my association with all of them. In the late 1940s and early 50s Dr. K.V. Gopalaswamy (for long time Registrar of Andhra University) and myself were quite close; in my earlier years at Andhra I received help, advice and encouragement from him. So did I from Principals Rangadhama Rao and Mahadevan. I got acquainted with Shri M.V. Rajagopal (now Vice-Chancellor of the Technological University at Hyderabad) when he was Registrar of Andhra University. Shri M. Gopalakrishna Reddy (present Registrar), one of the very bright old students of Dr. Krishna, is one of the most successful Registrars I know.

I had cordial relations with Vice Chancellors A. L. Narayan, K. R. Śrīnivasa lyengar and L. Bullayya. The present Vice-Chancellor Shri M.R. Apparow and myself have been friends since the early forties. No one felt happy more than myself when he became the head of Andhra University. I have not come across a more perfect gentleman. My acquaintance with Dr. B. Gopala Reddy dates from the time I was a student and I may claim it developed into friendship. Telugu literature and scholarship have not had a greater patron than him in the last three decades. He has been famous for long for his Tagore translations, but he is now emerging as a creative writer of high order. Dr. S.B.P. Pattabhirama Rao is another old and esteemed friend. He contributed to the growth of Andhra University and had a role in establishing Śrī Venkateswara University. He tries to live up to the ideals which C. Rajagopalachari and C. R. Reddi inculcated in him. Since 1959 or so when I became a member of the Mansas Trust created by him, Dr. P.V.G. Raju (Rajah of Vizianagaram) and myself became intimate friends. The Rajah Sahab stands head and shoulders above most politicians of Andhra Pradesh in philanthropy, integrity and intellect. As Education Minister he made the position of affiliated colleges stable and secure. All these three, who for many years served as Pro-Chancellors of Andhra University, have always given me advice and support.

In 1956 I was a member of the first study team on general education to U.S.A. and U.K. of which my old Principal Dr. S. Bhagavantam (then Vice-Chancellor, Osmania University) was leader. During our many weeks abroad, we came close to each other. In these he shed much light on the history of Andhra University, the working of Osmania University, and problems of higher education in general.

In the sixties, myself and Dr. Lakkaraju Subba Rau, who was a Syndicate Member for several decades and acted as Vice-Chancellor a number of times and who contributed quite substantially to the development of Andhra University, developed mutual regard and friendship, and till his passing away he lavished much affection on me. From him I came to know many details relating to the history of Andhra University. Under Drs. S. Bhagavantam Krishna and Lakkaraju, I virtually made a case study of Andhra University and developed insight into problems of University governance.

My sojourn in Śrī Venkateswara University since October 1975 has been so far happy and many inform me, successful; this is because of the cooperation and goodwill I have been receiving till today from the Syndicate, Faculty and Senate. Yet, I look back with nostalgia to the decades I spent as a teacher in Andhra University and sometimes wish that I had not left that University. But which Indian academic, excepting a Raman or a Seshadri, has resisted the lure of administrative office when it was possible to get it ? (Wrote when Prof. Murty was the VC of S.V.U., Tirupati)

ANNEXURE-III

Contemporary Trends of Thought in Europe

Prof. K. Satchidananda Murty (1956)

During my recent European tour I had occasion to visit six West European countries and had the privilege of discussing philosophical problems with some. Leading world- thinkers. I find that the main schools of thought prevalent at the present are four: Existentialism, Marxism, Empiricism and Catholic realism. Among the Existentialists are to be found both theists and atheists. And among theists we have Catholic Existentialists like Augusto Guzzo of Torino and Gabriel Marcel of Paris. Among the atheists are to be found philosophers like Heidegger who was for some time a supporter of Hitlerand Jean Paul Sartre now almost a Communist. There is of course no unanimity about Heidegger's views about God. For example Gabriel Marcel told me that Heidegger was, so to say, in suspense between atheism and theism. Karl Heim of Tubingen and Buber (now in Jerusalem) are theistic Existentialists outside the Catholic fold. Bultman, probably the most important theologian next to Barth, is an Existentialist. Then, of course, there is Karl Jaspers, one of the most important philosophers now living and to whom almost all present-day continental philosophers have acknowledged their debt. It was he who first coined the phrase "Philosophy of Existence."

It is in England, the Scandinavian countries, Holland and Austria that we find philosophers who have been influenced by "Logical Positivists." I do not think any one important in England would care to call himself a Logical Positivist. Bertrand Russell, to whom Logical Positivism owes not a little, is too big to be labelled by such a name. C. D. Broad has never been a slave to the philosophical methodology, which solely consists in dissecting sentences and phrases. G.E. Moore, though his signal contribution to philosophy is in daringly asking the question, "New, what the hell do you mean by this?" never made his pages unreadable by indulging in chains of logical equations and formulae. Gilbert Ryle. The most fashionable philosopher now in England, told me that the sort of thing which Quine and others do, though a very valuable instrument of thought, could never be philosophy wholly by itself. Price, author of the classic book on "Perception," is too many-sided a man to be concerned solely with linguistic analysis. What I wish to emphasise is that if English philosophers as a whole have to be classified under one name, the most suitable term is" Empiricists." No important philosopher in England at present is an Idealist. There are in Scotland some Idealistic philosophers and in Manchester there is Emmet, who is a student of Whitehead. Another characteristic feature of English philosophers at present is none of them is a believer in God. Russell and Broad; are confirmed atheists; Ayer thinks that God- propositions are nonsense. Wisdom believes there is some sense in theological language, though he is not sure what it is. The country of Locke, Berkeley and Hume remains true to the Anglo-Saxon tradition of affirming nothing that is not rooted in empirical experience. In Germany also there is some interest in Logical Positivism. In Munster there is an institute of mathematical logic; in Munich there is Britzelmayer, and Rintelen at Mainz.. All these are confirmed logicians.

Marxism is an avowed philosophy adhered to by some thinkers in every country; but wherever it is to be found it is of a stereotyped pattern, with little or no innovation. Not that it has not influenced philosophers and theologians, Antonio Bomfy in Italy is an important Marxian thinker, and Miss Jeanne Hersch, a rising philosopher of Geneva, has been influenced by Marxism. In France, Sartre, the man who made Existentialism fashionable, is himself a half- Communist now. And it is with reference to Marxism, that Albert Camus has now developed his philosophy. The late Archbishop William Temple has tried to introduce dialectical method into theology and Bouquet shows evidence of his wide acquaintance with Marx in his many writings. And from his suggested classification of religions into world-transforming and world-affirming, we find that he is thinking of religions which can answer the challenge of Marxism and religions, which cannot.

I was surprised to find that in the West European countries Catholicism is a live force. I visited the ancient Gregorian University at Rome, the Fribourg University in Switzerland, the Munich University, and the Berchman's College at Munich and the St. George's College at Frankfurt. I was amazed to find the depth of scholarship and the range of originality exhibited by the Catholic priests. In Rome I met Drs. Naber and Ledrus of the Gregorian University. At the university they are not merely content in expounding and commenting upon St. Thomas and St. Augustine. Philosophy in its true sense, development through criticism and interpretative correlation, is much in progress in the Catholic Universities. Brugger of the Berchman's Kolleg at Pullach has vigorously criticized the foundations of mathematical logic and the format of his paper reminds us of Wittgenstein's aphoristic sentences, brief and numbered. Grillmeier of Frankfurt is engaged in developing a theology of his own, moored, no in the fundamentals of Christian thought, but through a criticism of Karl Barth and Bultman. In the Benedictine monastery of Maria Laach, where I spent a day, I found Rishi- like priests, oblivious to all the external world, possessed of encyclopedic learning and engrossed in specialist studies. There is, for example, the Pole, Krasinski, who has written a huge to me on the Medicine-philosophy of Tibet; who can give an off-hand talk on Sattva, Rajas and Tamas and Kapha, Pitta and Vayu. The priest Burkhard can elucidate any point in St. Thomas without referring to books. Krasinski surprised me by telling that there was little difference in the Metaphysical experience of mankind, as in mystical experience. Then there was the unforgettable Bochenski, another Pole, a Dominican, whom I met at Fribourg, who told me boldly that India had little to learn from modern Europe. He said that philosophical salvation of India lies in recapturing the true Indian tradition. "What India can get from Sankara and Ramanuja is much better than what it can from Russell and Ryle in England," he told me.

I think it would be best that I take each of the countries which I visited one by one and bring out the dominant trends of thought with reference to some of the important thinkers whom I met. In Rome, for example, I had the privilege of having a long talk with Prof. Ugo Spirito of the Rome University, the successor of Gentile, who has been also Minister for Education, under Mussolini. Spirito was nurtured upon the thought of Croce and Gentile. He has however now broken away from his masters, and is a Problematist and is not sure of any truth at all anywhere. His is the Religion of Research, as he calls it and eternal quest of truth is what he is engaged upon. He is not sure whether he will find anything at all in the end or what he will find if at all he finds. He told me that he had read the Veda and the Upanishads and that his thought was very close to Indian thought. He does not like the dualism between man and nature, of which too much is made of in Europe. He likes the Indian capacity to feel nature, and not to make much of man and think of the whole universe anthropocentrically. His colleague at the University is Antonio, a Crocean.

In Switzerland, I found the University of Geneva still much under the influence of Calvinism. The Emeritus Professor of the University, Charles Werner, is a lovable old man who is much respected throughout the French-speaking world. In a recent book of his, he has classified the entire modern philosophy under the head of the Philosophy of man, while he calls ancient Greek thought the philosophy of universe. The guiding principle of modern philosophy is what he calls the principle of Interior. He says that while the participation of man in the Divine is a valuable insight of modern philosophy, its fault lies in thinking of man as independent, of the universe. He thinks that a complete theory of Freedom is yet to evolve. There is a psycho-conscious difference between men and animals, according to him, and he says that Freedom is the essence of consciousness and independence from external things. Werner says that it is evident we are finite; what is lost sight of is that we mirror the infinite. The task of philosophy is to show man's infinity. In Geneva I came across a young Jewess, Miss Jeanne Hersch, who did much in popularising Jaspers through a recent book of hers and is now engaged in writing a book in which she will try to work out a line of thought showing influences of both Existentialism and Marxism. In general, her theory of philosophy is that philosophy is an illusion; for everybody who philosophises thinks that he can give something, but he cannot, for it is not permanent. But unless this illusion is nursed, one cannot contribute something of temporary value at least.

Basle University has the distinction of having in Karl Jaspers one of the most, important living philosophers. It was he who first gave rise to the phrase "Existential Philosophy" in a book of his in 1932. In that he tried to elucidate "Existence" by meditating on it, so that he, and following his method others, can communicate with each other to clarify, stimulate and strengthen the striving for Existence in actual conduct. The Transcendent, he says, can be attained by meditating on traditional symbols and Existential means. Having been married to a Jewess in Hitlerite Germany, Jaspers had to undergo terrible persecution, and towards all totalitarianism, whether Nazistic or Communistic, he is uncompromising. He told me that in the present-day world there is only one problem for philosophy in all the countries to oppose Communism. "All modern philosophy which fails to do so ceases to be creative." Jaspers has a deep acquaintance with Indian and Chinese thought. He has read the Upanishads, the Moksha Dharma, the *Gītā*, and Shankara's Bhashyas. He emphatically told me that there was nothing superior to Indian meta-physics; but he thinks that Indian theism is inferior to Biblical theism. Voicing his disapproval of the view of some philologists that the *Gītā* is a patchwork, he said that the *Gītā* contains contradictions; but they constitute its greatness and it is evident that it is a valuable source of truth.

In Basle, I surprised old Karl Barth, the great Protestant theologian, by calling on him. Though over 70, Barth is not a spent-fire. He told me that in his young days he was fighting the eclectics and other thinkers who said there was no speciality in Christian Revelation and now he had to fight Bultman and others who are bent upon existentially interpreting the scriptures. While he is modest enough to concede that God's ways may be mysterious, he is sure that Christianity is the Road to God, while other religions are distortions. When I specifically asked him whether he would deny salvation to a Hindu or a Confucian who leads a saintly life, Barth told me that he sets no store by saintliness. No man is perfect and in the eyes of his Maker every man is a sinner; Grace alone can save man. Barth exercises very wide influence in theological an philosophic-theological circles in Europe and America.

At Zurich, in the famous polytechnic, in which Einstein was for some time a professor, there is group of mathematicians interested in evolving a new philosophy. Gonseth and Bernays are the leading lights of this group. Gonseth calls his philosophy Open Philosophy. He says that knowledge is not a structure with notions which are definitely closed. All notions and ideas are Open. An idea or meaning is Open, according to Gonseth, when it has the possibility of being developed. Metaphysics being a portion of knowledge and knowledge being constantly in evolution, metaphysics also should evolve itself. A closed system of metaphysics deserves to die and will die. He thinks that none of the existing systems of metaphysics Existentialism, Neo-Scholasticism, etc., are Open. He told me that India, which has been confronted by new knowledge, ought not to be content with her old traditions but must develop an Open philosophy.

Zurich is a place of pilgrimage for many psychologists, because Jung still continues to preside over the institute located there. As often asserted by him, Jung is no philosopher. But from a long talk with him, I could gather that he is a Kantian in outlook. According to him the main point in philosophy is to know the limits of human cognition. You can come thus far and no more to come to this standpoint is real philosophical achievement and, according to Jung, K and did that. Philosophy must be based on psychology and he told me that the kind of mathematics which Russell knew was not enough for philosophy, and in his opinion Kierkegaard and Heidegger are neurotics. He says the Existentialists are stupid, as they deny the reality of Psyche.

In Germany I had a profound disappointment. There is no philosopher worth the name except Heidegger. He sits atop on the mountainous peaks in Black Forest near Freibourg. There are many people who say that they cannot discover sense in what Hidegger writes. Hans Barth of Zurich and Miss Aebi, a distinguished philosopher and authority on Kant, told me. That they never could understand what Heidegger was talking about. He had been a supporter of Hitler and after the fall of the Nazisalso, he continued for some time in office but then retired into his mountain seclusion. Heidegger does not believe in God. God is a myth created by people so that they can throw their responsibility on it. Heidegger thinks that man is not a Fact. Man is what he has to become. This shows that man has absolute freedom because he can become anything. Phenomenologically Heidegger has tried to show this is possible.

In France Sartre has become a legend. I was fortunate enough to meet Madame Colette Audry, a co-worker of his and a friend since his Normandi days. Sartre was primarily influenced by Heidegger, though, Gabriel Marcel told me, Heidegger disowns Sartre. Sartre is a vehement atheist. Being a successful novelist and playwright, he has produced valuable books on the psychology of imagination. Sartre is of late concerned, exclusively with socio-political problems and has allied himself with communists.

Alber Camus is the one man who has most successfully battled with the Sartrean theorists and followers. In his "The Revolt of Man" Camus has shown how it is possible that freedom can remain a permanently cherished goal of mankind, with-out his being enslaved by any kind of dictatorship.

In Greece I found a great deal of similarity with India because like us over here, Greece has a very ancient philosophical tradition. Over a cup of Turkish coffee, Theodoracopoulos, Ex-Education Minister and at present professor of philosophy at Athens University, told me that in Greece, though there was acquaintance with prevalent schools of European thought, usually people cling to Plato and Aristotle. He thinks that if the Schoolmen and modern Western thinkers can develop thought systems out of what Plato and Aristotle said, there was no need why they of Greece should entirely ignore their ancient heritage. Though Heidegger and Jaspers are known, there is no influence of Sartre or of Russell in Grece. (Account of Prof. Murty's visit to Europe in 1956).

ANNEXURE-IV

Non-Technical Account of My Work While receiving D.Litt., Martin Luther University, Germany

Prof. K. Satchidananda Murty (1987)

मान्या: विद्वत्तल्लजा:, सुहृद:,

विश्वविख्यातस्यास्य विश्वविद्यालयस्य कुलपतिमहोदयेन, अन्यैश्चाधिकारिभि: ममाद्य महान् सम्मान: कृत इति तेभ्य: सर्वेभ्योऽपि मे हार्दिकीं कृतज्ञताम् आविष्करोमि ।

यूरोपखण्डे लब्धप्रतिष्ठानां विश्वविद्यालयानाम् इतिहासेन समासादितपरिचय: सर्वोऽपि जानात्येव - कियद्वा महत् कार्यं साधयत्ययं विश्वविद्यालय: सर्वतो विश्राणने ज्ञानामृतस्येति । शास्त्रानुसन्धानेन साकम् अधीतिबोधाचरणानां सम्पादने तत्प्रथमतया कृतसफलयत्नोऽयं विश्वविद्यालय: अन्येषामपि विश्वविद्यालयानां पथिप्रदर्शक आसीदिति विदितचरमेव सर्वेषाम् ।

Long ago when I was a young lecturer I wanted to know about the nature of a university, types of universities and how universities evolved. One of the books which I then read was Friedrich Paulsen, The German Universities and University Study. From it for the first time I came to know that the first modern university originated in

Germany and it was that of Halle. It was the first university which was founded on the principles of freedom of philosophising and of free research and teaching. It and the University of Gottingen welcomed into their portals modern philosophy and science as well as enlightenment and culture and made them an integral part of the life of the German people. They were the earliest universities to give up the assumption that truth had already been given and teaching had to do with transmission only, and to accept a new assumption, namely, that truth must be discovered and that, it was the duty of university teaching to qualify and guide students in this. It has been rightly observed that integrating teaching with research and thereby creating the very model of the modern university and thus becoming the fountain-heads of much of modern scholarship and science was their achievement.

Reawakening interest in the study of antiquity with the aim of self-development and to achieve a cultivated personality through Wissenschaft: These became the working ideals of the universities after the pattern first set by Halle and somewhat later by Gottingen.

It was pointed out by those in charge of the Integrated Socialist Education System of GDR that "bourgeois humanist ideas" were not thrown overboard in the formulation of this system, but that retaining what was valuable in them the direction of the New Education Policy was actually determined by the spirit of "Socialist Humanism". (Alexander Abusch's speech, Education and Training in the German Democratic Republic, 1966).

The indebtedness of universities everywhere to these German models is obvious. So this honour which this great university has done me today overwhelms me with pleasure and gratitude. But I realise that I have been selected for this honour as a representative and spokesman of the great and immemorial philosophical tradition of

India, by a university which was the first in Europe to proclaim that theoretical philosophy should seek truth free from all assumptions and that practical philosophy should be based upon rational knowledge. I cannot adequately thank the GDR Ministry, the Rector and other authorities of this university for making me an honorary member of this august body of scholars and scientists.

With your permission, I may now mention in brief what I have tried to do in a few fields. I will begin with my work relating to the analysis of Indian culture and showing that Indian ethos and religion have always been positivistic, rational and in accordance with socialism (*The Indian Spirit*, Waltair, 1965). The last aspect may be enlarged upon: A study of Indian classics leads to the conclusion that their ideal state was a planned welfare state based on autonomous democratically governed villages. Government was considered as a means to achieve social good and promote prosperity. The business of the state was not merely to rule but to ensure also public morality as well as welfare. While cities and villages, castes and professions could make their own laws and customs be autonomous and govern themselves, the state had to ensure that they all worked harmoniously and did not clash with the good of all. A government is for the sake of the people, for preserving Dharma (righteousness) and for promoting welfare and prosperity. When it fails to do so it would have no justification to continue (Op.Cit.,)

I have argued that the only ideology which would be in tune with Indian ethos and religion is socialism. It is interesting that even modern Indian liberals like Dadabhai Naoroji, S.N. Banerjee and M.G. Ranade were not in favour of either capitalism or colonialism. According to Ranade collective well-being, the social good, should be the ideal of economic theory. Indian social institutions do not encourage concentration of wealth; Indian religious ideals condemn the ardent pursuit of wealth. He was perhaps the first liberal in India to advocate planned economic development under the auspices of the state. It is well known that Swami Vivekananda was perhaps the first Indian to call himself a socialist, while Shri Aurobindo was the first to talk of Asian socialism based on spirituality. The distinguishing characteristic of Indian socialism is its emphasis on individual freedom, personal ethics and repudiation of regimentation and mass culture. Authentic Indian Weltanschauung can only support an ideology which approves work and welfare, social progress and material well-being, but which would not make unlimited personal wealth and economic prosperity the sole worthwhile ends. (*The Indian Spirit*).

I may now refer to my work in another field, viz. ethics and relations among states. As far as democratic countries are concerned, to promote national interests is the duty of a politician in power. National interests are not immutable, they change because of international developments, existing state of society in one's own country and other countries and the progress in knowledge and techniques of production. There are, however, two paramount interests which remain unchanging though ways of preserving them vary. They are : external security and internal stability, the twin conditions necessary for national welfare and happiness. Dictatorship, territorial aggrandizement, domination of other countries, or colonization cannot be identical with real national interests, and today world peace is a real major national interest of all countries.

If there are ethical principles they must apply consistently and equally to states, i.e., men who run governments, as well as to citizens, and if any state must be bound by morality and law, so must all states be. As the good life is impossible without citizenship in a state and as it is a state which confers on individual's security, freedom and other benefits, and as a stateless person's rights are insecure, the citizens of a state have a duty to support and serve it. This prima facie obligation towards one's own state overrides one's obligations to humanity at large, if and when there is a conflict between the two, just as the prima facie obligation towards one's own family is greater than towards others. In most cases, however, there is no such conflict and generally in promoting the real good of one's own state i.e., the welfare and happiness of the people that constitute, if one serves the whole world, just as by discharging one's familial and civic obligations one serves one's state too thereby. While one's own country and nation have greater claims on one than others, the statesmen and the citizens of every state must take into consideration the interests of other states and not violate the lives, liberties and happiness of other peoples, because a state ought to behave towards other states as it thinks they ought to towards itself. But whereas individuals and groups within a state cannot resort to violence or take the law into their own hands, because the state is there to protect the legitimate interests and rights of every one of its citizens, a state may have to go to defensive war, as there is yet no international authority to guarantee and protect the integrity and independence of all states. It follows from all that has been said that one's obligation to obey the government of one's own state is not absolute, if it is not a moral government and if its actions are not solely devoted to secure the liberty, welfare and happiness of all its citizens. Thus it may become an individual's duty to disobey and defy an aggressive, dictatorial, or totalitarian government, and try to change or overthrow it. It must also be recognized that a government has the right to promulgate legislation in accordance with the freely expressed wishes of the majority of its citizens, unless this violates natural rights. It is a citizen's duty to follow all the democratically and duly enacted laws of the land

and strengthen the state. (For above *vide* my book: *Indian Foreign Policy*, Calcutta, 1964).

In May 1987 I had occasion to express the following ideas: peace, justice and prosperity could be achieved only if international relations are based on politics infused with morality. We have in India a line of thinking going back to very ancient times which maintained the doctrine of inseparability of artha and dharma – of material gain and the moral law, and of the superiority of righteousness to material gain and of the desirability of achieving victory without war. The state and its rulers are for the sake of dharma; nothing is a greater good for them than dharma. But in contrast to this there has been another school which advocated that politics need not be tied up with ethics, statecraft should not be subordinate to morality, and that national interest must come before human interests. If the first is a school of principle, the second is that of expediency.

There have been conflicts and wars not only for the sake of material gain, but for the sake of ideologies considered to be immutable, universal and absolute truths and for ways of life based on them. Even in modern times wars or conflicts to vindicate or demolish religious and political ideologies have not ceased. This situation will be transformed if the following are accepted : Universal truths are the concern of science and free untrammeled scientific inquiry will establish from time to time which they are; whatever is anti-scientific or irrational cannot be universal truth; and whatever is supranational and demonstrated to be neither true nor false by scientific inquiry may be absolute truth for one who accepts it as such, and while he may live by it and die for it, he has no right to impose it on others. It follows that no way of life or socio political organization is perfect, as every one of them is based on truth taken to be absolute by some; and absolute truth is indemonstrable. The 'anekantattva' (multifacetedness/multidimensionality) of truth, the mistake of taking a fragmentary truth as complete truth and the idiocy of fighting over fragmentary truths, have been pointed out in many Indian works. Only when this is put into practice the world will be saved.

In July 1964 I wrote: "A policy which refuses to take any ideology or way of life as final, perfect and worthy of being imposed on the whole world which believes that peaceful coexistence is possible on the basis of mutual respect and cooperation without any insistence on conversion to what is considered to be the truth and the right way of living, is very much needed today." (*Indian Foreign Policy*, p. xxiii.) In a speech at Columbia University in October 1985 Shri Rajiv Gandhi declared that "the world cannot be made in the image of a particular gospel". In a speech in the Kremlin in February 1987 Mr. Gorbachev asserted: "We do not claim to know the ultimate truth". He called for an end to "the isolation of politics from ethics". This is what some great Indian thinkers (e.g., Vamadeva, Utathya) have been urging from ancient times.

Lastly, I may refer to views I have expressed in 1985 on philosophy and the philosophical task: In ancient India at one time philosophy was conceived as the rational, critical and illuminating review of the contents of theology, economics and political science and also as the right instrument and foundation of all action and duty, which helped one to achieve intellectual balance and insight as well as linguistic clarity and behavioural competence. No one has been able to give a substantially better definition of philosophy. But in India over the centuries this conception receded due to the domination of the concept of philosophy as essentially ontology and metaphysics conducive to salvation.

If philosophical teaching inculcates in the students the habit of reflecting on one's life, thought and action, on what is happening in the society of which he is a member and in the world-community of which his society is a component, it is surely doing something practical and purposeful. The best philosophical training may indeed enable one not only to judge and decide for oneself on religious, moral, social and political problems, but to express oneself appropriately, and, hopefully even to act meaningfully in different situations.

Philosophy teaching should not give scope for any kind of endoctrinassions, religious or political, or even propaganda for a particular philosophical method or system. On the other hand, adopting a totally neutral viewpoint philosophy teaching should not bewilder the student by a mere exposition of various methods, doctrines and systems, without laying bare the starting-points of and the different ways and circumstances in which particular modes of procedure for solving problems developed, and the bases, implications and consequences of different doctrines and systems for individuals and social life.

While a philosopher as a philosopher may rightly concern himself with concrete realities and current problems, and it would be good if a considerable number of philosophers concern themselves thus, there is no duty or obligation on the part of every philosopher to do so either wholly or occasionally. Those who are completely engaged in ontology, metaphysics, analysis or formal logic, or history of philosophy are doing equally valuable work. But there seems to be a moral and professional obligation on the part of a philosopher to conduct his enquiries relating to religious, moral, social and political matters in a free and impartial manner with a critical and rational spirit, to come to whatever conclusions his intellectual pursuit leads him, and to express them without fear or favour, though this last may be more difficult than in the case of technical questions. It does not, however, appear proper for a philosopher in his capacity as a teacher or a research supervisor to present his metaphysics, religious faith or political ideology, if he has one, as the absolute truth with a view to converting his students and research workers, or to even try to make them all the practitioners of his own philosophical methodology. While it is not meet for a philosopher to set himself up as a prophet, a preacher, or a propagandist, because of his intellectual and moral integrity and/or the merits of his philosophy, a school may form itself around him or he may gain followers, in his own life-time without any effort on his part or after his death. F.H. Bradley, G.E. Moore, Wittgenstein and K.C. Bhattacharyya appear to be of this type. The *Bhagavad Gītā*, after outlining its metaphysics and ethics, concluded: 'Reflect critically on this fully and then do what you like (*Vimrsyaitad asesena yathecchasi tatha kuru*). After setting forth various philosophies, religious and secular, the Jaina philosopher Haribhadra concluded: Let the import of these be critically reflected (*paryalocyah*) upon by persons with pure reason (*subuddhibhih*). This is the right philosophic attitude. The standpoint of a true academic philosophy teacher may be that of Kant: "So far, there is no philosophy that one could learn. For where is it? Who has got it in his possession, and by what characteristics can.it be recognized? One can only learn to philosophize." (*Critique of Pure Reason*, 'Architectonic').

I have been informed that on an occasion like this it is the tradition for the recipient of the degree to present a general non-technical account of his work. Accordingly, I have presented briefly three aspects of what I sought to do over the years. Besides what I have mentioned, I have also laboured in the fields of history of philosophy, systematic philosophy, philosophy of religion and comparative philosophy. But I do not propose to say anything about them.

I would only like to reiterate how highly honoured I am by the degree you have chosen to confer on me, and how deeply beholden I am for this to the authorities of this University. In May 1987 your State along with other Warsaw Treaty States has called for "a new way of thinking, a new approach to the issues of war and peace, disarmament and other global and regional problems". (Vide "Documents of the Session of the Political Consultative Committee of Warsaw Treaty States", Berlin, May 1987). May I submit that the advocacy of such a way of thinking and approach is in accordance with the "humane and progressive component of ancient Indian tradition and with the views of Gandhi and Nehru". The Delhi Declaration of the Governments of India and the Soviet Union bears witness to this.

Some of us in India are attempting to develop and bring out the implications of this "new thinking", which is not really new, for non-violence and truth, as Gandhi said, are as old as the hills.

Permit me to conclude by expressing the hope that each one of us will seek ardently to aspire for and cultivate what has been expressed in two very old Indo-Aryan books, which some in India consider as scriptures : May I behold all beings with a friendly eye! (*Mitrasyaham cakshusha sarvani bhutani samkikshe*). Yajurveda/36-18.May I have goodwill towards all I know and do not know. (*Yamsca pasyami yamsca na teshu ma sumatim krudhi.*) Atharvaveda, (Customary Speech While Receiving Honoris Causa Degree at Martin- Luther University, Halle- Wittenberg, Sept. 8, 1987).

ANNEXURE-V

CITATION

Presented by Martin Luther University, Germany (1987) to Prof. K. Satchidananda Murty

The Philosophical Faculty of the Scientific Council of Martin Luther University. Halle- Wittenberg confers today, the title of honorary Doctor of Philosophy on Prof. K. Satchidananda Murty. This honor is bestowed on a great personality of India, who commits himself in word and deed to peace and international understanding in accordance with the principles of foreign policy of India. It is also meant for the Scientist, who has substantially contributed to the development of Philosophy in his country and beyond. We honor a personality who has integrated since more than four decades his own philosophizing, historical philosophical research and teaching with the responsibility of preserving the great spiritual goods of mankind to a harmonious unity. We regard highly the broadminded and moderate science policy maker, who is steering from a decisive position the affairs of university education of his country. The foundation for the scientific approach and the political sense of Satchidananda Murty, was laid already in his young years. He was born on 25th September 1924 in the family of a well-to-do farmer in Andhra Pradesh. His father, whose whole love was for his then still colonial suppressed motherland, took care that the talented son could acquaint himself early with the rich spiritual and cultural heritage of India.

Even before the entrance into the college he acquired an extensive knowledge of Sanskrit. After he completed his studies with a doctorate at the Waltair University, a career in comprehensive academic teaching followed, particularly at the Andhra University, where Prof. Murty was the Head of the Department of Philosophy for many years. His teaching talent and equally the intellectual charisma of Prof. Murty are testified by his extensive visiting professorships, both in his own country and in foreign countries, like U.K., U.S.A., Egypt, Italy, FRG, Pakistan, Iran, Turkey, Austria, USSR and in 1985 also in the GDR. Besides being university teacher Murty has soon created for himself an image of a university policy maker, as member of the planning committee for research at the Universities of India, as member of the National Committee for Central Asian Studies, of the Society for Asian and Comparative Philosophy and o. the Indian National UNESCO Commission. Since 1980 Prof. Murty is Chairman of the Indian Philosophy Congress and is presently working as Vice- Chairman of the University Grants Commission.

Notwithstanding this voluminous commitment to teaching and university policy making Prof. Murty is one of the prominent creative philosophers of his country. To his credit there are more than 20 books in English and in his mother tongue Telugu, several writings in Hindi besides several essays and small publications. Characteristic for the philosophical creation of Prof. Murty - I quote a word of Debi Prasad Chattopadyaya, the Chairman of the Indian Council for Philosophical Research- is the combination of the "best elements of today's thinking with the classical wisdom of the Indian Culture". In recognition of his services in philosophy he was awarded the B.C. Roy National award, the highest possible distinction of India for the achievements in the field of Philosophy, and also the Padma Bhushan award from the President of the Republic of India. The six honorary doctorates conferred on him by the Indian Universities to prove the high estimation of Prof. Murty's works. Prof. Murty's attention is primarily focused on two theme complexes which I want to highlight. Firstly, it is the re-interpretation of the rich philosophical heritage of India in connection with the current philosophical problems and secondly the problematic of war and peace from the philosophical perspective.

In 1952 appeared the book "Evolution of Philosophy in India" in 1965 "The Indian Spirit", in 1982 "Indian Philosophy since 1498" All this research pertains to the first mentioned theme- complex, linked with translations, commentaries and many-sided editorships. As quintessence of this research one can name the book "Philosophy in India: Traditions, Teaching and Research", which appeared in 1985 and became the standard work of the Indian philosophical history. The important thought of this work - this definition may be daring considering the abundance of the conceptional ideas and observations in this treatise is the evidence that Philosophy, understood as rational and critical thinking, has built long traditions in India. It means that rational and critical thinking knows no national barriers, therefore it cannot be the monopoly of a nation, or a culture and it could not recognize any limitations, built through historically developed diverse cultural, religious, or ethnic relationships. It is great merit of this book that on the one hand it describes the philosophical works of Indian Muslims, Christians, or Parsees along with those of the Hindus and on the other hand it introduces the Philosophy written in other Indian languages.

In a country like India, where through social contradictions and religious differences the endangering of the national identity has become a latent problem, such a balanced representation of history of philosophy, which comprehends the diverse multiplicity, can also contribute towards the internal peace of the country. With this, you, respected Prof. Murty, have amply demonstrated that rational and critical thinking has to be applied to the political and social reality.

The talks with Betrand Russell and Karl Jaspers in the fifties and also the sight of the ruins of the Second World War gave Prof. Murty the decisive impetus to concentrate on the problematic of peace, a topic, which has nice then occupied the mind of Prof. Murty incessantly. Together with A.C. Bouquet, Satchidananda Murty subjected the question of international relations and the rolc of the state in the tension area of war and peace to a rigorous verification test with the help of an informative description of the European and Indian intellectual history virtually on this problem. It is written down in the work "Studies in the Problems of Peace" which appeared in 1960 (New edition of the parts of the book written by Prof. Murty in 1986). Prof. Murty put before a critical examination of the Indian foreign policy in the book "Indian Foreign Policy" which was edited by no less a person that the American political scientist Harold D. Lasswell.

Your book on Peace, honorable Prof. Murthy, is a great, a warm, an important book. You defend and justify the thought, that wars are a social and not anthropological phenomenon, and with that you back up the conviction that they must be banned. The reorganizing of the society in terms of removal of economic inequality and of the capitalist profit endeavor are considered as important prerequisites for that but also as positive basis of a peace society, the free development of all men must be guaranteed. From this perspective it becomes clear, why Prof. Murty in his thinking on peace does not ignore the

Marxism and does not want to ignore it at all. For the ideal of free development of all human possibilities in the human sense is essentially an ideal of Marxist theory of society and - how it could escape the notice of a philosophical historian Prof. Murty- and main motive of the history of philosophical thinking.

Prof. Murty stresses the problems of responsibility of scientists and philosophers for the world which has been highly relevant in the past as well present, in which they live. Prof. Murty sees the risk of blind scientism in the separation of scientists from the social responsibility and in the too-narrow subject specialization. It is his idea about the creation of a 'Republica Litteraria', a kind of world academy as voluntary organization of scientists with the task of propagating peace-oriented world view all over and of keeping the world conscience always awake. This suggestion, even though in another form, has found its realization in the various Scientists organizations which are acting as critical and constructive partners for the decisive question of world politics.

We gladly endorse, revered Laureate, that your work in philosophy and political theory is for us, for Marxist Philosophizing not only of external interest, like how the humanistic works have a priori concurrence on their side (about the idea of peace). A look at the publication years of your philosophical peace studies - 1960 - shows that the intention lay farther from some kind of a fashion theme. The cold war had inflicted deep spiritual wounds. And hardly were those of the hot war healed up scantily. The world situation looked to be again irreconcilable and above all developmental opportunities of the countries which were liberated from the colonial yoke, collided with the contradictions of the capitalistic world. There was not yet any global fear, which was being spread by the waves of armaments in the fifties, but the escalation of the destruction arsenal was fearful enough. Without pessimism, but with un-ignorable warning Prof. Murty raised the voice of rationality and combined the analysis of the spiritual peace potentials of the world culture with the demand that this arming world civilization must learn at least to put the correct questions to itself and to its future, if it does not want to meet its doom. Prof. Murty formulated very accurately that the matter of peace is not a private affair and like the belated insight of Durrenmatt's physicist Mobius, that every attempt of an individual to solve things for himself, which concern all, must fail necessarily, so he appealed to all concerned, who are ready to think together. And totally in the sense of Kant's Peace philosophy, which aims at a controllable status of a world peace community. Prof. Murty advocated in a committed way the need for a universal ethical understanding thereby knowing very well that there is also a disastrous interpretation of Kant's ethics of conviction, whereby the good will may be good for a good deed, which however threatens to push the ethical act of peace itself to the second place. Only that will be ethically good, which effects the good. With this Prof. Murty declares war against the nihilism of values without a superficial assessment of value hierarchies of ideologies and cultures, which are certainly diverse in nature. This is in the same manner, in which Carl Friedrich Von Weizsacker once formulated that, he, who understands himself as neutral vis-a-vis certain values, could be put at every one's service.

Prof. Murty's metaphysics of peace made me very pensive. Please compare here also the interview which Satchidananda Murty has given to the Chief Editor of the "German Magazine for Philosophy" (SZfPh, 1 (34) 1986, P. 58-61). Prof. Murty differentiates there three dimensions of peace, which are formed differently in different human cultures, but which are indispensable. There is, firstly, the internal peace of the individual, secondly the relations between the individuals and groups of a society, of a nation or a country. Thirdly, the relations between nations and countries. The first dimension is lacking more strongly in the countries of industrial consumerist culture, so writes Murty than in other cultures. The truth of this observation, whereby I do not want to go into the terminological questions I consider as absolutely prudent. It also aims at the mission of Philosophy, which is lost at least in the philosophical literature of our country- to promote the individual acquisition of individually effective knowledge. Philosophical knowledge makes sense, only when it reminds one of one's personal consequence, when it becomes ethics. I need knowledge not only about the world as such, but knowledge about my situation in this world and about myself - in some cases also only about me alone. The inner peace in our quarrelsome and outwardly so restless life - do we have any such philosophical category for this? Do we have humanism of the individual, internalized speech, the in which understands itself as Microcosmos?

The modern humanism, if seen in this way, is seemingly old fashioned in many points. It rises above the value - ascetism of positivism, in so far as the latter bears any such and wins supporters, and it understands 'itself as rooted in the spiritual traditions of all great thinking. We do not think when he ventures to believe cautiously and precariously in power of ideas and ideals and thereby sees the horrible word of Nietzsche that the criterium of truth lies merely in intensifying the fleeing of power? Who does not remember the great old Greek (Platos) reliance on the creative function of ideas, a thought, which has over Hegel also influenced Lenin's thinking? Who does not remember the anguish of the scholastic, often wrongfully discredited, thinkers, who sought to bridge rationally the gap between intellect and reason, between knowledge and belief, in that they demanded that one should also necessarily comprehend that, what one believes? A theme, which is recurrently peculiar to the Marxian dictum of scientific self-understanding of the historical mission of the proletariat? Naturally, ideas and longings for peace alone do not move this world, but nothing would be more preposterous to ignore the great force of ideas, of the rationally supported belief in the peace. I believe, we are again in need of more philosophy, retrospective and forward looking, balancing, and reprimanding, full of wisdom and rich in knowledge, and that of Satchidananda Murty comes in here.

The world conscience is commensurable with ideas and deeds, and deeds are after blind without ideas. It is also a kind of a rediscovery of the power of reason, which means the new thinking and binds our Philosophy by commitment we understand it now in the broadest sense. Satchidananda Murty's work points in this direction. It is pointed against the madness of this century, as Heiner Muller characterized the living at the nuclear abyss, and with clear insight for purification and activity. Thereby it observes self-love - it BID would be quite modern to say self-organization in a sceptic way. Non-violence as Indian vocable has lost all its apathetic meaning particularly in Prof. Murty's work. But there is something human like active force Homonoia, i.e., in Prof. Murty's diction tolerance and universal ethics, which is capable of consent beyond all cultural limits. It is obvious that the philosophy practices its profession and not that of the politician, but this profession distinguishes itself through that measure of universality, which guarantees that something more than piece-work would emerge. It claims the whole length and breadth of the spiritual development of man, which while developing has also to achieve records of preservation. This I have learnt from Murty - the faith in the power of argument stands on the shoulders of the best traditions of history of reason. Therefore, no to the value nihilism, and no to the history-nihilism! Naturally, it does not have anything to do with the much-abused pure spiritual history. History of reason is nothing without the history of rational historical actors. Karl Marx has cast this idea in a concept, which stresses the radicality and caution of a historical qualitative change - it may be quoted here since even for the social philosophy of Satchidananda Murty a wise dialectics of preservation and change is necessary for a leap into the realm of freedom". If a great revolution has mastered the results of the bourgeois period, the world market and the modern productive forces and subjected them to the common control of the most developed peoples only then the human progress will no longer be like that hideous deity who wanted to drink the nectar only from the skulls of the slain.

Progress as progressing of the whole mankind - a utopia. It is a task of the future. And exactly therein culminates Prof. Murty's social philosophy, which unites the history of thinking with the positive knowledge about something practical as product of the marriage of philosophy and political experience of life. It is logical that for Prof. Murty peace problem could not be a more object of philosophical observation. It results from the aforesaid. Satchidananda Murty took part in 1982 in the world conference of "Religious Representatives for the Preservation of Sacred Gift of Life from a Nuclear Catastrophe" and in further meetings of religious peace workers in Moscow. In his contribution Prof. Murty stressed the Hinduistic teaching of the Unity of all being and the human life as the highest form of life and the conclusion evolving from that, to stand up actively against the atomic threat. A peace which is based on determent is unreliable here I am reminded of the talk of the General secretary of Sodium yesterday evening and lets the mankind exist only in fear and terror. The energetic demand for nuclear disarmament and cooperation of all, who have committed themselves to this aim irrespective of their ideologies, is one of the political premises of our Laureate. In this sense he actively promoted the international cooperation of philosophers and supported actively the formation of centres for the study of Marxism at the Indian Universities.

The International Conference on "Philosophy Peace and International Understanding" organized by the Indian council for Philosophical Research on your initiative and under your Directorship in December last year corresponded also to your concern, Prof. Murty, to promote practically the thought of peace through international exchange of opinions. In your keynote address you had again emphasized that the nuclear deterrent can never ensure peace. You gave expression to your confidence, and we are in total agreement with you that a world without nuclear weapons shall be in no way an insecure world and that the goal formulated by your Prime Minister, Mr. Rajiv Gandhi and the General Secretary of the CPSU, Mr. Michail Gorbatschev in Movement 1986 in Delhi would not be a pipe dream, a dream to step into the year 2000 without any atomic weapons.

Honorable Prof Murty! Scientific exactness, Philosophical creativity, peace activity and a great human charisma are united excellently in you as a person. You are a universally recognized University teacher and an esteemed and often a critical promoter of the new scientific generation in your country. In all the parts of India you are enjoying scientific recognition and human appreciation. On many international events you have represented in a dignified way your country, whose policies which are aimed at peaceful co-existence, detente, disarmament, and friendly association of peoples based on understanding, enjoy a high reputation in our country. In this sense may I be permitted, highly respected Prof. K. Satchidananda Murty, on behalf of the Philosophical Faculty of the Scientific Council of the Martin- Luther-University, Halle-Wittenberg to confer on you the honor of a Doctor Philosophiae honoris cause:

With this conferment we express our best wishes for your personal well-being and for a further fruitful cooperation of our both countries.(A Citation presented by Martin Luther University, Halle-wittenberg, Germany On the Occasion of Honorary Doctorate Conferred on Prof. K. Satchidananda Murty).

Works of Prof. K. Satchidananda Murty

(Authored/Edited)

IN TELUGU

1936: *Sangameśāṣṭakam,* Sangam Jagarlamudi:Ananda Ashramam Grandha Mala (Self).

1937: *Nāma-saṅkīrtana-mahima* (Translation of Śrī Prabhudatta Brahmachari's Hindi work), Guntur: Śrī Rāma Nama Kshetram.

1938: *Śrī Hanumad-Vijayamu,* Tenali: Janakirama Press, (with the financial assistance of Smt. Jampala Narayanamma, self published) Republished by Emasco Books Pvt. Ltd., Hyderabad 2023.

1941: *Śrīmad Bhagavad Gītā-Savyakhyanamu* (The Song Of Celestial), SangamJagarlamudi: Ananda Ashramam Grandha Mala (Self published), Republished 2024: Emasco Books (P) Ltd., Hyderabad.

1943: *Saptaślokī Bhagavad Gītā,* Sangam Jagarlamudi: Ananda Ashramam Grandha Mala (self published).

1946: *Iśopanishattu-Sa-vivaranamu*, Tenali: Sundaram and Sons.

1947: *Kāru Mabbulu* (Essays on Philosophical, Political and Social Problems), Tenali: Krishna Book Depot.,

Republished by Hyderabad: Emasco Books Pvt. Ltd.

1948: *Divya-Jīvitamu* (Translation of Edward Leen's The Church Before Pilate), Guntur: St. Michael's Press.

1950: *Rāma Tīrtha Vedanta Darshanamu,* (Translation of Vol. VI of Swami Rāma Tirtha's Complete Works), Guntur: Śrī Rāma Tirtha Seva Ashram.

1951: *Rāmānuja Darśanamu,* Guntur: Śrī Rāma Tirtha Seva Ashram, Republished by TTD, Tirupati: 1995.

1959: *Pramāṇa Paddhati Pai Prasangamu,* (Translation of Descartes' Discourse on Method with an Introduction, and in collaboration with Dr. K.V.R. Narasimham), Waltair: Andhra University.

1962: *Vijñāna Sarvasvamu — Matamulu, Darsanamulu,* (Editor, 'Religions and Philosophies', Volume VII of Telugu Encyclopaedia that presents in 849 pages the entire Western and Eastern Philosophies and Religions with contributors from all over the world), Telugu Basha Samithi, Madras, Hyderabad, Waltair.

1970: *Maniṣi-Mukti,* (Translation of Metaphysics, Man and Freedom; draft by Śrī M.V.N. Swami and revised by the author), Vijayawada: Navodaya Publishers.

IN HINDI

1962: *Samakālina Bhāratīya Darśan* (Edited), Akhila Bharatiya Darsan Parishad, Faridkot, Punjab.

IN ENGLISH

1947: *Hinduism and its Development*, Tenali: Sundaram and Sons, 1947, Republished by New Delhi:D.K. Print World (P) Ltd.,New Delhi, 2007.

1951: *Thought and the Divine*, Guntur: St. Michael's School Press.

1951: *The Rhythm of the Real*, Rajahmundry: Saraswati Power Press.

1952: *Evolution of the Philosophy in India (A Brief Sketch)*, Guntur: Industrial School Press, Republished under the title *Evolution of Indian Philosophy*, New Delhi: DK Print World (P) Ltd.,: 2007.

1957: Trans., *Ṣad Darśana Samuccaya by Haribhadra* (A Compendium of Six Philosophers), New Delhi: Eastern Book Linkers, 1986(Originally printed in 1957, Tagore Publishing House, Tenali).

1959: *Revelation and Reason in Advaita Vedanta*, (Originally published by Waltair: Andhra University Press,and USA: Columbia University Press,1959 and Republished by Motilal Banarsidass, Delhi, 1974.

1960: *Studies In The Problems Of Peace*, Co-author with AC Bouquet, Calcutta: Asia Pub., House.

1963: *General Education Reconsidered* (Ed.), Bombay: Asia Publishing House, 1963.

—— *Metaphysics, Man and Freedom*, Bombay: Asia Publishing House.

1964: *Indian Foreign Policy*, Calcutta: Scientific Book Agency.

1965: *The Indian Spirit*, Waltair: Andhra University Press.

1967: *Readings in Indian History, Politics and Philosophy* (Ed.), London: George Allen and Unwin, 1967 and Bombay: Allied Publishers.

1971: *Nāgārjuna*, Delhi: National Book Trust ; Reprinted in 1978 and 1983.

1972: *Current Trends in Indian Philosophy* (Ed.), with K. Ramakrishna Rao, Bombay: Asia Publishing House.

1973: *The Realm of Between*, Simla: Indian Institute of Advanced Study.

1976: *Far Eastern Philosophies*, Mysore: University of Mysore.

1980: *Andhra Contribution To Buddhist Thought*, Hyderabad: International Telugu Institute.

1982: *Indian Philosophy since 1498*, Waltair: Andhra University Press.

1984: *Niśreyasa Dharma*, Varanasi: Central Institute of Higher Tibetan Studies.

1985: *The Advaitic Notion*, Śrīngeri: Śrī Śrīngeri Sarada Pitham; Reprinted as *The Advaitic Vision*, Bombay: Bharatiya Vidya Bhavan, 1990.

1985: *Philosophy in India: Traditions,Teaching and Research*. Delhi: Motilal Banarsidass for Indian Council of Philosophical Research; Reprinted in 1991.

1986: *The Quest for Peace*, Delhi: Ajanta Publications. (Originally published in 1960 as chapters in the *Studies in the Problems of Peace*, co-authored with A.C. Bouquet).

1990: *Radhakrishnan: His Life and Ideas*. Co-author with Ashok Vohra. New York(Albany): State University of New York.

1991: *Ethics, Education, Indian Unity and Culture*. Delhi: Ajanta Publications.

1992: *Gita Bhāṣyatraya Vivechana*, Bologna Nations Symposium.

1993: *Vedic Hermeneutics*, New Delhi: Shri Lal Bahadur Shastri Rashtriya Sanskrit Vidyapeetha, and Motilal Banarsidass.

1995: *The Divine Peacock: Understanding Contemporary India* (Ed.) , Delhi: Indian Council for Cultural Relations and Wiley Eastern Limited.

1996: *The Perennial Tree* (Ed.) , New Delhi: Indian Council For Cultural Relations and New Age International (P) Ltd..

1999. *History, Culture and Truth*, Kalki Prakash, New Delhi.

2000: *Be A Lamp Unto Yourself*. Chennai: The Theosophical Pub., House.

2002: *Life, Thought and Culture in India* (ed.) , Project of History of Indian Science, Philosophy and Culture (PHIPSC), Centre for Studies in Civilization (CSC).

2024: *Towards A New Philosophy*. New York: Routledge.

2024. *Vedānta And Bhagavadgītā*. New York: Routledge.

2024. *Hinduism, Yoga And Indian Culture*. New York: Routledge.

2024. *Buddhism, Taoism, Confucianism and Shintoism*. New York: Routledge.

2024. *On Education And The Philosophy of Education*. New York: Routledge.

Works on Professor K. Satchidananda Murty

1975: *Collected Criticism of K Satchidananda Murty*, (Ed.) Ramakrishna Rao, K. Et al., Machilipatnam: Triveni Publishers.

1995: *The Philosophy of K. Satchidananda Murty*, (Ed.) Sibajiban Bhattacharyya and Ashok Vohra, New Delhi: ICPR.

1996: Prof. K.Satchidananda Murty (*A Brief Biography*), Dr. M. Surya Kameswara Rao, in Telugu Vachakam, IX Standard, Tamilnadu Textbook Corporation, Madras (now Chennai).

2011: *Vedartha Mimamsa*— K. Satchidananda Murty (Telugu translation of *Vedic Hermenutics*) Tr. Vadrepu China Veerabhadrudu, Hyderabad: Emesco books.

2013: *Acharya Kotta Satchidananda Murty* — Biography, M. Rajagopalan Rao, Guntur: Bouddha Sahithi Pracharana.

2013: *Acharya Kotta Satchidananda Murty - Biography,* M. Rajagopala Rao. Guntur: Bouddha Sahithi Pracharana.

2013: *Philosophical Perspectives of K.Satchidananda Murty,* Dr. Pusuluri Boaz, D.K. Printworld (P) Ltd., New Delhi.

2016: *Adarsha Tathvavetta, Mahamahopadhyaya Kotta Satchidananda Murty,* Raghunath, K. Vijayawada: Sahithi Pracharanalu.

2016: *Prof. Kotta Satchidananda Murty Complete Works in English (Vol. I),* EMASCO Books, Hyderabad, 2016.

2016: *Telugu Rachanala Sankalanam (Vol. I), Acharya Kotta Satchidananda Murty,* EMASCO Books, Hyderabad (Telugu).

2017: *Jnana Yogi Acharya Kotta Satchidananda Murty,* Ed. Padma Bhushan Yarlagadda Lakshmi Prasad, Raithu Nestham Publications, Hyderabad (Telugu).

2018: *Gandhian Philosophy — An Appraisal, Prof. Kotta Satchidananda Murty,* Ed. Padma Bhushan Prof. Yarlagadda Lakshmi Prasad, Sahithi Publications, Vijayawada.

2018: *Mahatma Gandhi Tattva Vivechana,* Kotta Satchidananda Murty, Sahiti Publications, Madras.

2019: *Thanaku Thanu Velugaina Vadu, Manavathavadhi, Padma Vibhushan Prof. Kotta Satchidananda Murty,* EMASCO Books, Hyderabad, (Telugu).

2020: *Reason, Revelation And Peace,* Ashok Vohra (Ed.). New Delhi: Motilal Banarasidass.

2021: *Samajikamsalapi Oh Dharsanakuni Vivechana, Acharya Kotta Satchidananda Murty,* Ed. Padma Bhushan Yarlagadda Lakshmi Prasad, EMASCO Books, Hyderabad (Telugu).

2023: *Idhi Mana Bharateeyam, Acharya Kotta Satchdananda Murty,* (Translation Dr. Kotta Raghunath), EMASCO Books Pvt. Ltd. Hyderabad, 2023 .

K. Satchidananda Murty

(September 25, 1924 – January 24, 2011)

A Brief Profile

- *Andhra University:*
    - *Alumnus of Andhra University-M.A., Ph.D.*
    - *Joined as Lecturer in Philosophy, 1949.*
    - *Professor of Philosophy: 1960-84.*
    - *Head of the Department for 20 years.*
    - *Chairman, Faculty of Arts*
    - *Principal, Andhra University Postgraduate Centre, Guntur; Andhra University, Orator etc.*
- *Vice-Chancellor, Śrī Venkateswara University, Tirupati, 1975-78.*
- *Vice Chairman, UGC, New Delhi 1986-89.*
- *Chairman (Chancellor), Central Institute of Higher Tibetan Studies, Sarnath, Varanasi (A Deemed University), 1988 - 1995.*
- *Visiting Professor, Princeton University, USA,1959.*
- *Spalding Lecture's, Oxford, 1963.*
- *Over the years (from 1950s to 1995) lectured at several universities in Europe, USA, China, Thailand, Japan etc. at different times.*
- *Visiting Professor, Indian Institute of Advanced Study, Simla, 1970.*

- *UGC: National Fellow 1973-75; National Lecturer 1978.*
- *ICPR: National Fellow 1984-86; National Lecturer 1987.*
- *General President, Akhila Bharatiya Darshan Parishad, Lucknow University Session, 1963.*
- *General President, Indian Philosophical Congress, Patna University Session, 1968-1980.*
- *Chairman, Indian Philosophical Congress, 1980-1995.*
- *Chairman, UNESCO Meeting of Philosophers of Asia and the Pacific, Bangkok, 1983.*
- *Member, Steering Committee, Federation International des Societies de Philosophie, 1988-1995.*
- *Founder- President, International Society for Indian Philosophy.*
- *Dr. B.C.Roy National Award (highest in India for Philosophy & the first to get it), 1982.*
- *Padma Bhushan award in 1982.*
- *Padma Vibhushan (Second National highest award) in 2001.*
- *ICPR Lifetime Achievement Award in Philosophy.*
- *First Indian Philosophical Congress National Award etc.*
- *8 Hon. D.Litt. Degrees of Indian Universities: from Kashmir through Kashi to Tirupati.*
- *Delivered Convocation Addresses at several Indian Universities.*
- *Hon. Dr. Phil., Universities of Halle-Wittenberg, Germany; Academy of Sciences, Moscow.*
- *Hon. Dr. Sc., Sofia University, Bulgaria.*

- *Mahamahopadhyaya, (Rashtriya Sanskrit Vidyapeetha, Tirupati 1995).*
- *Hon. Professor:*
  - *Andhra University*
  - *People's University of China, Beijing.*
  - *Jawaharlal Nehru University, New Delhi*
  - *Benaras Hindu University; and University of Hyderabad, Hyderabad.*
- *Over the years Organized/Presided over/ Inaugurated/ Valedicted many Seminars/ Workshops/Conferences in India and abroad.*
- *Delivered Endowment Lectures in Universities all over India.*
- *Addressed by invitation Plenary sessions of international conferences of Philosophy at Jakarta & Nairobi, Russia, USA etc.*
- *Director, International Conference on Buddhism (organized by ICCR-ICPR), New Delhi, 1984 (inaugurated by Smt. Indira Gandhi).*
- *Chairman, Organizing Committee, International Seminar on 'Peace, Philosophy & International Understanding', New Delhi, 1986.*
- *Chairman, Organizing Committee, International Seminar on Sankaracharya, New Delhi, 1989 (under auspices of Culture Dept., HRD Ministry).*
- *Chairman Project on India Studies, (GOI).*
- *Vice-Chairman, Sub-commission on Education (1985-88),*
- *Chairman, Sub-commission on Social Sciences (1988-90), Indian National Commission for UNESCO.*

- *Member, Press Council of India (1988-1994).*
- *Vice President, International Federation of Philosophical Societies (FISP), a global organization in the field of Philosophy (1993).*

Pictures – for Ambience

Sri Anjaneya Temple in his own Lemon Orchard.

Near Sri Sangameswara Swamy Temple, Sangamjagarlamudi.

His ancestral house at Sangamjagarlamudi.

His ancestral house at Sangamjagarlamudi.

KSM as a young man

At Princeton University office

Teaching at Princeton

Near Liberty Statue, New York

At SV University office

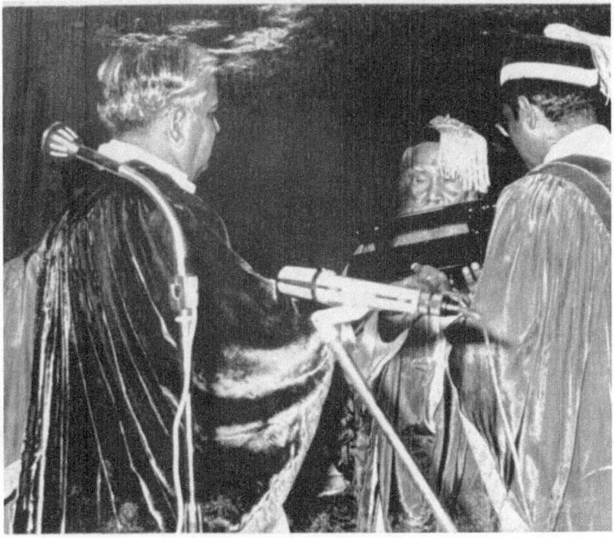

Honouring his guru Sri Palle Purna Pajnacharya with D. Litt., at SVU

In Puja at Sri Sringeri Sarada Peetham with his wife

Riding a Horse

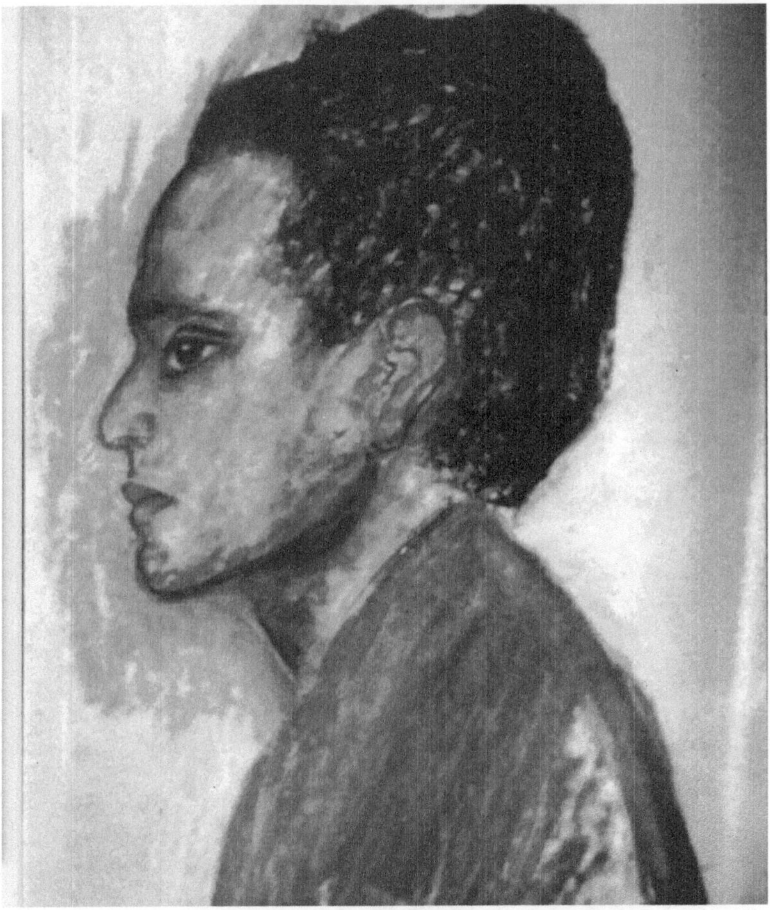

French Artist imagination of KSM

With Dr. Raja Ramanna and his grandson Udayana at Andhra Cottage, Andhra University.

Near Great Wall of China

Near Kremlin, Mascow.

With his grandchild Veda at Tushita, Vizag house

With Sri P. V. Narasimha Rao and his grand child Udayana at Andhra Cottage, Andhra University.

Unwinding at Andhra University.

At UGC Office, New Delhi

In his house with Sri NTR at New Delhi

Without spectacles in Rome

Convocation address

Riding horse with grandchild Veda

Centre in his name at Acharya Nagarjuna University, Guntur

Centre in his name at Andhra University

Bust at Acharya Nagarjuna University, Guntur

Darshan Bhavan in his name at Andhra University

DR. B. C. ROY NATIONAL AWARD FUND

Medical Council of India

Citation

At very young age, Dr. Satchidananda Murty received his Sanskrit education from eminent traditional Pandits which made him fully equipped for the study of Indian Philosophical works in their originals. He took first class honours degree in Philosophy in 1946 from the Andhra University and later his Ph.D from the same university. Joining as a Lecturer in Philosophy in 1949, he soon rose to an eminent position and obtained the national fellowship of the university Grants Commission in 1973 and became the Vice Chancellor of Venkateswara University, Tirupati in 1975. He has been a visiting professor in several universities in the United States and has visited a number of foreign universities. He was a visiting professor in the Indian Institute of Advanced Study, Simla in 1970. He was General President, Akhila Darsan Parishad, Lucknow University Session in 1963, General President, Indian Philosophical Congress, Patna University Session, Member, Board of Advisers, Council for the study of mankind from 1959, Member, National Committee on Central Asian Studies, Government of India; in 1969-70 Member, Society for Asian and Comparative Philosophy) Member, Indian National Commission for UNESCO.

He was also a member, Board of Studies and Examiners in several universities and on the Selection Committees also. He was a member of the Assessment Committee of the Centre of Advanced studies in Philosophy in the Universities of Visva Bharti, Banaras and Madras and also a member of the University Grants Commission in their plan committees. He was a member of the Sahitya Academy, Andhra Pradesh.

Professor Murty is also the author of about sixteen books in English and eleven in Telugu and also edited one Book in Hindi, and the range of his interest covers not only Philosophy and religion but also History, Politics and International affairs.

His brilliant academic career and the contributions he has made to Philosophy and literature have won the admiration of outstanding scholars both in the East and West.

The Management Committee of the Dr B C. Roy National Award Fund have great pleasure in selecting him for the award under the category "eminent person in Philosophy".

(Dr. V. B. Krishnan)
Secretary
Dr. B. C. Roy National Award Fund

(Dr. B. N. Sinha)
Chairman
Dr. B. C. Roy National Award Fund

Martin-Luther-Universität Halle-Wittenberg

Unter dem Rektorat
des Ordentlichen Professors für Ökonomie
der Land- und Nahrungsgüterwirtschaft,
Dr. agr. Werner Isbaner
verleiht die
Philosophische Fakultät
des Wissenschaftlichen Rates der
Martin-Luther-Universität Halle-Wittenberg
durch ihren Dekan, den Ordentlichen Professor
Dr. sc. phil. Reinhard Mocek,

Herrn
Prof. Dr. K. Satchidananda Murty
geb. am 25. September 1924 in Andhra Pradesh

in Würdigung seiner hervorragenden wissenschaftlichen
Leistungen auf dem Gebiet der Philosophie und seiner
hohen Verdienste um den Frieden in der Welt und um die
freundschaftliche Zusammenarbeit der Völker

die Würde eines
Doktors der Philosophie ehrenhalber
(Dr. phil. h. c.)

Zum Zeugnis dessen ist diese Urkunde ausgestellt
und mit dem Siegel der
Martin-Luther-Universität Halle-Wittenberg
versehen worden.

Vollzogen zu Halle (Saale) am 8. September 1987

Prof. Dr. W. Isbaner

Prof. Dr. sc. R. Mocek

German University D. Litt.

In Appreciation

Southern Connecticut State University is honored to welcome the distinguished philosopher, author, and scholar,

Dr. K. Satchidananda Murty,

a man of deep wisdom and learning, you have had a profound effect on many students and thinkers throughout the world. In your books and lectures, you explore the human mind as it struggles to understand reason and revelation, metaphysics and freedom. You bring a special insight into the study of Indian thought and convey that insight, not only to citizens of your native country, but to students and colleagues in many other countries, as well, including Europe, Asia, and North America. You have also been deeply committed to peace for many years and have kept that commitment at the heart of your life and your work. You have been praised for your brilliance and celebrated for your accomplishments. And as the prestigious Vice Chairman of the University Grants Commission, you continue to play a crucial role in setting the directions for future research and discovery in your country. We feel privileged to welcome you to our campus, and we extend to you our most sincere greetings.

Michael J. Adanti, President
April 9, 1990

Southern Connecticut University - Appreciation

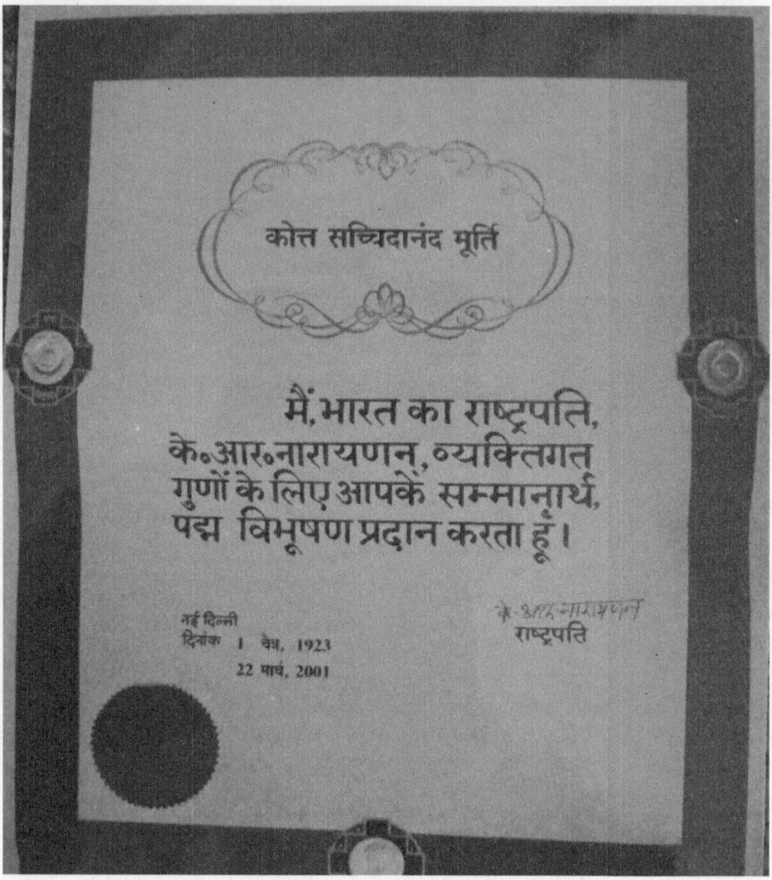

Padma Vibhushan Award

कोत्ता सच्चिदानन्द मूर्ती

मैं, भारत का राष्ट्रपति, ज़ैल सिंह, व्यक्तिगत गुणों के लिए आपके सम्मानार्थ, पद्म भूषण प्रदान करता हूं।

राष्ट्रपति

नई दिल्ली
दिनांक 24 मार्च, 1984
4 चैत्र, 1906

Padma Bhushan Award

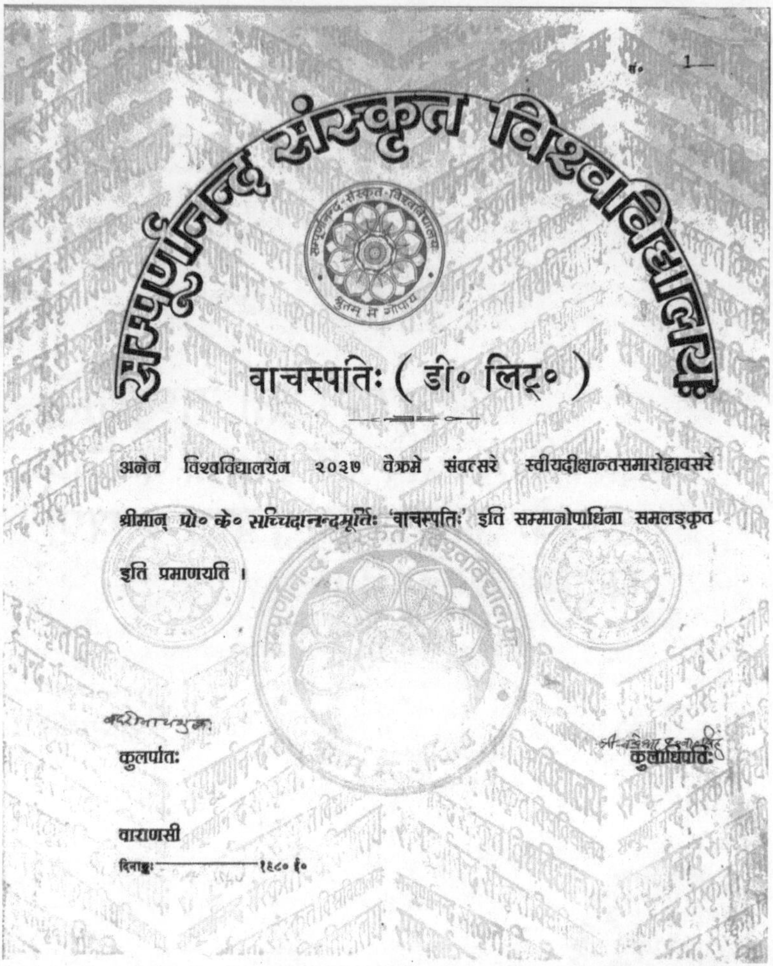

सं० 1—

सम्पूर्णानन्द संस्कृत विश्वविद्यालयः

वाचस्पतिः (डी० लिट्०)

अनेन विश्वविद्यालयेन २०३७ वैक्रमे संवत्सरे स्वीयदीक्षान्तसमारोहावसरे श्रीमान् प्रो० के० सच्चिदानन्दमूर्तिः 'वाचस्पतिः' इति सम्मानोपाधिना समलङ्कृत इति प्रमाणयति ।

कुलपतिः

कुलाधिपतिः

वाराणसी

दिनाङ्कः ———— १९८० ई०

Sampurnananda Sanskrit Vishwavidyalayam, Varanasi - "VACHASPATI " (D. Litt.) award

राष्ट्रियसंस्कृतविद्यापीठम्, तिरुपति

मानितविश्वविद्यालयः

राष्ट्रियसंस्कृतविद्यापीठम्, तिरुपतिः
(मानितविश्वविद्यालयः)

महामहोपाध्यायः

अनेन विश्वविद्यालयेन १९९५ ई० संवत्सरे प्रथमदीक्षान्तसमारोहे
आचार्यः के. सच्चिदानन्दमूर्तिः
भारतीयविद्यासु निरतिशयां वैशारदीमभिलक्ष्य
महामहोपाध्यायः
इति सम्मानोपाधिना वि इति प्रमाणयति ।

कुलपतिः
तिरुपति
युव-आषाढशुक्लतृतीया
दिनाङ्कः १ जुलै १९९५ ई०

कुलाधिपतिः

Rashtriya Samskruth Vidyapeeth (National Sanskrit University), Tirupati - "Mahamahopdhyaya" (D. Litt.) award.

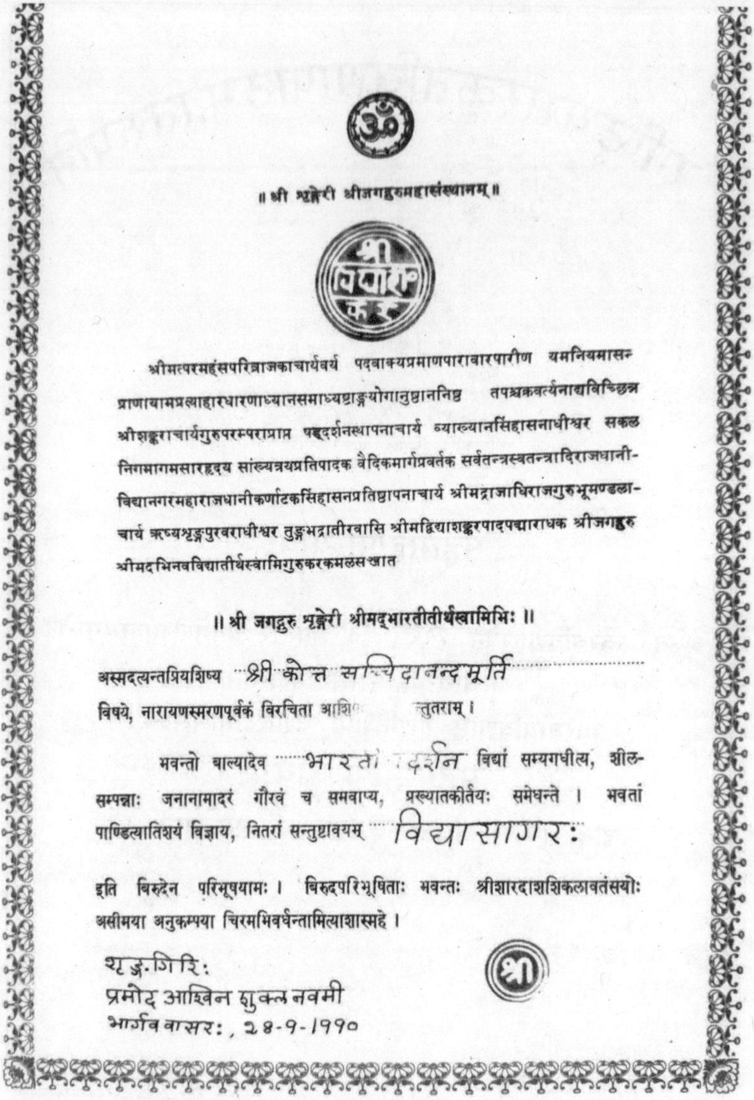

॥ श्री शृङ्गेरी श्रीजगद्गुरुमहासंस्थानम् ॥

श्रीमत्परमहंसपरिव्राजकाचार्यवर्य पदवाक्यप्रमाणपारावारपारीण यमनियमासन प्राणायामप्रत्याहारधारणाध्यानसमाध्यष्टाङ्गयोगानुष्ठाननिष्ठ तपश्चक्रवर्त्यनाद्यविच्छिन्न श्रीशङ्कराचार्यगुरुपरम्पराप्राप्त षड्दर्शनस्थापनाचार्य व्याख्यानसिंहासनाधीश्वर सकल निगमागमसारहृदय सांख्यत्रयप्रतिपादक वैदिकमार्गप्रवर्तक सर्वतन्त्रस्वतन्त्रादिराजधानी-विद्यानगरमहाराजधानीकर्णाटकसिंहासनप्रतिष्ठापनाचार्य श्रीमद्राजाधिराजगुरुभूमण्डला-चार्य ऋष्यशृङ्गपुरवराधीश्वर तुङ्गभद्रातीरवासि श्रीमद्विद्याशङ्करपादपद्माराधक श्रीजगद्गुरु श्रीमदभिनवविद्यातीर्थस्वामिगुरुकरकमलसञ्जात

॥ श्री जगद्गुरु शृङ्गेरी श्रीमद्भारतीतीर्थस्वामिभिः ॥

अस्मदत्यन्तप्रियशिष्य श्री कोत्त सच्चिदानन्दमूर्ति
विषये, नारायणस्मरणपूर्वकं विरचिता आशि[illegible] [illegible]तुतराम् ।

भवन्तो बाल्यादेव भारती[illegible]दर्शन विद्यां सम्यगधीत्य, शील-सम्पन्नाः जनानामादरं गौरवं च समवाप्य, प्रख्यातकीर्तयः समेधन्ते । भवतां पाण्डित्यातिशयं विज्ञाय, नितरां सन्तुष्टावयम् विद्यासागरः

इति बिरुदेन परिभूषयामः । बिरुदपरिभूषिताः भवन्तः श्रीशारदाशशिकलावतंसयोः असीमया अनुकम्पया चिरमभिवर्धन्तामित्याशास्महे ।

शृङ्गगिरिः
प्रमोद आश्विन शुक्ल नवमी
भार्गववासरः, २४-९-१९९०

Sri Sringheri Sarada Peetham, Karnataka - "Vidyasagar" award.

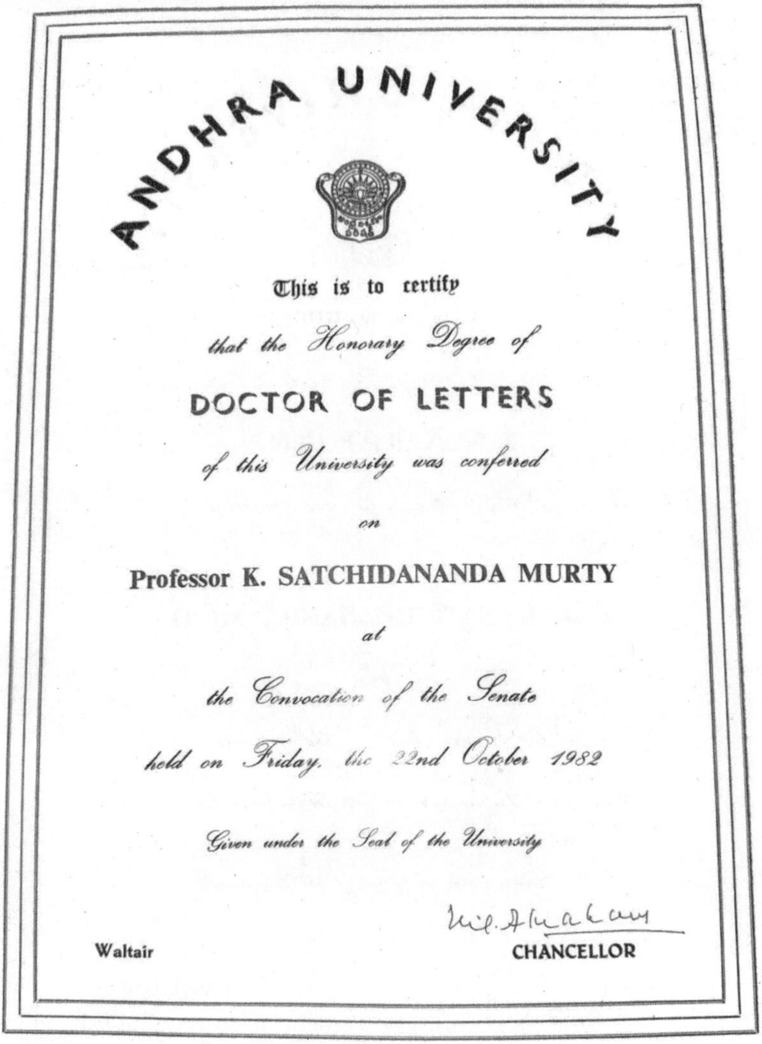

ANDHRA UNIVERSITY

This is to certify

that the Honorary Degree of

DOCTOR OF LETTERS

of this University was conferred

on

Professor K. SATCHIDANANDA MURTY

at

the Convocation of the Senate

held on Friday, the 22nd October 1982

Given under the Seal of the University

Waltair

CHANCELLOR

Andhra University D. Litt.

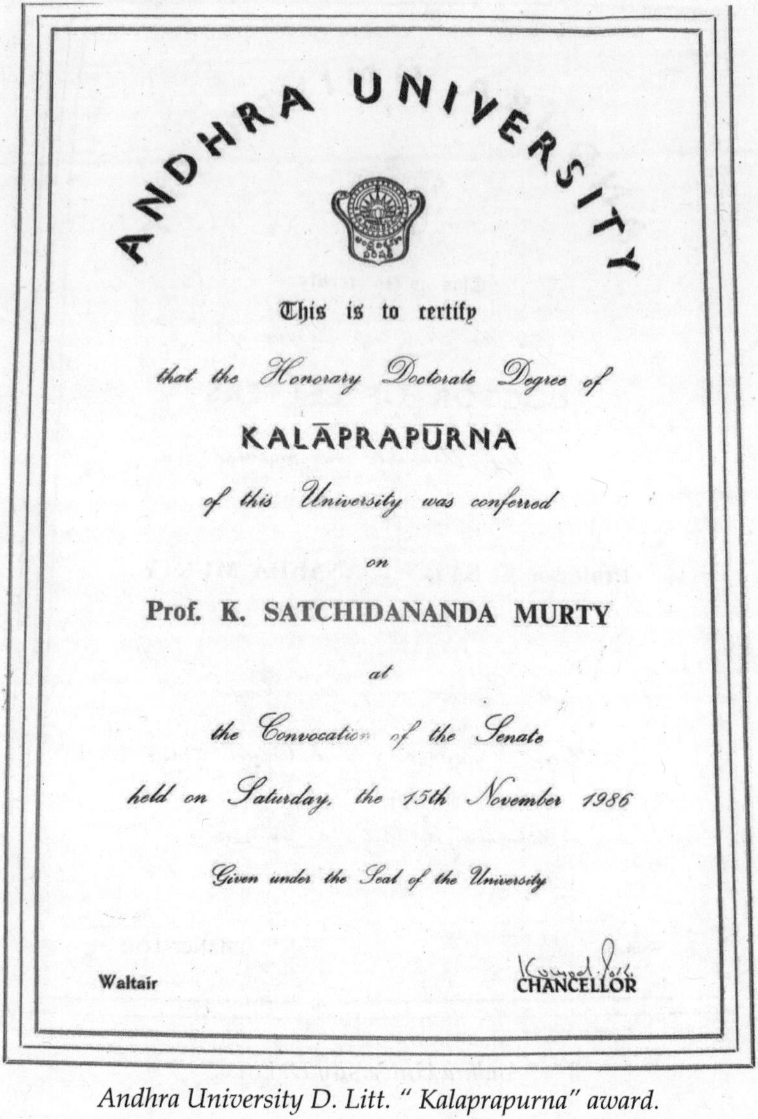

ANDHRA UNIVERSITY

This is to certify

that the Honorary Doctorate Degree of

KALĀPRAPŪRNA

of this University was conferred

on

Prof. K. SATCHIDANANDA MURTY

at

the Convocation of the Senate

held on Saturday, the 15th November 1986

Given under the Seal of the University

Waltair

CHANCELLOR

Andhra University D. Litt. " Kalaprapurna" award.

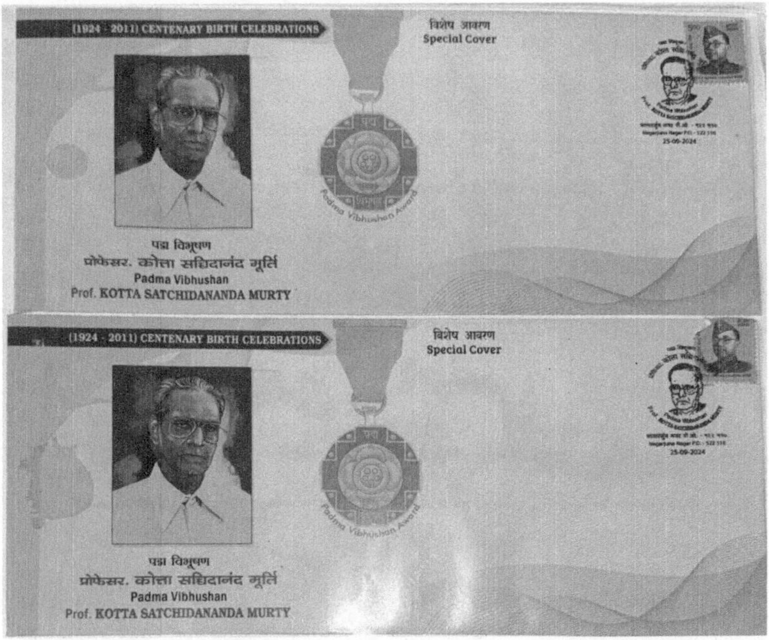

Postal First Day Cover to commemorate Centenary Year.

Professor K. Satchidananda Murty

The Research Project Committee of the Council voiced the need to institute a National Award for distinguished work in Philosophy in India, namely, "ICPR Silver Jubilee Award for Distinguished Life Time Achievement in Philosophy" to be awarded to a living Indian Philosopher and which does not require any project to be carried out by the recipient of that award. Considering that the year was the Silver Jubilee Year of the ICPR, the award was called the ICPR Silver Jubilee Award. The award amounts to Rs 1.00 lakh cash. The first such award was conferred upon Professor K. Satchidananda Murty.

'Samadhi' at their lemon orchards.

Index

N